Trust in Food

Trust in Food

A Comparative and Institutional Analysis

Unni Kjærnes, Mark Harvey

and

Alan Warde

First published in 2007 by
PALGRAVE MACMILLAN
Houndmills, Basingstoke, Hampshire RG21 6XS and
175 Fifth Avenue, New York, N.Y. 10010
Companies and representatives throughout the world.

PALGRAVE MACMILLAN is the global academic imprint of the Palgrave Macmillan division of St. Martin's Press, LLC and of Palgrave Macmillan Ltd. Macmillan® is a registered trademark in the United States, United Kingdom and other countries. Palgrave is a registered trademark in the European Union and other countries.

ISBN-13: 978–1–4039–9891–0 hardback
ISBN-10: 1–4039–9891–4 hardback

This book is printed on paper suitable for recycling and made from fully managed and sustained forest sources.

A catalogue record for this book is available from the British Library.

Library of Congress Cataloging-in-Publication Data
Kjærnes, Unni.
   Trust in food : a comparative and institutional analysis / Unni Kjærnes, Mark Harvey, Alan Warde.
      p. cm.
   Includes bibliographical references and index.
   ISBN 1–4039–9891–4 (cloth)
      1. Food consumption – Europe. 2. Food – Quality. 3. Nutrition policy – Europe. I. Harvey, Mark, 1943– II. Warde, Alan. III. Title.

HD9015.A2K65 2007
338.1'94—dc22   2006044836

10 9 8 7 6 5 4 3 2
16 15 14 13 12 11 10 09 08

Printed and bound in Great Britain by
Antony Rowe Ltd, Chippenham and Eastbourne

Contents

List of Tables

List of Figures

Acknowledgements

This book has been written on the basis of a research project, the European Study of the Social and Institutional Conditions for the Production of Trust, which was funded by the European Commission Research Directorate-General 'Quality of Life and Management of Living Resources', Key Action 1 on 'Food, Nutrition and Health' (EU-contract number, QLK1-CT-2001-00291).

The research was a collaborative effort of six teams located at the National Institute for Consumer research (SIFO) in Oslo, the Royal Vetinary and Agricultural University of Denmark, the Federal Research Center for Nutrition (BFE) in Germany, the University of Porto, the University of Bologna and the University of Manchester. The people involved were Laura Terragni, Christian Poppe, and Randi Lavik from Norway; Lotte Holm, Bente Halkier, Annemette Nielsen, and Terkel Møhl from Denmark; Pedro Graça, Mafalda Domingues and Maria Daniel DeAlmeida from Portugal; Corinna Willhöft and Torsten Lenz from Germany; Roberta Sassatelli, Paolo Magaudda, Maria Paula Feretti and Armando Salvatore from Italy; Corinne Wales, Florence Bergeaud-Blackler and Modesto Gayo Cal from the United Kingdom. We are grateful to them for having been able to draw freely upon their insights, reports, drafts and published materials. Their work forms the empirical foundation of this book. Explicit reference to their written reports appears throughout the text. We would like to express our warm appreciation and gratitude to all. We are particularly indebted to Bente Halkier and Lotte Holm who provided preliminary written material, especially for Chapters 6 and 8. We, however, are responsible for the final account, having re-written and re-interpreted the material throughout. We hope that the result will not surprise our colleagues too much!

We would also like to thank Tricia Dennett for much effort devoted to preparing the manuscript.

A special word of thanks goes to Anne Murcott who far exceeded her responsibilities as an advisor, who read parts of the manuscript and who has been a constant source of encouragement and wise advice. Warm thanks as well to Jukka Gronow and Alan Scott, also from our Scientific Advisory Panel, for their contributions throughout the development of the project.

Unni Kjaernes, Mark Harvey and Alan Warde
June 2006

1
Introduction: Problematizing Trust in Food

1.1 Food on the agenda as an issue of consumer trust

Consumer distrust in food has emerged as a pressing issue on the political agenda over the last decade or so. Many have tried to understand this, employing a variety of approaches and explanations, most of them concentrating on what is happening to consumers. But if you look at pan-European public opinion-poll data, there are systematic variations in levels of trust which cannot be attributed either to universal distrust among consumers, or to their inability to understand or evaluate risk. We have to look elsewhere than individualistic explanations. There is obviously something distinctive about each country; but it cannot be some sort of national character, since levels of trust also vary significantly over time. So it has to be something in the way each country or region has dealt with food issues and crises, and the way their governments, markets in food, and so on are organized. This is our main interest in this book. What is it in our modes of food consumption and their social and institutional environment that sustains trust in food in contemporary Europe? What is it that nurtures scepticism and distrust among food consumers and provokes intermittent crises? To answer these questions, the book will present a study of opinions, organizational structures and strategies in six European countries, based on an extensive research project conducted between 2002 and 2004.

People have been eating, digesting, delicately tasting, cooking, fashioning, needing, desiring, being disgusted by, stealing and buying food through history, but only recently have we been trusting – or distrusting – food, or at least so it is often observed. Is there something new about food in the 1990s that has resulted in its emergence as an object to be trusted or distrusted? There have certainly been fairly major historical

1

changes and the late twentieth century has been blessed with new vocabularies of good and evil: junk food (dangerous food), unnatural (GM) and hyper-natural (organic) food, fast and slow food, and food dedicated to healthy eating. Food has, of course, gone through many historical transformations, but the recent past has certainly witnessed the highlighting of new sensibilities and moralities.

Major technological changes in the way food is produced, transported, prepared, packaged and sold have also resulted in totally new journeys from farm to plate. Many of the activities previously undertaken in the home – like chopping vegetables, washing salads, preparing ready to serve meals – have increasingly been shifted into new commercial processes. Although there has been a long history of the rise of the supermarket, the all-embracing one-stop shop has increasingly heralded the end of the daily shopping round of baker, butcher, grocer and market stall. Across Europe, the pattern has been uneven, but the progress seems relentless. The big brand manufacturers that had become the family favourites of the mid-twentieth century – from Kellogg's to Heinz, Nescafe to Coca Cola – have been knocked off their pedestals by the supermarkets' own-brand labelled produce. Increasingly, food does not come from farmers and markets, but via integrated supply chains. As a result of global sourcing, food has almost ceased to be seasonal (you *can* have fresh strawberries in mid-winter), and instantly transported exotic fruits and vegetables from across the world have rapidly become commonplace, compared with the torrid and tortuous centuries it took the potato or tomato to become accepted as normal to European palates.

And food is probably more regulated now than it has been throughout history. There are labels with long lists of ingredients and additives; There are trading rules on a global scale that define what is safe to eat, sounding like a twentieth-century food Inquisition: the *Codex Alimentarius*. There are global rules, European rules and national rules, in various states of harmony and disharmony. Traceability and control at every point of the food process has become mandatory, but it is difficult to cope with disparate food systems across the world, or with ingredients sliding beneath easy detection. Policing of food has become increasingly complex, and food is governed differently, subject to new political accountability, with shifting responsibilities between farmers, retailers, distributors and manufacturers.

Last, but not least, consumers and patterns of food consumption have changed dramatically over recent decades. The death of the family meal has been widely declared and bemoaned, replaced by micro-waved instant meals for whoever wants what when. Lunch-breaks and mid-day

meals being replaced by sandwiches make their supply the fastest growing business area in UK food production in the 1990s. 'Grazing' and
snacking, TV dinners, eating out displacing eating in, all suggest the
emergence of new social habits embedded in different lifestyles.

Then, on top of, or perhaps arising out of, these changes, there have
been major food scandals and scares – which is where trust and distrust
have been seen to arise. Not all of these are of the same kind, and indeed
different scandals highlight different dimensions of trust. Some relate to
food quality, as when hydrolysed protein masks exactly what meat consumers are being sold. Others, like E. coli and salmonella outbreaks, are
a consequence of contamination and inadequate hygiene regimes
which become much more urgent with the escalation of size and dis-
tance. Yet, the dioxin scandal and the contaminated olive oil scandal
were strictly 'national', the former specific to Belgium and the latter to
Spain. The GM controversies have raised issues ranging from environmental damage by genetic pollution to the implications for human
health, but with uneven reactions in different European countries. The
introduction of the euro had possibly its most conspicuous impact on
everyday purchases, above all of food, rather than purchases of large
consumer durables. Being associated with accusations of unfounded and
unfair increases in food prices, it constituted an economic 'scandal',
affecting many European countries. Outbreaks of foot and mouth disease or swine-fever, and equally the controversial and distressing ways of
suppressing them, make especially manifest the consequences of carniv-
orous consumption, modern intensified farming and the spread of disease through international channels of transporting and rearing
animals.

And, most notorious of all, BSE was exemplary of a scandal that combined many different features: a scientific scare in industrial farming
revealed by the little-understood prion; catastrophic consequences for
neo-liberal market deregulation; and political failures in scandal management. Lack of confidence in beef, the sales of which instantly plum-
meted, was seamlessly intertwined with distrust in politicians and their
expert advisors because government was seen to have concealed for a
considerable length of time scientific advice which would have required
difficult – and economically costly – intervention. In the context of the
integrated market the first response of several governments was to seek
to ban imports of British beef. In the face of unilateral trade bans, EU
officials felt compelled to act to impose a more consistent resolution,
initially to prohibit British exports. It was a rapidly internationalized
crisis, becoming an issue that seriously challenged European and other

national regulatory institutions as well as those of world trade. Moreover, it was a particularly contagious scandal which proved difficult to close down or contain. Hence, these different scandals expose different dimensions of trust in food – safety, nutrition, economic value, quality, and environmental and animal welfare ethics. We can also add a social and political dimension, appearing, for example, as boycotts of food coming from particular companies or countries.

Yet we might pause to wonder whether, however spectacular and consequential the BSE episode may have been, it deserves so prominent a role in understanding public anxieties. It had some distinctive features, but it was far from unprecedented. Food has always been contentious (Argenbright, 1993; Burnett, 1989; Helstosky, 2004; Levenstein, 1988; Smart, 1986; Thompson, 1971; Tilly, 1975; Wong, 1983) – not surprisingly, given its importance to life, health and well-being – but the grounds for contention alter in gravity with the passage of time. As Europe modernized the security of food supply, the price of food, its purity and its cleanliness, its composition and its provenance were issues which successively exercised public concern, requiring state intervention to maintain social order, challenge fraud, and to define and police standards of hygiene and authenticity. If we look at the historical record, these issues arise at different times, with different degrees of strength and at different stages of social and economic development.

What we have presented here are the types of questions and issues from which we started in setting out to do our study. If the conflicts are not new, the contemporary issues still seem to have some distinct characteristics. In particular, they seem to be framed as a question of 'consumer distrust'. This expression has become part of contemporary political discourse and of our everyday language. However, because the trust/distrust dichotomy is so commonly used and because it is so politicized, we first need to take a closer look at what we mean by these terms. This will then allow us to present our questions and to outline our ideas about how we can analyse the contemporary dynamics of trust and distrust in relation to food consumption.

1.2   How can we understand consumer distrust in food?

A British consumer will 'trust' her local butcher or the advice given on food labels, but have little 'confidence' in the safety of irradiation processes. A German will have '*Vertrauen*' in other persons and in institutions. But there is a stronger word, '*Sicherheit*', which has many aspects, like certainty, being safe and feeling safe. Similar distinctions are found in Scandinavia. In Danish, trust will be translated into '*tillid*', a state of trusting something or someone. But in relation to food, Danes often use '*sikkerhed*' – feeling secure and '*tryghed*' – feeling safe. In Norwegian, the idea of '*trygghet*' is widely used and strongly politicized, encompassing this feeling of safety and protection as well as the provision of trustworthiness by institutional actors. Less often used in relation to food is '*tillit*', which is more relational, to trust someone. The German proverb '*Vertrauen ist gut, Sicherheit noch besser*', translated by Seligman into 'trust is good, confidence is better', may in Norwegian (and Danish) be '*tillit er bra, men trygghet er bedre*'. The Latin languages don't have this distinction between trust and confidence – or rather, a generalized idea of confidence does not seem to be conceptualized in the same way as in Northern Europe. '*Fiducia*' covers the first, more or less, but '*confidenza*' has a different meaning, overlapping with 'familiarity', indicating something that is more limited, perhaps even confidential. The literal translation of the German proverb does result in an acceptable meaning if '*Sicherheit*' becomes '*esser sicuri*'. Instead, '*Fidarsi e'bene, non fidarsi e'meglio*' – 'trust is good, mistrust is better' – seems to catch the Italian sentiment better. Similarly, in Portuguese trust is translated into '*confiança*', but then indicating something a bit different, namely a personal belief, a conviction or familiarity. From the word '*confiar*' comes '*fiar*': '*Não é pessoa em quem possamos fiar-nos*' – 'he is not a man to be trusted'. A notion of confidence/*Sicherheit* seems to be missing even in the Portuguese language (Salvatore and Sassatelli, 2004).

Already we see here that trust is multi-faceted and that it may mean different things in various countries. Many more expressions could be added, each with a distinct meaning in various languages. Perhaps food is a special domain, because conceptualizations of trust so often are intermixed with issues of food safety and security. However, the importance of trust is not at all restricted to food. On the contrary, trust has been emphasized as a key phenomenon in modern societies, ensuring social coherence and collective commitment, allowing cooperation, and making everyday practices possible in a very complex and ever-changing world (Barber, 1983; Luhmann, 1979; Misztal, 1995; Pharr and Putnam, 2000; Seligman, 1997). In many situations that we encounter trust stands as a very flexible alternative to direct control – or to the exercise of power and coercion. For example, people will much more willingly pay their taxes, a basic element of functioning welfare societies, if they trust their fellow citizens to contribute their due share and trust the state authorities to use them as promised. Contracts cannot control and predict every detail in cooperation between and with business corporations, trust makes it easier. When people put their health and their lives in the hands of medical institutions, it is very burdensome and scary to do so without believing that the hospital, with its doctors and nurses, equipment and medication, will do its best to give proper treatment. Perhaps less personal, it is risky to board an airplane. We have to trust that the airline, the pilots, the control tower and the mechanics all have sufficient competence, resources and commitment to bring us safely down to earth again. All of these arenas are dominated by big, complex and quite abstract institutions, where personal contacts represent, at best, a very partial substitute. We have to trust the whole institution (or even system) as such.

Still, food seems also to contain special qualities and challenges. Food is necessary on a daily basis, a diet is a very complex matter and the relevant dimensions are multiple. And it is truly integrated in the complex and dynamic structures of modern societies. There has been considerable academic interest in people's worries about food, very often framed recently as a question of dealing with risks, usually concerning health and environmental hazards. Two – very different – approaches seem to have been the most influential.

First, there is a large volume of research within the framework of 'risk perception' (Frewer, Scholderer and Bredahl, 2003; Hansen et al., 2003; Poortinga and Pidgeon, 2005; Renn and Rohrmann, 2000; Slovic, 1999). Risk perception refers to cognitive, psychological processes of understanding and probability assessment. Differences between 'lay' and 'expert' views have been at the focus of attention, with the sub-text that the laity is either ignorant or irrational. With a cognitive frame of reference, information and communication play a key role. People's worries emerge from information they receive about problems, for example media scares. Correct and understandable information is necessary as an input to establish a more realistic perception of risk and thus reduce worries. Trust in the informant and the ability to distinguish between trustworthy and non-trustworthy information are therefore important. The 'risk communication' literature does increasingly recognize that the social and cultural context for what people think ought to be considered. Distrust is a problem for risk communicators if it interferes with the message and general aims. One problem is the misconceptions that can lead people to worry too much or make the wrong decisions. They may, for example, stop buying a food item because of the health risk, even though the calculated probability of being harmed is extremely low. One example is the Alar scare, others are BSE and GM. Increasingly, however, risk communication research seems to link to research on risk regulation, thus focusing more on institutional characteristics (Ballantine, 2003; Leach, Scoones and Wynne, 2005; Löfstedt, 2004). It is recognized that consensual models based on implicit, non-participatory and non-contingent forms of trust are no longer working. The notion of 'critical trust' has appeared, indicating that trust and scepticism may coexist (Poortinga and Pidgeon, 2004). Critical citizens indicate more engaged people, which may be a good thing and increase trust. But participation and institutional transparency may be ambiguous in terms of building trust. So also are initiatives to increase institutional independence, for such strategies may also nurture uncertainty and distrust. Yet, is all of this only about communication and media scares? Increasing institutional distrust is recognized, but the major structural changes and conflicts over food that we have described are rarely touched upon. Are there any links between institutional change and trust? And how can we understand variations in trust?

The second dominant perspective starts with the notion that we all now live in a 'risk society', introducing a macro-level and more critical approach to the question of risks, where it is exactly the questions about causes which are discussed (Beck, 1992, 1999; Beck, Bonss and Lau, 2003; Beck, Giddens and Lash, 1994). The emergence of a risk society signifies a transition from the primacy of conflicts over the distribution of material goods and values to contestation over the distribution of risks. Risk society is associated with, among other things, the development of new technologies, globalization processes, and new divisions of labour and responsibility. In this view, 'risks' entail mainly health and environmental hazards. Modern risks typically arise from unintended side-effects of ordinary economic and social processes and call into existence a distinctly new form of reflexivity and contingency. These risks are difficult to detect and measure, the effects may be very long term, and they are not limited to a particular space or social group. The politicization of side-effects leads to crises of legitimacy, as for example with BSE. The role of science and experts becomes more crucial and more contested. Responsibility for managing risks is increasingly accorded to the individual. 'Uncertainty' is a reflection of the conflicts that these processes raise for the individual. Distrust seen as an outcome of increasing reflexivity and uncertainty has formed the background for discussions on food, risk and trust (Almås, 1999; Brown and Michael, 2002; Michelsen, 2001). It is not difficult to see that aspects of this general description fit well for the food sector. However, is contemporary distrust in food a matter of individual uncertainty as a consequence of reflexive modernization? That would imply that we will find the same tendencies everywhere, variations perhaps depending mainly on individual resources to handle the new responsibilities and the uncertainty. Is that the case? What about the conditional nature of trust?

It is evident that 'trust' is a problematic concept with a number of different connotations. Several questions emerge where established approaches seem to be insufficient to understand and explain the current situation:

- Is trust in food only a question of safety (and environmental hazards), what about other aspects of food?
- Are individual perceptions, decisions and strategies the most central issues?
- Is trust in experts and science the key? Or the authorities? What about market actors? Are there distinctions according to roles and expectations?
- What about the conditionality of trust? How is trust affected by what other actors do?
- What in modern societies 'creates' trust in food? Is it the same in all countries, for example throughout Europe?

These questions form the background for the study of social and institutional conditions for consumer trust in food presented in this book. Our aim is to explore consumer distrust in food and the importance that this issue has had in Europe over the last couple of decades. Trust is usually recorded through public opinion surveys. Such surveys can reveal, for example, variations between individuals and social groups and across countries. However, we explore consumer trust in food as something more, or different from, individual risk perception or uncertainty. As a critique of individualistic approaches, we see trust as a property of the collective organization of social relations, as part of processes of institutionalization. 'Institutionalization' is thus a key concept in our analysis, indicating not only the establishment of formal organizations, like companies, legal or contractual rules, and the setting-up of food agencies, but also of stable informal entities like households and organized interaction, like shopping, meals and citizen relationships to the state. Institutionalization provides organizational and normative frameworks that in most cases are seen as taken for granted, 'normal' procedures which strongly influence what we do as consumers and the expectations that we have. Institutions provide us, as researchers, with a macro-level, panoramic vantage point from which to account for the regularities of collective conduct.

In trying to understand current issues of trust in food, we therefore consider expressions of public opinion as only part of the story. We also need to look at other actors who are involved, and in particular those interacting directly and having the power to influence conditions, Through studies of institutional actors, like market actors, authorities and non-governmental organizations (NGOs), we directed attention towards the interrelations between those actors and the consuming public. In the process, we studied structural arrangements as well as various key actors' understanding of food issues and trust, including food authorities, farmers, processors, retailers, food experts, the media and consumer organizations. In order to enable us to identify critical elements and issues, we compared six European countries: Denmark, Germany, Great Britain, Italy, Norway and Portugal. An important point in our analysis is how institutional actors relate to, and interrelate with, ordinary people as consumers, individually and collectively. In trying to understand consumer trust and distrust, what exactly is meant by the word 'consumer' becomes crucial.

1.3 Different ways of understanding what 'a consumer' is

For most of human history, the main problem of food has been one of obtaining sufficient food for the population. During and after the Second World War, for example, this remained the principal consideration. In the face of real or potential shortages, governments encouraged the mass production of food because it promised a secure and regular supply in sufficient quantity. Distribution of enough food at acceptable prices was the foundation of production-oriented agricultural policies throughout Europe. Safety was an issue between state authorities and producers, so consumers did not have to bother their heads about it. Overall there was little controversy and Europe witnessed scarcely any collective action over food. The threat to social order posed by public reaction to shortages of food or to its hazardous composition disappeared. Nutrition re-emerged as an explicit problem in the 1980s as, thereafter, did matters associated with the industrial manufacture and preservation of foods. At the same time, partly driven by New Right doctrines of economic liberalization, attention became directed towards consumers and consumer choice. The previously almost automatic preference given to the interests of producers began to be questioned, and the interests of 'the consumer' found a place in the discourse of the food system.

Perceptions of food as problematic in the current period are profoundly influenced by notions of 'the consumer'. There is nothing new about food being exchanged through markets, though there has probably never been a period in Europe when a larger proportion of the food consumed has been commercially provisioned. However, it is not accidental that references to 'consumer' society, or 'consumer' culture, are increasingly common ways to capture in a word the distinctiveness of the contemporary period. Consumption and consumers are central topics. People are addressed as consumers, and come to think of themselves, in some situations, as consumers. Many people develop what Bauman (1988) called 'the consumer attitude'; they expect their wishes to be made real and all their pressing problems to be resolved by purchasing remedies through markets. Their expectations come to be conditioned by the sense of rights afforded by the role of consumer.

The current dominant understanding of the term 'the consumer' derives from neoclassical economics (Gagnier, 2000; Winch, 2006). It characterizes the consumer as sovereign; its theory of demand posits autonomous individuals choosing items in accordance with a preference schedule that reflects personal utility. This notion has played a theoretical role in estimating the value of exchange in economics; but as a comprehensive basis for understanding *social* processes of consumption, it is obviously wanting. Indeed, for the purposes of our argument, it is important to recognize that there is a different, and older, genealogical root for the term 'consumption', which emerged from Latin into early English and meant 'to destroy, to waste, to use up', a sense long predating the neutral sense developed in the eighteenth century to describe market relationships – whence the distinguishing of consumer from producer and, analogously, consumption from production. The more recent meaning signalled greater interest in the changing values of items in exchange, rather than the purposes to which goods and services might be put. These two meanings have existed in tension ever since, even though it is the consumer as purchaser (or, more broadly, as 'chooser') rather than as user which currently predominates (Bennett et al., 2005, 58). With little interest in what commodities are used for, economics offers no account of why people choose the items they do, because the explanation from utility is formal rather than substantive. Nevertheless, the concept of the consumer has achieved wider and wider circulation in recent years. It has been extended to describe and prescribe an orientation to action which extends far beyond the purview of individual choice in market situations. Most obviously, citizens have been encouraged to approach the state and its provision of public goods from the point of view of the consumer role. The social construction of the character of the consumer, and the extension of the terrain upon which (consumer) the attitude is deemed appropriate, is a major impetus and a fundamental backdrop to understanding crises of trust in food.

Much that happened in the field of food in Europe could be read as the consequence of a more demanding consumer. Key actors – the European Union, national politicians, corporations and mass media – increasingly frequently and explicitly attended to consumers and their putative interests. A series of movements and campaigns gave a new political gloss to concerns of consumption in general and food consumption in particular – global anti-capitalism, Fair Trade, opposition to GMOs, the Slow Food Movement, observing 'no-shopping' day and concern with food miles come to mind (Micheletti, Follesdal and Stolle, 2003; Miele and Murdoch, 2002; Sassatelli and Scott, 2001). American contributions like those from Marion Nestle (2002) and Naomi Klein (2000) have received considerable attention as a reference point for mobilization. These are new forms of activism, though they may still be less widely supported than the primarily instrumentalist and practical consumer associations, like the British Consumers' Association, the Norwegian Consumer Council and the Italian Altroconsumo (Cohen, 2003; Hilton, 2004). But whether wider publicity implies greater power is disputable. After considering the question in the context of the institutionalization of consumption, a somewhat unorthodox approach, we argue that populations exert influence to some degree because of publicity accorded to consumer interest, but that this is not indicative of a transfer of power sufficient in itself to command major changes in the organization of food supply.

1.4   Trust as social and relational

Trust is subject to much philosophical dispute. Following from the questions that we posed and the problematization of 'the consumer' and consumer choice, we will explore trust not only as social (i.e., not a matter of individual psychology), but also as relational. This means that instead of trying to contextualize individual opinions of trust, we study trust and distrust as emergent properties of on-going relationships between social actors. For example, in the case of food, the relations that people have *vis-à-vis* a producer or a retailer will be different from those they have towards government bodies. Mostly people want access to food which is safe, nutritious, gives fair value for money, is consistent, tasty and so on. Trust could be seen as an expectation, a practical confidence, that other relevant actors in the food system will behave in such a way as to ensure that some or all of these objectives are met. The main point is that it is *actors* who can be trusted or mistrusted. Trust is thus a strand, or a dimension, of a relationship between actors. Trust depends on who they are, what they do, and the interaction involved.

In order to undertake a comparative institutional analysis of trust and distrust in food that takes account of complex interrelations, we maintain that it is best to examine the trust relationships between the key actors or agents involved within given food systems. We consider three sets of actors particularly important because they are directly involved – market actors who supply food, state agents responsible for regulation and governance, and consumers and their representatives. Above all, it is the extent to which consumers find these various actors trustworthy which concerns us. These are, theoretically, the key institutional formations from which public trust in food emanates.

In part, the question of trust in food is one of the divisions of responsibilities over food and its provisioning. If the matter was to be left to households and markets alone, trust would be a matter between buyers and sellers, and the responsibilities of the consumer would be those of the utility-maximizing individual; ranking issues of safety, price, aesthetic quality, nutritional value in relation to different food items in an economist's calculus of preference. The contentious debate over school meals in the United Kingdom represents a recent example in an age-old history of controversy over the consequences of the market provision of food. Another example is the long-standing question of obligatory versus voluntary nutrition labelling. As in other major areas of consumption – transport or health care, for example – there have been many more political and academic debates over the respective role of state and market in provisioning. Food being an 'essential' item, states have long assumed the responsibility for regulating its production, marketing and consumption. In the contemporary period, a range of issues has emerged beyond those of food safety and price, to include various aspects of quality, health claims, and claims as to origin, like those concerning champagne or different kinds of cheese. Labelling of food has become a focus of regulatory activity: how much information, and of what kind, should be displayed about a given food item. Esping-Andersen's (1990) *The Three Worlds of Welfare Capitalism* is typical of a vision in which the relative balance between public or private provisioning and of goods and services, commodification and de-commodification, privatization and

nationalization, have positioned state and market as essentially antago-
nistic forces, often sustained by contrary ideological perspectives and
political strategies. What is interesting about the issues raised by trust in
food is that it slices this question of the relationship between state and
market in quite a different way. It is widely taken for granted that there
should be a governmental role in the regulation of food markets, and
that the provision of food cannot be left to the market alone. But
equally, it is clear that the complexity and scale of contemporary food
provisioning requires that food suppliers and retailers assume major,
publicly accountable responsibilities for standards of trading, and that
these cannot be left to the forces of market competition. For example, a
radical down-loading of risk to the consumer by removing a safety floor,
and giving the consumer the right to choose between price and safety
usually appears as very problematic; like selling cheap eggs that have to
be thoroughly cooked because they may contain salmonella. With the
extension and globalization of markets, it is also evident that what were
previously national regulatory systems have had to change accordingly.
The need to consider food safety when the GATT agreement was
extended to agricultural products is a prominent example (Micklitz,
1992; Vogel and Kagan, 2002).

Comparing different countries, however, raises the question of
whether the division of responsibilities for key aspects of food (safety,
quality, nutritional value, economic value, environmental and animal
welfare) is the same in all of them, and if not, as seems likely, how do
they vary? So the question 'what sustains trust in food?' led us to investigate just what differences there may be in the relationships and
responsibilities between state and market actors, and how much and
what kind of responsibilities are assumed by consumers in different
countries. How does the model of a market-oriented Anglo-Saxon political economy versus a continental European social state play out in this
respect? What about the Scandinavian welfare state solutions?
Moreover, given the integration of a European market and the Common
Agricultural Policy, how does a new layer of supra-national regulation
and governance impact on different national state – market relationships?
This in turn led us to explore how the division of responsibility was
expressed in the institutions of the state itself. For example, how is a
consumer voice represented, if at all? Is control over issues of food
practised in a 'productionist' manner, within ministries of agriculture
and fisheries? Or does it lie in the ministries of health? Or are consumer
matters instead handled as part of trade policy? Or, indeed, is it divided
between all three? And what is the significance of the emergence of new,

more autonomous agencies across Europe, such as the European Food Safety Authority? We explore variations in terms of the different divisions of responsibility, but also in terms of governmental efficiency, transparency and accountability – broadly, modes of governance – as they vary from country to country.

The same kinds of issue apply equally to market provisioners and consumers. Any tourist knowledge of food provisioning in different countries – experiences of buying food, or eating out – gives hints of major differences in the roles of street markets, farmers' markets, processed and branded food, and retailers, both small and large. Going into these differences in greater depth, we aim to examine how the market provisioners, especially farmers, processors and retailers, are organized and institutionalized differently across Europe. Whether responsibilities are or are not divided makes a difference. A retailer can be responsible for, and organize, the whole food chain from wherever in the world food comes. In other cases, a farmer sells food to a wholesaler, who sells it on to a processor or retailer, who then sells on to the final consumer, where there is no overall responsibility assumed by any one of these actors. We explore this kind of variation.

If we consider these two aspects of the division of responsibility and governance together, we can see how the complex relationships between state regulation and market responsibility are differently institutionalized in different countries. Some economic sociologists have chosen to call this the 'embeddedness of markets', stressing how markets operate within different societal frameworks. We prefer to emphasize both the ways in which different provisioning systems are organized as interdependent markets and the ways in which these articulate with the state – which itself, of course, is organized in different ways in respect to the division of responsibilities between different state agencies and modes of governance.

Since our main concern is to explore the issue of consumer distrust, consumers constitute the third major type of actor in our analysis. Above we discussed how the notions of 'consumption' and 'consumers' may be problematized. In order to be able to include consumers in our comparative, macro-level analysis of trust in actors, it has been crucial that we deliberately and explicitly break with the tradition of analysing consumers as individuals and consumption as a matter of (individual) consumer choice. Instead, consumption is seen as the outcome of processes of institutionalization, including several sets of everyday practices, such as cooking and eating, buying food, reading about food, and more. Similarly, consumers are seen as actors with reference to a complex bundle of roles, such as being a carer, a customer, a citizen. Such practices and roles will vary. And, as one element affecting this, we know, for example, that the institution of the family and the gender division of labour is quite different throughout Europe and has also changed considerably in recent years.

We have suggested that the state, market provisioners and consumers may be differently institutionalized in different countries. When we talk of the institutional basis for trust in food, therefore, we consider that the core of any explanation requires an analysis of the relationships between these three 'poles', a triad of relationships, or what we name 'triangular affairs'. All three poles may vary from country to country, but to understand trust, we need to understand the relationships between them: between consumers as purchasers of food and food provisioners; between consumers or citizens and those responsible for the regulation and governance of food provisioning in the state; and, finally, between market provisioners and state authorities. We do not wish to argue that this is the basis for a complete or closed explanation. Any brief consideration of the food scandals that have shaken trust in food across Europe in recent years provides evidence for many other influences, notably the role of the media, science and technology, international trade and competition, to name but the most obvious. But we will argue that this triangle of three poles is central to any plausible explanation, if only because these food scandals have critically upset the 'good relationships' between them. The trust crises were not restricted to a relationship between consumers and provisioners. The BSE crisis, as analysed in our different countries in this book, and the respective roles and responses of state and market actors, suggest that trust is tri-polar, that trust in food rapidly became an issue of trust in public authorities, including public scientists, regulators, and most certainly politicians. Because the different countries have developed each of the three types of institutions along historically different trajectories, and because the origins and impacts of different crises or scandals have been so uneven across Europe, we believe that this 'deep institutional' account is well placed to understand the huge variation in food experience within Europe and the emergence of distrust in food as a late twentieth-century phenomenon.

To summarize, to see trust as social and relational means that we should seek to understand the dynamics of 'who trusts whom in regard to what'. By this expression we do not want to indicate that we are looking at rational decision-making processes. We are looking first of all for aggregate effects in terms of variations in institutionalization processes. Seeing distribution of responsibilities as a central issue, both in respect to states and markets and in respect to private and public spheres, we concentrate on macro-level interrelations between three poles: the provisioning system, the regulatory system and consumers. We use both survey and institutional data as inputs to this analysis. In doing this, we see consumers and consumption in a particular way, where 'the institutionalization of consumption' is a key concept, a concept that directs attention towards distinctive patterns of how consumption is organized and normatively founded.

1.5   Outlining the structure of the book

As already noted, trust is a tricky, multi-dimensional concept. We therefore start our analysis by giving some attention, in Chapter 2, to theoretical understandings of 'trust', and of 'consumer trust' more specifically. We also give some consideration to what trust in food might imply. We review the relevant debates and indicate where our own study fits. After outlining our conceptual orientation, we discuss in Chapter 3 the implications of our approach for the design of the study, presenting briefly the methodologies for data collection and the empirical analyses. Thereafter, we present and discuss a large body of empirical findings. In Chapter 4 we give an overview of the large and consistent variations in public opinion observed in the survey in relation to trust in food across Europe. The survey data also form the basis for a more extensive analysis of factors that affect trust in food items presented in Chapter 5, focusing particularly on beef as a central and contentious issue in debates over trust in food in recent years. This analysis provides an even stronger indication that institutional and structural explanations are needed to understand variations and changes in trust in food. As a first step towards this, we take a closer look in Chapter 6 at what the survey revealed about the consumer. The roles of citizen, active consumer and the market consumer are explored, the evidence pointing even more strongly towards national and societal differences between consumers in different countries.

This leads us directly to the institutional perspective, introducing a new range of empirical data concerning how consumers in their food related practices, provisioning systems in their delivery of food to the consumer, and states and governments in their regulation of food matters, differ from country to country. This argument is built in two steps. First, we look at the relationship between consumers and provisioners, on the grounds that in all modern societies, the main channel for food provisioning is exchange between market providers and households.

We find that there are systematic differences in how households are organized in their consumption of food, but also that provisioning systems, people buy their food which determine how, vary from country to country (Chapter 7). We find, though, that the relationship between societal consumers and national provisioning systems is insufficient to account for the differences in levels of trust discerned in the survey. Hence, in Chapter 8 we bring the state and regulation into the picture, showing that here, too, there are significant differences in the ways that states operate with respect to market actors, and also in how consumers are engaged in, or represented by, state regulatory systems. We conclude this stage of the argument by constructing 'triangular affairs of trust', between consumers, market actors and the state.

Having completed our main empirical analysis, we then reflect on what this means for our understanding of trust as an emergent aspect of social relationships, returning to questions raised earlier. We consider what the nature of the changing social basis of trust might be, following the major scandals certainly, but also following the longer-term shifts in the nature of the food we eat, how we behave as consumers, and the effects of 'modernization' and the increasing dominance of supermarkets (Chapter 9). We emphasize the significance and, indeed, positive role of distrust, and how distrust may be institutionalized in different countries. This completes the journey so that, finally, in Chapter 10, we give an overview of both the major surprises and the most significant outcomes of our research, and how these have changed our views of what constitutes 'trust in food'.

2
Trust and Food Consumption: Theoretical Approaches

'Trust', though part of our everyday vocabulary, is used for very specific analytical purposes in a number of academic disciplines. In Chapter 1 we indicated that the theoretical approach to trust is critical for an understanding of contemporary issues of distrust in food. In this chapter, we will delve into major contributions to academic debates in order to develop a conceptual framework for analysing trust associated with food consumption. First, we argue that individualistic, and often cognitive, approaches are insufficient and perhaps even misleading in relation to understanding contemporary consumer worries about food. We seek to problematize the link often drawn between (dis)trust and individual perceptions of risk. Second, we review critically some approaches to social accounts of trust. We discuss two, quite different, types of approaches to trust; cultural and normative theories, on the one hand, and theories of institutional performance, on the other. While the first finds trust arising from embedded social relationships around routines of consumption, the second focuses upon the effectiveness of political and administrative procedures for the establishment and reproduction of trust. These approaches are then used to frame an account of the role of inter-relationships between significant actors in the emergence of different types and degrees of trust. Within the field of food, consideration of the relationships between processes of provisioning, consumption and regulatory arrangements are of particular importance. Trust is analysed as an emergent property of the institutional configuration constituted by the articulation of these three processes. Next, we examine different types of trust and the conditions of their existence. We take issue with some contemporary social theory by suggesting that an understanding of trust, at least with respect to consumer trust in food, requires recognition of no more than two types – familiarity and confidence. Finally, we advance the hypothesis that different forms of configuration generate distinct forms of trust.

2.1 Cognitive trust: Individuals and the role of information

Why is it that people seem so concerned about issues related to food? Is it a reaction to the recent 'media scares'? Why are people so sceptical when scientific experts and authorities say there is no reason to worry? These questions have dominated the research agenda about risk perception and risk communication. Trust is mainly seen as an element in or outcome of cognitive processes[1] associated with evaluations of risk, most often safety hazards. Numerous studies have analysed people's reactions to technological hazards and media crises, often focusing on issues such as GM food and BSE. Perceptions and probability assessments involved in risk perception and risk-taking behaviour can be characterized as 'judgements under uncertainty' (Löfstedt and Frewer, 1998). An important topic has been the lack of correlation between lay and expert perceptions and assessments of risks. Food experts and policymakers often judge consumer unease to be excessive, unwarranted and irrational. If people's reactions are not in accordance with experts' evaluations of risks, the main reason is often seen to be lay ignorance. What has been called the 'deficit model' (Wynne, 1996) is a truly technocratic approach where consumers' distrust is to be avoided by administrative and technological means, particularly through (one-way) information programmes (Scholderer and Frewer, 2003).

Departing, however, from earlier assumptions that 'objective' information about scientifically assessed risks is misinterpreted by ordinary people, a large body of literature has emerged on people's perceptions of risks, seeking general mechanisms underlying consumer attitudes (for example, Fife-Schaw and Rowe, 1996; Slovic, 1999; Sparks and Shepherd, 1994). Avoiding the distinction between objective risks and subjective perceptions, risk assessment should be regarded as inherently subjective, representing a blending of science and judgment influenced by psychological, social, cultural and political factors. This holds for lay people and experts alike (Slovic, 1999). Diverging views are linked to differing cognitive frames of reference. The perception of risks is thus found to be multidimensional (including even factors unrelated to human health), varying with the degree of personal control; evaluation of risks versus benefits is complex and perception varies according to specific hazards (Hansen et al., 2003).

In this school of thought, trust is associated with the ways in which individuals perceive, evaluate and act upon, risks. It has been suggested, however, that trust may be as much a consequence as a cause of variations in risk perception (Frewer, Scholderer and Bredahl, 2003; Poortinga and Pidgeon, 2005). Trust is involved because most aspects of food risks at the product level, 'credence characteristics', cannot be identified or controlled by consumers. In communication about risks, therefore, 'source credibility' emerges as an important factor, understood as 'whether an audience perceives a speaker to be making assertions that she or he considers true or valid' (Hansen et al., 2003). Moreover, lack of success of one-way information has led several to suggest two-way communication programmes and consumer involvement in debates and regulatory decision-making (Foster, 2000; Slovic, 1999; Scholderer and Frewer, 2003). Even though participatory or dialogical in nature, these contributions still adhere to the cognitive focus on communication. Leading representatives of risk research now accept that their approach can be criticized for its 'lack of integration' with the 'social and cultural context' and are trying to find ways of considering the institutional sphere (Löfstedt and Frewer, 1998). But so far, empirical work conducted within this tradition often concludes only with a catalogue of typified individual attitudes towards risk.

A general feature of all these studies is that distrust emerges from communication on food risks. How can trustworthy information be established? Research on risk *communication*, which developed with reference mainly to chemical and environmental hazards across the board, is directed more towards institutional strategies. Being more 'managerial' in nature, often evaluating communication programmes or the handling of specific media crises, new and more active modes of building trust are sought in order to counteract assumed declining levels of public trust toward industry, regulators and science. The decline is linked to the dramatic rise in access to information through television and the Internet, to the centralization of government, and to the amplification of risk by the media. The main concern is how organizations communicate and are perceived, rather than what they actually do. Studies typically focus on regulatory scandals in the media, including those with a major impact, such as GM food, BSE and the dioxin scandal in Belgium, but also less prominent ones, such as the cases of alar and acrylamide (Löfstedt, 2004; Jensen, 2004; Miles and Frewer, 2001; Siegenst and Cvetkouitch, 2001).

More critical, Wynne sees a repeated need among major institutional actors to reinvent new 'public deficit' modes (Wynne, 1996, 2005). Risk assessment by experts is a crux to the conflicts and a major source of public concern and distrust (Hoffmann-Riem and Wynne, 2002). From being generally ignored, public concerns do get attention. But a simplification of scientific knowledge and downplaying of the 'unknown unknowns' is taking place which, rather than being comforting and pacifying, instead raises public scepticism. People are not necessarily risk obsessed and fear driven, incapable of handling 'uncertainty', individualized and atomized. Their scepticism is rather associated with performative issues, control of science, scientific contingencies and the handling of the unknowns. Public (or 'lay') involvement is seen as a key: 'In order to overcome some of the distrust and suspicion expressed by lay publics *vis-à-vis* expertise, it is essential to institute regular occasions for such interaction, thus making expertise more open, transparent and accountable to a wider audience' (Gough et al., 2003).

There are obvious lessons to be learned from these studies, telling us about different rationalities and perceptions, about the importance of what organizations (especially authorities) do, and also about how controversies unfold. However, consumption, and trust related to it, is problematically assumed to be a matter of individual, rational decision. Also problematic is the restriction of trust issues in relation to food to specific safety hazards and expert evaluations. Finally, a cognitive understanding of trust concentrates on transmission of information as the major conduit of trustworthiness. However, such a cognitive account of trust easily becomes tautological: trust is based on trustworthy information and trustworthy information is information that which is trusted. The actual interaction associated with the food items as such and its associated practices tend to be overlooked. We argue that interaction and practices related to the food should be the focus of attention in explaining conditions for trust, not communication about risks.

2.2 Distrust in risk society: A question of uncertainty?

In cognitive accounts uncertainty and ignorance are cited as a major reason as to why problems of distrust emerge. Uncertainty has also been considered important in some sociological contributions, which address macro-level social change. One example is the much vaunted 'risk society' hypothesis of Ulrich Beck (1992) which suggests that the nature of responses to danger and hazard has changed in recent years. Beck points to two major features of what he calls 'the second modernity' to which trust is relevant: risk society and individualization (Beck, 1999; Beck and Beck-Gernsheim, 2002; Beck, Bonss and Lau, 2003). Paradoxically, however, although clearly a macro-social analysis, trust remains within the frames of individual and cognitive considerations of safety and environmental hazards, though Beck explicitly does not presume rationalistic assessment of risks. People, it is argued, are increasingly forced to take individual and personal responsibility for their everyday lives and lifetime careers. This responsibility gives freedom, but it also represents pressures, dilemmas, frustrations and uncertainties. Structural constraints influence how individuals take on these responsibilities; lack of knowledge and insight, asymmetrical power relations and distribution of resources all affect freedom of manoeuvre. These dilemmas and uncertainties appear in all areas of everyday life, not least in the labour market. But in relation to issues like food, safety and environmental hazards predominate. The notion of 'risk society' implies that modern risks (like GM food and BSE) are typically difficult or impossible to estimate, and have consequences unlimited in time and space. The feeling of uncertainty in the face of these new forms of risk, combined with a lack of power and control, form the background for Beck's understanding of contemporary issues of distrust linked to food.

Beck's theory is a general one aimed at understanding major processes of social change and it has formed an interpretative frame for understanding contemporary issues of distrust in food (Almås, 1999; Breck, 2000; Brown and Michael, 2002; Michelsen, 2001). Modern risks, among which food issues figure high on the agenda, and the consequences of individualization, imply that distrust will be prominent in the most advanced societies. The increasingly complex and dynamic character of modern systems of food provisioning, knowledge and regulation is frequently said to lead to unpredictability, fragmentation and contradictions, themselves core features of contemporary consumption (Busch, 2000; Gabriel and Lang, 1995). Such features may in turn challenge trust by increasing uncertainty (Almås, 1999).

Several objections can be made to this approach to trust in food. To begin with, even though the framing is very different from the theories discussed in the previous section, the individual, cognitive understanding of trust is retained. Uncertainty, which is linked to assessments of safety and environmental hazard and conflicts between lay and expert evaluations, is seen as the outcome of macro-social processes, but distrust seems to remain at an individual level. Second, contentious issues extend beyond health and environmental hazards. People may be sceptical about, or deceived with regard to, for example, quality and flavour, price, nutritional composition, as well as various aspects of production and distribution (such as animal welfare or child labour). These issues may be 'new', like GM food or animal welfare, or quite well known, like fraud, salmonella or poor nutritional composition. Third, distrust may be less a matter of uncertainty than an inability to exert practical control over the outcome of these issues. In our view, improving trust will not only be a matter of eliminating feelings of uncertainty or reducing potential hazards, but involve actual improvements in the quality of food or of demonstrating social justice. If this is the case, there is no need to assume a long-term trend toward greater distrust. It may very well be that after a period of rapid shifts, new institutional arrangements may, if successful, provide legitimate solutions to conflicts of interest and power imbalances, or find ways to handle the asymmetric information. Indeed, the historical record shows that changes in the food sector have often been accompanied by consumer distrust and activism, which in turn have resulted in new forms of organization (Hirdman, 1983; Kjærnes, 1995; Levenstein, 1988; L. A. Tilly, 1983). From this perspective the question of trust can be addressed as a primarily social phenomenon, immediately and particularly relevant to consumption.

2.3   Trust as social

Trust can be, and frequently is, considered to be more than an individual attitude, or a private and personal judgement. Instead, it is something that structures social life and is a collective orientation. Trust then refers to a set of moral values, social cohesion or a cultural community in an abstract sense (Misztal, 1995). The background can be formulated in rational terms, as when Elster regards trustfulness as the expression of norms that makes everyone better off than they would be without it (1989a, 113–23). Focusing on cooperative settings, he suggests that norms generate common lines of action that make other people's behaviour predictable. Norms guide social action and contribute to social stability; they create credibility to promises and threats. Norms are motivations that provide 'the cement of society', without which 'chaos and anarchy would prevail' (Elster, 1989b, 50; Gambetta, 1988, 162) seems to agree with Elster's understanding of trust as norms which create predictability, a prerequisite for social cohesion to emerge. The opposite may be disastrous: '(T)he unpredictability of sanctions generates uncertainty in agreements, stagnation in commerce and industry, and a general reluctance towards impersonal and extensive forms of co-operation' (Gambetta, 1988, 162).

Others, Parsons being a prominent example, have also focused on the normative foundations of action, seeing trust as a prerequisite for maintaining social order. Distrust erodes the cohesive basis of society by alienating the individual, inciting a search for alternatives, often found in shady or illicit identities of deviant subcultures or criminal gangs. Thus, theorists who at first glance are quite divergent, seem to share the idea of trust as fundamental to social order, but at the same time consider it fragile, such that distrust and disorder are a constant threat to society (Mistzal, 1995).

Recent contributions in this vein have focused more on the dynamics than the functions of trust. Shared norms and predictability are still central, framed for example as issues of solidarity or cooperation. But attention is directed more towards what people do, their participation in social networks, in social mobilization, and in interpersonal contact. It is argued that confidence develops only very slowly, starting out in primary socialization with the development of basic, trusting personal relations, and continues into secondary socialization processes where young people and adults engage in social networks and organizations. The formation of trust thus requires shared and relatively stable norms within society. Trust in institutions is regarded as an extension of interpersonal trust, projected on to political institutions and therefore conditioning the assessment of political performance (Inglehart, 1997; Putnam, 1993; Uslaner, 1999). These ideas are typically taken in two directions. Some, like Putnam, emphasize trust as a form of social capital which is intertwined with an unequal distribution of social resources, thus varying in kind or degree according to social status and demographic characteristics. Others, like Luhmann, see trust as intrinsically embedded in local or national cultural superstructures or systems (Luhmann, 1979).

We maintain that trust emerges, and ebbs and flows, in accordance with a dynamic associated with social activities. To say that trust is social is to emphasize shared norms and expectations, the predictability of cooperation and the constitution of everyday practices. Trust is associated with how people normally relate to each other, how they interact in social networks and how they develop their relationship to political institutions. A basic condition of trust is its emergence from, and embeddedness in, processes of institutionalization. By 'institutionalization' is meant the processes whereby different sets of actors mutually recognize and typify habitual actions (Berger and Luckman, 1976).

Because of their mutuality, such habitual actions appear in the form of institutional arrangements. Institutions develop historically, but appear to the individual as an objective reality, apprehended through processes of socialization. In that way, institutionalization processes make cooperation less dependent on personal relations and specific evaluations. Often, but not always, institutionalization will mean the emergence of organizations (such as businesses, public bodies and households) and formalized interaction between them (such as regulatory or contractual arrangements). These conditions for trust change only slowly, and are usually tacit and taken for granted within a given context. Appreciating this aspect of the sources of trust in food requires attention to two sorts of institutionalized activities, socially embedded practices and relationships, and political and administrative frameworks of regulation. The first aspect directs us towards food consumption and market interaction, the second towards the structure and performance of formal organizations, such as the food industry and regulators. We deal with each in turn.

2.4 The institutionalization of food consumption: Habits and routines

Studies linking trust to food consumption often have a basic economic understanding of the consumer as a 'shopper', a customer. An economic perspective usually takes, implicitly or explicitly, consumer sovereignty as axiomatic, assuming consumers' free choice, based on their preferences and the information they received (for example, Scholderer and Frewer, 2003; Böcker and Hanf, 2000). Criticism from sociologists who maintain that economic transactions should be understood as 'embedded' in social relations and context (for example, Granovetter, 1985) seems especially pertinent when analysing consumer trust in food.

There have been different strands in the new economic sociology of markets, some emphasizing the importance of the embedding of economic transactions in social networks, where buying and selling are shaped by an interpersonal social context (Granovetter, 1985; Krippner, 2001; Lie, 1991–92). This more micro-social conception of embedding can be contrasted with a more institutionalist, neo-Polanyian view, where social or economic practices become 'bedded down', or routinized in institutions, be they tangible like market-places or shops, or intangible like norms or conceptual frames (Block, 2003; Boyer, 1997; Harvey and Randles, 2002). Trust, in this light, can be seen as a critical condition for consumers when they enter into routinized and stabilized patterns of buying, self-provisioning and consuming. Different societal ways of institutionalizing the buying and selling of food are exemplary cases for this analytical perspective. Markets cannot work without minimal conditions of trust between buyers and sellers. So much is implicit and non-contractual in market transactions, whether in small shops or supermarkets. When we speak of the 'institutionalization of the consumer', it is within this neo-Polanyian conceptual context.

However, to recognize the social character of food consumption requires reference not only to the situation of purchase. Food consumption involves a much greater variety of aspects in our dealings with food as individuals and households, not only from acquisition through cooking to eating and clearing away, but also in exchange of information and knowledge and in our position and participation as citizens with reference to such activities. Consumption is deeply rooted in our everyday lives, influenced by cultural norms and social status, the organization of the labour market and household structure. Food norms and expectations reflect conventions, which express social group affiliation as well as local and national identity. Patterns of food consumption therefore vary in time and space, shaped by, and in turn shaping, the specific context formed by the food-provisioning system. This is why we argue that food consumption should be analysed as processes of institutionalization. The ways in which consumption is institutionalized – the daily routines, the directions and priorities of food consumption, as well as the responsibility, power and resources of 'the consumer' – have impacts on trust and the forms of trust relations. The socially embedded consumer role forms the foundation for individual and collective action and mobilization, as well as influencing how consumers appear in broader political alignments. Without making allowance for this possibility, our approach would be incomplete.

The notion of institutionalization points to the importance of routine and conventional action. Of course not all activity is institutionalized and some is unconventional. We cannot dismiss choice altogether. Among the abundance of foods available, we are forced to select between them. But we mostly do not reconsider our decision each time we purchase milk or bread, nor can we choose something that is not on offer. Rather, most often we buy 'the usual thing'. Food related practices, as part of everyday life, are usually highly routinized. Everyday routines are neither explicit, individual acts of decision-making, as assumed in cognitive approaches, nor are they mere unconscious, predetermined acts (Gronow and Warde, 2001). Routines normalize practice. They are the 'way things are' done (by 'Us' if not by 'Them'), and they are also 'the ways things should be done'. Strongly normative, routines are the consequence of social interaction and are embedded within, and as, social institutions. But this understanding of routinized and normatively regulated practices does not preclude agency or strategic considerations. In some situations, routinized practices become explicit and contested, routines can intermittently break up – an exception, or new and alternative, often ideologically justified, habits may be established – often gradually – again to become tacit and taken for granted (Swidler, 1986).

The habitual, tacit character of everyday practices like food consumption often sustain an unreflective trust. Repetition makes a practice second nature. Referring to Bourdieu, Misztal has characterized one form of trust as *habitus*: 'Trust as habitus is a protective mechanism relying on everyday routines, stable reputations and tacit memories, which together push out of modern life fear and uncertainty as well as moral problems' (Misztal, 1995, 102). Because Bourdieu's concept of habitus has a number of connotations not directly relevant to our discussion, we will not employ this expression directly. Still, and following Misztal (and others, like Luhmann and Giddens), it is important to recognize the role of trust in facilitating routinized practices in situations characterized by lack of control, and, at the same time, to acknowledge the routinization of daily life as itself an important source of trust. Within this context, trust can be understood as embedded in, and also expressed through, tacit engagement in daily routines.[2] Trust then becomes part of the taken-for-grantedness that characterizes many of our daily practices. This is not necessarily 'blind trust' – trust that is without any foundation – because trust is typically being confirmed by experiences and the normative and institutional framing of the practices. Trust therefore includes both particular and conditional dimensions and unconditional, systemic dimensions (Cvetkovich and Löfstedt, 1999, 175). The conditional dimension is not easily explored using perspectives emphasizing shared norms and tacit, taken-for-granted routines. We will, therefore, in the next section consider some very different approaches, where conditionality is a core feature.

2.5 Trust and institutional performance

As opposed to theories of trust emphasizing norms and routines, which Mishler and Rose (2001) call 'cultural' theories, so-called 'institutional' theories propose that trust is derived from institutional and political performance.[3] Trust hinges on citizen evaluations of institutional performance. Institutions that perform well generate trust, while those that perform badly generate scepticism and distrust. Institutional theories seem to deny a direct causal relationship between the development of interpersonal trust, on the one hand, and institutional trust on the other. Trust in institutions is rationally based, and most contributions within this tradition seem to be founded in a rational choice perspective, thus emphasizing the role of rational calculation of self-interest (Coleman, 1990; Mishler & Rose, 2001; Rothstein, 2000; Sztompka, 1999). This approach anticipates that variations in national levels of trust will be associated with the satisfactory performance of particular institutions (typically measured as economic performance or degrees of transparency/levels of corruption), either as an aggregate output or as individual experiences. A number of useful studies have explained trust as a result of satisfaction with the performance of political and regulatory institutions (Kaase, 1999; Klingemann and Fuchs, 1995; Levi and Stoker, 2000; Listhaug and Wiberg, 1995; Miller and Listhaug, 1998).

However, trust is not always limited to a matter of acceptance of outcomes. It may also be an effect of participation. Trust links citizens to regulatory bodies that are intended to govern on their behalf, and thereby enhances the legitimacy and effectiveness of governance (Hardin, 2001). But this does not imply that political distrust necessarily has the opposite effect. Scepticism is assumed to have a constructive role in democracy, in the sense of requiring sufficient evidence or reasons for trusting (Braithwaite and Levi, 1998). The conditional character of citizens' trust may be accepted as a part of a legitimate democratic framework, and does not necessarily contest governance. People *should* question the performance of politicians and governmental bodies, and a healthy scepticism is a prerequisite to democracy (Sztompka, 1999). But scepticism which gives way to distrust can also be subversive to governance. Where distrust affects the legitimacy of existing institutional arrangements, governance itself becomes contested. Distrust can also become a problem for governance; for example, when it leads to non-productive increase in government regulations as a means of building or regaining trust (Majone, 1999).

Cultural and institutional theories are often presented as mutually exclusive explanations of trust, but their opposition should not be exaggerated, as indicated by the point made above about varying roles of distrust. Some empirical studies suggest that while cultural explanations may be important under stable conditions marked by general consensus about values and solutions, explanations related to the performance of specific institutions are needed for an understanding of trust under conditions of turbulence and social change. Social networks may also come to have more importance when institutional trust fails on a general basis (Guseva and Rona-Tas, 2001; Völker and Flap, 2001). But even under more stable conditions, evaluations of performance cannot be seen only as a rational consideration of self-interest. On the one hand, there are variations across sectors and countries that suggest considerable path dependency, where institutional performance is part of a comprehensive, dynamic process embedded in a cultural and historical setting (Rothstein, 2000). On the other hand, norms, resources and skills developed within personal social networks may influence the ways in which interaction with formal organizations is experienced and handled, thus being mutually reinforcing. So, structural and cultural frames influence both how institutional actors operate and how people relate to, and react upon, them.

Cultural and institutional explanations refer to different social mechanisms for the generation of trust. Culturally based trust, developed outside the formal spheres of markets and politics, will be less affected by poor performance of institutions and therefore less directly conditional. This is relevant in our case through the institutionalization of food consumption. Trust derived from institutional performance may be more volatile and sensitive, as trust will vary according to evidences of success and failure of public performance in a much more specific way. In the next section we will take a closer look at food institutions and consider how changes in the food sector which affect relations with consumers have implications for the fluctuating, conditional facets of trust. These different mechanisms point to different sources, different dynamics and different roles of distrust. But, as suggested above, they cannot be completely separated. High levels of culturally founded trust can represent an effective buffer against negative responses to instances of institutional failure. Yet, this generalized high trust can hardly be sustained if institutional performance is continually inadequate. Likewise, generalized distrust in other people and in institutions will be a major obstacle to the development of trust in particular organizations and institutional procedures.

2.6 Institutionalized relationships of trust

It would seem, therefore, that it is necessary to consider both learned habits and organizational performance in order to understand the social sources of trust in food. In both instances trust is mediated through other actors. The consumer, as an individual, has no control over the qualities of the food offered for sale, beyond a capacity to select among goods available in the market-place. From the consumer point of view, he or she, most of the time, trusts or distrusts some*one* rather than some*thing* (Kjærnes, 1999). Trust inheres in the relationships between actors. There are many relevant actors, including scientists, mass media, and so on, but the most immediate from the point of view of the consumer, the retailer, is probably the most important. We therefore pay particular attention to trust in the exchange relationship.

The consumer at the point of market exchange has, first and foremost, to trust the provisioning system and the actors inhabiting that system. Because the consumer has less power than the organizations providing food, judging the latter trustworthy generally requires shared, or at least clear, norms and expectations, as well as the ability and competence of the latter to meet those expectations. This is then not simply a matter of knowledge and information, but also of the reliable delegation of practical control. This delegation requires the existence of trust. It is necessary that other actors assume and comply with certain responsibilities. In such a situation, the consumer must be clear about what those responsibilities are, and that these other actors are competent and capable in their capacities to meet those responsibilities. A social division of responsibilities is a key feature of any set of impersonal trust relations. Trust emerges from the establishment of social responsibilities and their fulfilment in practice. Where this occurs, one often finds non-reflective reproduction of trust which delivers, relatively efficiently, other benefits too. Failing performance, by contrast, may lead to trust being questioned.

Trust is not always relevant, but does facilitate interaction in situations where an actor lacks control, where the outcome is not fixed, or where information is incomplete. This lack of control refers not merely to imbalances of knowledge and information, but as much to material outcomes, to lack of practical predictability and reliability. We depend on others to supply us with food, but the interactions with them will mean that we lack control in many respects. Food is a basic necessity, but potentially a serious health hazard. Moreover, food is very important as part of our everyday lives and has many facets and ramifications, thus raising other issues, such as those related to quality, taste and economy, as well as a number of wider normative and social concerns related to proper conduct, including fairness, cultural values, animal welfare, environmental issues and the like. Controversy and lack of control may be associated with all of these aspects. Its multi-dimensionality makes food different from many other commodities.

Seligman, among others, observes that uncertainties and lack of control may be overcome by the simple reliance on the ordered workings of existing institutional arrangements (Seligman, 1997, 25). Referring to Luhmann (1988), he characterizes this as 'confidence' in a system and its institutions, that is the continued functioning of patterned, normative role expectations (ibid., p. 20). One basic condition for consumer trust must be that the supplier will live up to shared norms and expectations regarding the activities for which the supply side should be responsible. It is important to notice that such norms and expectations cannot be understood as individual preferences on personal value hierarchies. Rather, these are genuinely social constructs, embedded in institutionalized practices. Reputation, based on the iteration of ordinary routine activities, becomes the basis for new or enforced expectations and hence for confidence in the system of interacting activities. Predictability is therefore important. Economists see organization processes (as opposed to personal relations) as a way of reducing uncertainty, leading to less reliance on trust (Guseva and Rona-Tas, 2001). To the consumer, organization may improve predictability and thus form a foundation for tacit and generalized trust relations. This does not remove, however, the consumer's basic underlying lack of power and control. Any market exchange between suppliers and consumers is characterized by asymmetries of power and information which invariably favour the former. That the supplier will conform to consumer expectations cannot be taken for granted. Suppliers depend on selling food so there is always the possibility of misuse of power. Institutional arrangements therefore often include various forms of social control and sanctioning, including regulation, which may serve to ensure reliable performance.

Trust will also be called upon, perhaps to an even greater degree, when this implicit and tacit mutuality of norms and expectations does not pertain, either because shared norms and expectations are not established or because the acts, the character or intentions of the other cannot be confirmed. If organizations are very dynamic, new technologies are incessantly introduced, and responsibilities are continually shifting, standards and expectations may need to be rapidly and repeatedly revised. In addition, it may not be clear to whom these expectations should be directed. This is, as we continue to argue, not necessarily a matter of individual uncertainty and worry, but it may imply that standards and relations are, at a social level, more open and subject to debate.

Ongoing changes in the European food sector have features that may both strengthen and challenge the foundations of trust. Integration, management systems and technological innovations can improve predictability and efficiency, thus supplying foods at a lower price, of a predictable quality, in a wider selection, and with lower risks for unintended (but known) safety hazards. On the other hand, many of the changes imply shifts in power and distribution of responsibilities, such as integration of markets along the food chain, more concentrated ownership structures, global sourcing and the like. The number and types of economic agents involved in interdependent exchanges is large and changing, including different types of retail outlet, food processors (branded and supermarket own-label), distributors, logistics, packaging, marketing, seed growing, farmers, agricultural services, technology experts, auditors, marketing consultants, and so on (Harvey and Randles, 2002; Lyon, 1998; Busch, 2000). The complexities of technologies and provisioning systems pose problems of understanding, such that consumers may not be convinced that their interests are sufficiently protected.

New and wider social issues are also being brought up. This is illustrated by the debate on genetically modified foods. But this debate also shows how normative and trust-related questions raised by institutional change depend on the social and political context. While American consumers saw this as relatively routine technological improvements, the framing of the European debate has been that this new technology is challenging the institutional order and thus also raising the issue of trust (Bruce, 2002; Pollack and Shaffer, 2000). While scepticism has referred directly to consequences for consumer health, a number of other issues have also been prominent, such as environmental effects, economic power, and consequences for Third World countries (Isserman, 2001; Powell, 2000). The debate eventually also came to consider the role and involvement of consumers as actors in policy formulation and implementation on both sides of the Atlantic (Barling and Lang, 1999; Light et al., 2003). In Europe, the issue escalated in such a way that it raised many questions about the organization of the food system.

Changes such as these have led some to argue for the emergence of new forms of trust. Giddens states that moderns forms of interaction require 'a leap into uncertainty' (1991). The extent to which trust is actively and reflexively attributed to actors is a source of considerable debate. It is a standard refrain of supporters of the reflexive individualization thesis (for example, Beck, Giddens and Lash, 1994, among many others) that Western populations have become more sceptical, less deferential, less trusting of authority, more likely to feel that it is their own responsibility to make decisions about their personal actions, commitments and careers. In such circumstances they are less likely to simply tacitly and routinely trust other actors to behave in accordance with their own or the general interest. For this purpose, several of the theories of trust have pointed to the importance of a type of trust which is more consciously and actively negotiated. Giddens coins the term 'active trust' to indicate a condition where trustworthiness is no longer taken for granted, but has to be actively argued and demonstrated (1994). Without the same emphasis on individualization and reflexivity, Seligman (1997) and Luhmann (1979, 1988) are also concerned with the instability, complexity and uncertainty of modern societies. They suggest that changes in modern societies represent a development from 'confidence' to 'trust', where reliable forecasts of consequences cannot be made (Luhmann, 1979, 25) and circumstances necessitate stronger belief in the goodwill of the other (Seligman, 1997, 41).

We take the view that a more parsimonious and economical vocabulary is sufficient and that the impression of the apparent newness, or much greater prevalence, of 'active trust' can be accounted for, in the field of the food system, by appreciating the development of new procedures and institutions for reassuring consumers. For while it may be the case that in mutual and reciprocal personal relationships there is an important element of negotiation that is worthy of the designation of the construction of 'active trust', the degree of inequality of power and control between provider and individual customer is such that the relationship cannot be well described as a form of negotiation. Certainly, the retailer does not have to trust the customer. The relationship is the very antithesis of the 'pure' type that Giddens depicts as coming to predominate in intimate personal relationships. Nor is the situation like that required in a business context between agents seeking a contract whether across firm boundaries or between colleagues (Deakin and Michie, 1997; Sako, 1992; Bijlsma, Frankema and Costa, 2005).

Many ongoing controversies in the area of food are associated with the establishment of the legitimacy of institutions and organizations, including systems of quality and safety assurance, a proliferation of independent audit systems, traceability and transparency, and new forms of consumer representation (Busch, 2000; Jacobsen and Kjærnes, 2003; Lyon, 1998). These are institutional solutions that aim at keeping imbalances of power and information in check. They are techniques for allaying consumer anxiety, dealing with suspicion or scepticism about the quality of food supplied. In more general terms, they may be characterized as 'institutionalisation of distrust' (Braithwaite, 1998; Levi and Stoker, 2000). This usage seems to be in accordance with Luhmann's even more abstract use of the same term (Luhmann, 1979). It must be emphasized that this may not be an even, predictable or consensual process. To the contrary, changes and institutional responses depend on the interests of, and power relations between, actors, on how the food system is organized, on how problems of distrust have been solved in the past, and so on. Therefore, we expect negotiations and balancing of values, interests and responsibilities to be handled very differently across settings. Ultimately, this is not only a question of defining and framing food issues, but also about control over food, and how people's lack of control (*qua* consumer or citizen) is handled institutionally when conditions change.

2.7   Determinants of trust in institutionalized arrangements

Different forms of trust have largely been identified by reference to macro-level modernization processes and temporal change (see, for example, Giddens, 1994; Luhmann, 1988; Seligman, 1997). A distinction is often made, as do we, between trust involved in personal or network-based relations, on the one hand, and trust involved in interactions with impersonal and formal organizations, on the other. Both forms emphasize stability and shared norms and expectations, but the character of the relationship means that these are established in distinctly different ways. Importantly, questions of the balance of power and information are very different.

Different types of social relationships and attendant forms of trust produce different kinds of normativity and rationality (Salvatore and Sassatelli, 2004) and different divisions of responsibilities. At one extreme, trust may be founded on the particular, network-based personal relations of the local community shop. We characterize this as 'familiarity' (re Seligman and Luhmann). Such a relationship between shopkeeper and customer will be built on a wide and versatile set of mutual obligations based on personal knowledge, experience and local networks. The imbalances of power and information will be limited, instead mutual dependencies are emphasized. As production and distribution is small-scale and not standardized, the relation is based on trust in the person's direct engagement in the network. Trust is associated with particularity, small-scale and limited distances of food provision in time and space. It will probably also be linked to consumption habits and culinary systems that are based on fresh foods, low degrees of industrial processing and home cooking, and a selection limited to what these local provisioning systems can provide.[4]

In general, functioning trust relationships based on personal networks in this basic form are rare within West European food-provisioning systems, which in most cases involve at least some degree of impersonal, formalized relationships (in the distribution chain, through regulatory interventions, etc.). Personal network-based relations are typically associated with very different forms of markets from those which now predominate in this part of the world (Lyon, 1998). We will therefore suggest that references to particular personal relations and distribution networks today mainly represent a reaction to a breakdown in impersonal trust in formal public and market institutions (Guseva and Rona-Tas, 2001; Völker and Flap, 2001). When people are generally distrustful of institutional actors and institutionalized solutions, one option is to search for much more particular and personal forms of interaction, with fewer imbalances in power and information and more emphasis on mutual dependency (Kjærnes, 1999). One may also find references to such localized or familiarized relations in the building of institutional identity, promoting a local region or particular sets of values (Murdoch and Miele, 1999; Salvatore and Sassatelli, 2004). Examples like the Slow Food movement and farmers' markets may, at least in part, be interpreted as attempts to emphasize the mutuality of norms and expectations within non-personal larger systems, perhaps as an alternative, or merely an addition to more formalized, institutionalized procedures of standardization and surveillance.

In contrast to trust associated with personal exchange, formalized organization represents the major mechanism for establishing contemporary trust in food. We characterize trust in institutions and institutionalized procedures as 'confidence'. Organizational efforts with the aim of ensuring predictability can form the basis for routinized and tacit consumer trust in increasingly impersonal and complex food institutions. This implies more reliance on generalized symbols, such as brands, generic labels, country or region of origin, and so on. These may lay the foundation for a non-contingent aspect of trust, trust in the institutionalization processes as such. In general, the *capability* of markets and regulators to produce predictability and shared symbols seems to vary, with important elements of competence and learning, as indicated, for example, by the unstable situation in the Russian food market (Berg et al., 2005). Earlier in this chapter, we contended that for buyers and eaters of food, organization does not replace trust, but instead implies different forms or qualities of trust. Impersonal, institutionalized relations also have to be based on assumptions tested by experience,[5] in situations where asymmetries of power and information may be very large. Contrary to the situation of personal networks, you need to trust a large number of unidentifiable strangers (Seligman, 1997; Shapiro, 1987). The trust relation must be general and impersonal. Inherent possibilities of limiting information and misuse of power may give rise to scepticism (Shapiro, 1987). This is not a recent issue. Extensions of markets have usually been accompanied by particular institutional solutions to ensure and demonstrate predictability and adherence to shared norms and expectations. A number of efforts made by corporate market actors can be perceived as serving such functions, such as branding and labelling, traceability, declarations of corporate social responsibility, and so on. In an unchallenged and consensual situation, this may work perfectly well. However, the situation can also be more contentious and the interpretation and prioritization of norms and expectations may become subject to controversy. What is expected and acceptable and what is not? Evaluations will inevitably be very complex. Moreover, businesses are, for competitive reasons, typically rather closed organizations. How can uncertain and sceptical consumers be convinced that the outcome is acceptable, and make them confident that they will be neither poisoned nor cheated?

The problem – and need – of signalling 'honest intent' or 'good faith' and acceptable performance is significant, often involving other institutional actors, such as control bodies, special interest organizations, experts and the media. The fundamental importance of third party involvement is shown throughout history, closely associated with the expansion of food markets from very early on, as intrinsic parts of processes of institutionalization (Coppin and High, 1992; Elvbakken, 1997; French and Phillips, 2000). In a stable situation, where such an institutional order is in place, negotiating and balancing norms and expectations and making clear divisions of responsibilities between various actors, supports the establishment of a certain mutual understanding. Market arrangements demonstrating clear standards, reliability and predictability, together with third-party audits and/or public and stakeholder involvement capable of promoting transparency and verification can provide a basis for considerable generalization of trust relations and, in turn, for the routinization of consumption – even when relations and the food selection are very complex.

We expect to find that trust relations are institutionalized in different ways in different countries and for various food items and issues, referring to specific normative expectations and social distributions of responsibilities. Institutional solutions are, therefore, context specific. Problems may, however, arise when consensus is not achieved and when powerful actors systematically fail to meet expectations. Apart from poor performance, there may be ongoing mismatches in expectations as well as upheavals and crises of legitimacy. As already noted, the changing character and increasing complexity of food-provisioning systems present new challenges. Among other things, this is reflected in the proliferation of internal and external control and audit systems.

2.8   Forms of institutionalization and forms of trust in contemporary food markets

Drawing together the main threads of our theoretical orientation, we intend to interpret evidence about variations in trust in Europe by using a social and relational, rather than a cognitive and individual, analytic framework. To do this we pay particular attention to processes of institutionalization, by which we mean the process of establishment and reproduction of rules, shared norms and expectations which facilitate the coordination of activities across relevant populations. Two types of institutional explanations of trust are separated out which emphasize the importance of socially embedded, practical routines of consumption and the performance of political and administrative organizations. We judge that both are relevant; but their relative importance is an empirical question which we will address in due course. However, their inter-relationship is equally important, for it is to be expected that patterns of consumer behaviour will respond in part to processes of regulation and, vice versa, that regulatory frameworks will be constructed in the light of particular patterns of consumption.

To analyse this inter-relationship, we begin from the view that trust in food is primarily the result of trust in pertinent and particularly powerful actors involved in its production, delivery and regulation. The conditions for trust and distrust in food depend on the character and functioning of a complex of relationships – in the market-place, in public regulations, and in civil society and public discourse – and on the interdependency between these arenas. It is assumed that different systems of provision, regulatory regimes and patterns of consumption will provide distinctly different roles of consumers and forms and levels of consumer trust. To capture these features we focus on processes of institutionalization within particular organizational, political and cultural settings in which the whole configuration of actors and their inter-relations are played out. Any one aspect, or any particular actor, cannot be understood in isolation from the rest.

Our focus on institutionalization directs attention towards stable, cultural elements of trust, expressed through norms and routinized practices as well as formal organizations, distribution of responsibilities and power relations. The conditional, more specific and performance-related elements must not be ignored, however. Trust and mistrust ebb and flow in response to events and interventions. This conditionality can in its turn result in new forms of institutionalization, like procedures to ensure transparency, third-party audits, representation, regulatory arrangements to check power imbalances, and so on. But conditionality is also manifest through public attention, mobilization and protest, as suggested in more institutional approaches to trust. These elements play out differently depending on the types of inter-relations and thus help to understand and analyse various forms of trust.

In this chapter we have argued that trust is not merely a self-regulatory device of the social system. Nor can it be reduced to a 'public good' consciously to be engineered – especially when 'the engineers' may be as much part of the problem as of its solution. Variations in institutionalization processes which generate trust are based upon strong cultural and normative foundations as well as depending upon specific organizational procedures and decisions. These develop in complex and path-dependent ways, the outcomes not only forming distinct social and relational references for trust in food, but also providing differing capabilities for producing consensus and generalized trust and to handle re-emerging problematic events and conflicts. Lack of trust may appear in different ways: as a generic feature expressing generalized distrust in food institutions which, if severe, may be accompanied by feelings of powerlessness and insecurity, or, if less severe, may be reflected in intermittent reactions, like shifts in demand. But distrust may be more systematically expressed and cultivated, providing a basis for action by the consumer (or, more precisely, by the public in relation to its role in consumption), like complaints, boycotts or forms of political action, which may generate new, perhaps less generalized trust relations in the market. The recognition of emerging distrust, and the needs for specific forms of its institutionalization, represent a reaction to the claims of consumers. Thus distrust may form an important basis for generalized, but at the same time dynamic and conditional, forms of consumer reassurance which can be considered to be productive and positive.

We contend that not only will the degree of trust vary between countries, but so will its types. Recent social theories of trust, especially when illustrated in accounts at the level of entire societies, have tended to distinguish three types of trust. Although different terms are used by different theorists, there is a common rationale behind making distinctions between familiarity, confidence and 'active' or 'reflexive' trust. While familiarity relies on particular personal networks, confidence refers to (more or less abstract and general) institutions and institutional procedures, We have indicated our scepticism, at least in relation to trust in food, about the value of a third type, whose importance tends to be emphasized in accounts like those of risk society or late modernity which postulate that the nature of risk, or the conditions for institutional legitimacy, have altered significantly in the last two or three decades. Our scepticism is grounded in several observations. *First*, it exaggerates the role of individuals and reflexivity in the establishment and reproduction of the fundamental core of everyday trust in people and procedures without which the pursuit of everyday life would be immeasurably more difficult than it appears to be across Europe. *Second*, distrust in the conditions under which food is produced and provided is in no way a novel feature of the contemporary period. It would require to be shown that distrust had substantively and fundamentally different origins now than in the past, an issue which would entail a historical interpretation of earlier protests and controversies of which we are unconvinced. *Third*, notions of reflexive trust potentially misread the processes of repair of trust after crises, processes for the reconstitution of trust. *Fourth*, increased institutionalization, if providing clarity and predictability, may also improve the conditions for producing confidence instead of new, more active forms of trust. *Finally*, and a rather weaker claim, but one absolutely central in relation to consumer trust in food, the mechanisms by which active trust is established and reproduced are accounted for through negotiation and monitoring of agents who are engaged in mutual and reciprocal relationships. In the case of the consumer as an individual, there is no reciprocity. The consumer must trust other powerful actors, but there is no requirement for the latter to trust the former.

Instead, we believe that we can operate adequately with the more economical distinction between familiarity and confidence, providing that we pay sufficient attention to the processes by which trust is reconstituted, in the context of episodes of contestation or potential crises of legitimacy, as with BSE for example. This is a process of re-institutionalization, which may involve reform of procedures, reallocation of responsibilities or establishment of new organizations, in response to distrust. We characterize this as a phase of 'reassurance'.

What might be new about the current conjuncture are new ways of responding to distrust via its institutionalization. In other words, the reconstitution of trust may now be achieved primarily through the establishment of new arrangements designed precisely to allay public distrust through explicit acknowledgement that there can be many grounds on which consumers may rationally doubt the trustworthiness of powerful actors in the food system. This process of institutionalization of distrust is the hallmark of recent reforms of the European food regime.

In sum, the provisional conceptual framework presented in this chapter has identified different types of macro-level explanations of varying levels of trust, distinguishing basically between cultural and performance related conditions. In the empirical analyses to follow, we will use these as complementary explanations, which potentially play varying roles in different institutional settings. We have also distinguished between two main forms of trust. These forms may coexist, the balance between them depending on the character of institutionalized relationships between actors and which combine into particular configurations which can schematically be represented as three major arenas; the provisioning system, consumers and regulatory arrangements. We seek to illustrate the utility and validity of these concepts by providing an empirical account of the variations in, and dynamics of, consumer trust in food.

3
Enquiring into Trust: Some Methodological Considerations

Our research project was devised to explore the basis and dynamics of trust in food in a context where the BSE crisis had pushed issues of food safety high up the political agenda in Europe. The prevailing ethos was one in which political authorities, but also market actors, perceived an erosion of confidence among consumers that food being produced and sold was safe to eat. Those in positions of power thought the consumers' fears, if not entirely groundless, much exaggerated; and irrespective of the real circumstances, considered it an urgent priority that trust should be restored. How that might be done depended partly on understanding how trust in food ebbs and flows. The main scholarly view, as described in Chapter 2, approached the matter in terms of changing perceptions of risk in the modern world and how these affected the behaviour of individuals, but we were unpersuaded that this was a plausible way of understanding variations in trust. It seemed to us that trust in food was based on much broader considerations than simply safety, and that an adequate account would have to pay much greater attention to the institutional context in which action occurred and opinions were formed.

In order to explore the impacts of institutional context on trust in food, we applied a comparative approach. We did this by recording variations in trust using population surveys and studying social and institutional contexts in six European countries (and at the EU level).[1] This, however, posed some methodological difficulties, associated with obtaining satisfactory explanations of variation through cross-national comparison of institutions where we had relatively few (six) cases. Our resolution of those difficulties involved unorthodox approaches to the understanding of public opinion, the linking of quantitative and qualitative evidence, and the character of explanations of national variation. Our study was, thus, exploratory. In the absence of systematic institutional analysis in this area we could not be certain which were the key factors in explaining trust, resulting in our collecting potentially relevant information across a wide canvass and subsequently sifting the data to identify hypotheses about causal processes.

In this chapter, after a presentation of the general outline of the study (Section 3.1), we discuss (Section 3.2) some of the general consideration about the value of institutional explanation. Then we consider some more specific methodological issues associated with comparison of a small number of cases (Section 3.3). Finally, we describe briefly the technical aspects of the survey and institutional studies (Section 3.4).

3.1   The project

Our principal aim was to explain variations in popular trust in food by distinct processes of institutionalization, at the centre of which are inter-relations between consumers and other actors. To measure variations in trust, we elected to undertake a population survey. The social and institutional context was studied using documentary sources and interviews at both country and EU levels. The analysis seeks to integrate survey data about how consumers perceive and handle challenges to trust and distrust in the course of their routines of everyday life with qualitative data at institutional level about the conditions for the production and maintenance of trust. This entailed a triangulation of data collection methods and multi-level comparative analyses.

At the onset of the project, focus was directed primarily towards food safety. However, it was soon realized that the scope needed to be wider. Starting to identify debates and conflicts which may be associated with consumer trust in food, these could not be delimited clearly to food safety, and nor did the issue of 'food safety' mean one and the same thing in the various countries included. Consumer trust and distrust needed to be analysed in relation to a variety of issues associated with food, food marketing and public discourse. We focused on five 'key food issues': safety, nutrition, quality, ethics and value for money. All are independent aspects of concern around which consumer trust wavers. As the aim has been to capture the variety and multi-dimensionality of trust in food, the contents of these issues have been treated as a matter of empirical observation rather than as a matter of definition.

In Chapter 2, we argued that trust is fundamentally a property of relationships between actors. It is likely to be an emergent property of ongoing relationships between partners where the partnership can be seen to be directed towards one or more concrete objectives. In the case of food, the objectives of commercial enterprises may be profit, of government the safe supply of food to the population. For the consumer, objectives will include access to food that is safe, nutritious, fair value for money, consistent, tasty, and so on. Trust could be seen as an expectation, a practical confidence, that other relevant actors in the food system will behave in such a way as to ensure that these objectives are met. In fact, the consumer might trust a particular retailer on some of these grounds, but not others. The main point is that it is actors who have to be trusted or mistrusted. Trust is thus a strand, or a dimension, of a relationship between actors. In this regard, the consumer is seen not as an atomistic individual, but as a social collectivity sharing some common norms and expectations, like shoppers in the supermarket or the small greengrocer, with consequential differences concerning the nature and scale of the trust relationships.

We consider that eight key categories of agent or agency are centrally involved in contemporary food systems in Europe: farmers, manufacturers, retailers, consumers, governments, food scientists, consumer organizations and mass media. Each of these actors is configured differently from country to country, and the differences will be greater or smaller between case studies. For example, the retailing system will exhibit different levels of concentration of firms, size of outlet, relationships between small and large organizations, amount of farm-gate sales, and so on. The differences between England and Scotland will be less than for England and Norway. Equally important, consumers are configured differently, in terms of their relative wealth, their culinary tastes, the level of food education, and any dietary recommendations they have been exposed to. Probably more important, there will be differences in terms of the organizations that claim to speak for them, whether they be quangos like SIFO in Norway or independent associations like the Consumers Association in the United Kingdom, and the social movements that mobilize around the quality of food, from the Slow Food Movement in Italy to the Vegetarian Society and the Soil Association in Britain.

Food systems are not coterminous with national boundaries, but for purposes of analysing trust relationships we can identify them in terms of jurisdictions of regulation; that is, those geographical spaces which are governed by the same laws. There are several spatial levels relevant to this account: global, EU, national states, and regional and local levels of decision-making. They are distinct because there are different sets of rules and regulations, and of official authoritative organizations, which frame and regulate the conduct of food production, manufacture/processing, distribution and retailing.

Relationships between actors also vary from country to country. For example, the power of the large supermarkets has increased greatly in the United Kingdom in the last quarter of a century to the extent where they now hold the greatest power and influence within the British food chain. They exert very considerable control over the activities of farming, processing and distribution, activities which were previously more autonomous. In so doing, however, they now assume a greater social responsibility for risks. Thus, as wholesale markets for food have declined, along with the small grocery store, so too did the divided and dispersed assumption of risk and narrow focus for trust. If farmers grow crops and animals to the specifications of the supermarkets, rather than take produce to market, and processors produce packaged foods bearing the brand name of the supermarket, the social locus of trust and assumption of responsibility of risk shifts. Methodologically, therefore, it is important to consider every relationship between each of these eight actors in every 'system' that we explore. Trust relationships of various sorts exist between all these actors. Some of these are tacit, some are contractual being based on written or informal contracts, some are the result of, and are reproduced through, personal connections, and so on. The relationships between these agents may also include ones of competition, conflict, cooperation, alliance, mutual constraint and reciprocal influence, and the like. 'Trust', what it consists of, how it might be identified, how it might be experienced as a feature of a social relationship, may itself differ between countries. Differential national experiences may lead to different criteria being used to attribute trustworthiness to actors and to some types of trust being more valued than others. As an effect of conflicts between different agencies, some criteria will confer legitimacy on the actors relevant to them, while casting doubt on the probity of other actors.

We explore systematically different national configurations of these eight actors and their inter-relationships. Consumers and governments vest responsibilities for the creation and monitoring of conditions for trust in different institutional arrangements. Degrees of separation between regulatory agencies and the food industry, systems of accountability between different actors, and the distribution of social responsibility for risk between actors are likely to be key aspects of variation in trust. Levels of commoditization of food also involve shifts in the distribution of social responsibility for risk. For example, whether food preparation (washing, cooking, preserving, etc.) is undertaken in the household or not will significantly affect the range over which trust is distributed between different actors. As we developed our analysis, we focused particularly on actors grouped under three relational poles: consumers, market actors and state actors.

The project concentrates upon relationships involving trust between consumers and the others. Whilst it is clear that relations between the other seven actors can also involve many of the dimensions of trust outlined above (governments and farmers, retailers and manufacturers, etc.), and would be worthy objects of analysis in their own right, our primary questions are which of these actors do consumers consider to be trustworthy, in what respects, and with regard to what sphere of action and influence? Different types of institutional relationship between consumers and other agents lead to different types and levels of trust in different societal configurations. By approaching trust as an emergent property of extended social relations the question is automatically raised of how their judgments about trustworthiness developed over time, and what were the principal influences on the formation of judgment. Institutional arrangements or configurations develop over time. They have a trajectory, a developmental path, the determinants of which can be identified and described. In a food system, the various agencies will each have their own particular paths of development resulting from both their own internal logic and their external relations with each other. The resulting dynamic configuration will be different from case to case. Among the consequences are, in some sense, unique configurations of trust relationships and possibly distinctive understandings and thresholds of trust. One major challenge is therefore to depict such configurations in their specificity.

It is particularly important to find ways of describing differences in the social constitution of consumers over time, and between countries. Whilst this proves difficult, the major methodological flaw to be avoided is to assume that consumers have remained the same, whilst all around them institutions have changed. In our assembly of eight actors, the changing nature of the trusters has to be considered alongside the changing nature of the trusted. Shopping patterns, commoditization of food and the nature of the food commodities consumed are amongst the characteristics employed to characterize institutional differences and changes in consumers, along with the ways in which consumers protest, mobilize and are represented.

Trust and distrust are affected by the occurrence and handling of food crises. The type and scale of distrust generated by a crisis is related to the institutional context of the risk and the distribution of social responsibilities and competences in relation to risk and risk reduction. Crises, in this sense, are as much a property of trust configurations and related to

systems of food provision, which in turn can provide the basis for institutional change, along with the restructuring of institutional trust relations and systems of food provision. Thus, in the case of BSE, several of
the main actors and their inter-relations were placed in question: the use
by farmers of animal protein for cattle feed; the regulatory regimes and
deregulation of safety standards; the competence of science, especially
in the face of new unknowns; the nature of food processing and the use
of animal body parts for food, and so on. The fact that each of these
were generalized throughout the food system contributed to the scale of
the crisis, and the scale of the trust and distrust at stake.

Food scares, episodes of contestation, political mobilizations around
food issues are collective expressions of mistrust. By their nature, opinion surveys can only elicit responses from individuals. But, it would be
an error to infer from a feature of the method that the opinions of trust
and distrust are therefore only expressions of individuals – the methodological individualist illusion. The reasons for this are many, but they
include that the opinions captured in the survey will be only the
opinions of the day upon which the survey is administered, that survey
questions are unable to tap all relevant aspects of trust and concern, and
they may elicit answers to questions about which the respondent is
uninterested or has never reflected upon. But most of all, mistrust is an
emergent property arising from collective behaviour.

We employed a survey, therefore, in order to explore the distribution
of trust among consumers through questioning their opinions about
food issues. The findings show that consumers are not uniform in their
attitudes and opinions, neither within single countries nor across countries. For theoretical and narrative reasons, we use evidence from the
survey less as a means to understand and explain the attitudes of individuals, than as a means to characterize public opinion. We are at least
as interested in the fact that German public opinion is more strongly
divided than the British with respect to safety as in the precise number
of persons expressing concern. The balance of opinion matters more
than the distribution of personal convictions. We therefore pay particular attention to comparison of the national aggregates of responses to
survey questions. Trust is not so much a result of explicit individual
calculation of exposure to risk of malfeasance as it is a tacit emergent
product of quotidian routines and mass media circulation of news and
feature stories.

In addition, trust is evidenced as much by what people do as what
they think. It gives pause for thought that, given the popularity of burgers among fast foods, only 4 per cent of Europeans said that they were

'very safe'. Hence, our survey included questions about practice as well as attitudes, and we draw upon other types of source material to discover how people behave in particular circumstances.

It is not just that food scares are likely to make people more suspicious at a later time in new circumstances, though of course that is a plausible hypothesis, but that particular institutional configurations make collective expression of opposition, or media amplification of problems, more likely. Crises are inherent to food systems and the management of such crises are an element in the constitution of the system itself. In order to treat 'crises' such as BSE, foot and mouth disease, e-coli, and so on, as key to dynamics of change, and yet as not exogenous, they might be analysed in terms of engagements of each of the eight actors. In this respect, crises can be seen as significant in the development of societal norms of trust, where expectations of risk reduction are raised, responsibilities are more clearly differentiated, and accountability made more transparent, so that trust and distrust thresholds are changed. Crises are in historical perspective normal and, moreover, are central to the analyses of institutional change, both as precursors and as more or less direct consequences.

3.2 The nature of the comparative institutional method

We will show that the survey revealed national variation so great that it is impossible to imagine that the causes of trust in food are anything other than features of the institutional arrangements of the different societies. Such great variation in the responses of individuals cannot plausibly be attributed in their extent or their entirety to the socio-demographic characteristics of the populations, as was demonstrated by Poppe and Kjaernes (2003). Nor is it likely that it can be attributed to the distribution of psychological traits across countries. Institutions matter. Thus our approach concentrates on institutional causes, distinguishing our work from that of others who attempt to explain mistrust of food in terms of risk perception, rational calculation or availability of information.

The six countries were selected not only to ensure geographical variation. They also represent substantively different types of settings, relevant to the analyses of societal institutionalizations of the handling of food safety and necessary for making qualitative generalizations (Blaikie, 1993, 176–81). They represent countries with a strong welfare-state tradition as well as countries with more liberal traditions. They represent countries where the food sector is a major contributor to national income, and countries where its economic significance is less important. Finally, they represent countries where the food sector is highly competitive on the international market, and countries where the food sector is protected by national policies.

Our objective is to try to identify key characteristics of institutions and, subsequently, the relationships between institutions which affect levels of popular trust. Our procedure required that we simplify and codify those institutional characteristics by means of a systematic review of factors that are thought to affect trust in the six countries. Simplification is on the basis of expertise with those cases, and subsequent discussion between teams of researchers. We consider this method valuable because the bases of comparison and judgments about the characteristics of cases are made totally explicit and are available to critical scrutiny.

The terms 'institution', 'institutional' and 'institutionalized' are widely used and with varying connotations across the social sciences. In our usage, institutions and processes of institutionalization imply the stabilization of mutually recognized rules and resources for social interaction. In order to analyse the institutional changes in the handling of food issues in the different societal contexts, we look at different cases with complex configurations of relationships between actors. Three analytical themes were prominent – social responsibility for food issues, institutionalization of consumption, and institutionalization of distrust. The theme of *social distribution of responsibility for food issues* addresses interdependent institutionalizations between actors of ways of thinking, ways of acting, and ways of relating to each other on the basis of particular organizational and material resources. Analysing the distribution of responsibility between actors involves looking at connections and entanglements between private market provisioning patterns, public regulatory systems and civil society associations, and arrangements within households. The theme of *institutionalization of consumption* involves looking at the patterns of food consumption and dietary habits in the six countries, including issues such as provisioning practices, cooking traditions, education of consumers and media usage. The theme of *institutionalization of distrust* addresses consumers' active expression of distrust; for example, in the form of consumer organizations and individual consumer action. It also involves looking at strategic solutions to consumer distrust, such as institutional independence, transparency within food regulation, and institutional incorporation of consumer interests.

The institutional studies involved primary-data collection in the form of documentary analysis and key informant interviews and also analyses of secondary data. Secondary data for the case studies were official documents from public authorities, market actors and organizations in the food sector. In addition, legal documents, policy documents, reports, web pages and statistical information were also consulted. This material was supplemented with media-texts and also with open-ended qualitative interviews (McCracken, 1988) with representatives of seven types of actor in the food sector; namely, producers, manufacturers, retailers, consumers' organizations, public authorities, scientists and the mass media.

The aim of the qualitative interviews was to identify concerns and priorities among selected strategic actors in the food system and their perception of each other. This also gave access to the informal workings of the food system, which could not be learned from documentary analysis. An interview-guide was used in all studies, covering: respondents own perception of important food issues; routines, strategies and policies in relation to beef and tomatoes; interaction with other major actors (including consumers) in respect of the five key food issues; and safety and quality policies. In each country 15–20 interviews were conducted which were tape-recorded and transcribed verbatim.

The concrete analyses reflect the fact that not all issues have the same salience everywhere, and neither were the conditions for conducting the empirical research identical. Moreover, the availability and variety of written material about the topics addressed varied considerably. Descriptive analyses of the food systems in each country and at the EU level were conducted, covering the main characteristics of the national food policy systems, national food market and consumer institutionalization. The EU-level institutional mapping covered institutional set-up and change and recent political developments in EU food policies.[2]

Given the complexity of the object of comparison, our methodology of comparative institutional analysis combined several approaches, in particular the more holistic methodologies of the 'societal effect' school (Maurice, Sellier and Sylvestre, 1986; Maurice and Sorge, 2000a; Maurice, 2000) and the 'orders of worth' approach(Boltanski and Thévenot, 2006; Lamont and Thévenot, 2000) with Ragin's use of qualitative variables as a tool for systematizing and quantifying qualitative data (Ragin, 1987).

The difficulty is to substantiate causal inferences on the basis of the evidence that we have compiled for the six cases. The problem has been specified reasonably clearly in a relatively long-running methodological debate in the social scientific literature, particularly in historical and comparative sociology, about the merits of case-oriented relative to variable-oriented research. A principal champion of case-oriented research is

Charles Ragin (1987,1992, 1994, 1995, 1997), who has pioneered what he calls Qualitative Comparative Analysis (QCA), which represents an increasingly sophisticated way of dealing with problems of causal explanation in situations where there are too few instances in historical experience for the application of standard statistical techniques. The principles underlying case-oriented approaches were criticized, very clearly and in some detail, in an essay by John Goldthorpe (1997). The main problem is that case-oriented work is often indecisive with respect to causal claims because of what is referred to as 'the small-N problem'. There are many more causal factors than there are outcomes, and so never enough cases to inspect the many possible different potential causal combinations generating high or low trust. We therefore attempt to specify, and then to illustrate, a pragmatic set of procedures with which to deal with the small-N problem. These procedures amount to being as explicit as possible about the steps we have taken to be methodical in our comparative analysis and, through that transparency, to be clear about the limits of interpretations which we submit for critical review.

Our original resource data generated by the country research teams involved qualitative descriptions of the main aspects of national systems of food provision, regulation, and consumer behaviour. Furthermore, critical events and crises were identified with the purpose of understanding drivers for change in institutional arrangements, legislation, and the emergence of new social or media forces for change (Halkier and Holm, 2006 Reference to *Appetite* special issue). A parallel descriptive and analytical task was undertaken at the European level, along with the impacts of European change in institutional arrangements and legislation on national configurations, and vice versa. A level of systematization of empirical data gathering and reporting laid the initial grounds for comparison, and a holistic qualitative analysis of societal differences in the institutional bases of trust was retained. Following Ragin, the qualitative national empirical analysis was then further systematized, using variation on key dimensions concerning systems of food provision, regulatory and governmental institutional arrangements, and institutionalization of the consumer.[3] These are combined with key statistical data used as descriptors for qualitative differences.

This preparatory phase of data generation and systematization was essential for enabling subsequent comparisons, even if the method is largely hidden in the final analyses presented here. The method was one of generating comparable features for different national systems, with all their peculiarities. This involved 'deconstructing' the societal wholes into quasi-variables and then creating discriminatory features variable by variable, but only during the data organization phase. The aim for subsequent analysis was to avoid comparison on a term-by-term basis, criticized for its assumption that terms are equivalent or comparable across different societal contexts. The 'societal effect' school has argued forcefully that 'the reciprocal, interactive constitution of actors and spaces' (Maurice and Sorge, 2000b, 2), where spaces are defined by processes and relations between actors, has the implication for comparative methodology that any term (such as 'an actor', or 'a process', or 'a relation') is defined by its interconnectedness with others. These specific interconnectednesses produce 'patterns of coherence' and these are the proper objects of comparison, in order to reveal 'societal effect'.

> If there is no such thing as term-for-term comparability, it is through their location within a societal space that the analytical categories can acquire meaning, namely that inherent in their very specificity. (Maurice, 2000, 28)

But we cannot insist too much on the need to generate systematic data in order to be able to subsequently compare societal configurations of variables, rather than variable-by-variable comparison. A similar approach to comparative methodology is adopted by the 'grammars of worth' approach, where different cultural systems are seen to be generated by different evaluative and justificatory principles. The particular interest for this approach to the analysis of trust is that these justificatory or evaluative principles may be seen to bear similarities with different 'grammars of trust', such as the dimensions noted above. The evaluative principles proposed by Boltanski and Thévenot ('market performance', civic solidarity, domestic and familial, inspirational and creative, and public worthiness), are easily recognizable as possible generators of different types of trust. But, methodologically, the object of comparison that derives from this ontology becomes the holistic one of the widespread and interconnected adoption of these generative grammars, singly or in combination, by constellations of actors in a given society (Lamont and Thévenot, 2000).

Applying a Ragin method for the construction of structural variables to the national data, therefore, is initially intended to reveal 'patterns of coherence' within and between the three main domains identified for comparison within each society (systems of provision; institutionalization of the consumer; regulatory and governmental institutions). Developing and generating empirical institutional data using a combination of the Ragin structural variable method and the 'societal effect' approach involved three phases of data organization.

Step I involved calculating and characterizing the balance of opinion in each country on a topic and then identifying institutional variables to identify or impute its plausible causes. For example, when Norwegians and Danes say they consider most foods safe, the similarities of their shared social-democratic political traditions are more likely to be an explanation than their very different food trade policies. The reasoning is that if there is a direct or approximate match between the pattern exhibited across the cases of both a characteristic item and the outcome variable, then it might be deemed a hypothetical cause and explored further. If patterns do not coincide, then it is less likely, though not impossible, that such an item would contribute to a causal explanation and it can thus be eliminated from further inquiry.

It is difficult to construct a conclusive account of the differences between countries precisely because institutional forces combine together in a complex fashion to channel behaviour and opinion. It is not to be expected that we will ever find single powerful causes of variation in levels of trust. Examining descriptive associations, item by item, in search of the causal factors that influence popular trust in food across all the cases and domains studied, has its limitations. However, that exercise, which we might call a horizontal cut at the available institutional data, is a *necessary* stage in the process of developing a satisfactory explanation of variation. There are sufficient similarities in the institutions operating on each country, and similar functional requirements regarding the management of trust, to justify inquiring whether specific forms of organization – say centralization of responsibility, or concentration in the retail market – have similar effects across cases. The systematicity and the transparency of the procedures might increase confidence in such an exploration.

The second step, profile-building, by contrast, put the institutional country variables back together to generate a profile of the societal 'whole'. The assumption is that each country has a particular profile which comprises specific combination or configuration of features, giving each case its unique character and generating identifiable effects like the degree of confidence in a national population in food taken home, trust in the safety of beef, or perceptions of improvement or decline in the quality and taste of food. Profiles were constructed for each country separately, inferring the importance of the component or constituent factors from comparison with other countries, but with the integrity of the institutions of each country asserted and posited as a real basis of the identifiable emergent effects. This is to follow closely the maxims of Maurice and Sorge (2000a,b) regarding the potential error associated with term-for-term comparability.

To construct a profile, relevant aspects of the three component elements of our theoretical model of relationships between societal actors – the institutionalization of consumers, provisioning system, and state regulatory systems – were compiled country by country. These were then put them together to describe the anatomy of the overall configuration of each country, discussing how each of the three component relationships are articulated together, and how the operation of, say, the regulatory system is intermeshed with features of the institutionalized consumer.[4] The effect is to identify the key structural features of each country, to describe their articulation and thereby to derive some explanation of emergent effects. This procedure has contributed to a powerful form of understanding of each case individually.

As acknowledged above, it is just not possible with only six cases to demonstrate statistically the power of particular causal factors. The profiles presume that institutional variables are better at characterizing both the integrity of each societal case and the basis of the differences between cases, thus implicitly suggesting the causal relevance of particular factors. In *the third step* we return to refine our understanding of the component elements that support the configurational accounts of country profiles, looking more systematically to see whether some causal factors are particularly important. We bear in mind that, as Maurice and Sorge caution, term-by-term comparison may be misleading. But it will not necessarily or always be so, because some processes and forces impact in common across the cases. On the basis of observations that countries more dependent upon supermarkets exhibit higher levels of trust, for example, we can begin to found an account of the causal mechanisms underlying trust.

Methodologies for projects like ours, with a relatively small number of cases (common in the research portfolio of the EU), mean that statistically grounded causal analysis is generally not the optimal technique (Mahoney, 2004). We require, instead, another type of systematic and methodical approach, rather than an intuitive or implicit one, to identify institutional factors that can serve as a basis for a narrative causal account. The step-by-step deconstruction and reconstruction provided a useful tool for eliminating unsatisfactory causal accounts based on considering correspondences between the outcome variables that are to be explained and institutional factors. It is a technique or tool for organizing qualitative comparison. It can be used over data of any kind, statistical and documentary. It is an unparalleled way of using team expertise from different countries to work on individual cases. There are benefits from this collaborative approach that could not be generated by solo or one-country based comparative research.[5]

3.3   The quantitative survey empirical approach

Studying trust, it is important to get a picture of public opinions. Giving priority to comparing countries rather than conducting extended analyses of social variation within a particular national context, we aimed for representativity and standardization rather than open design. We used CATI –that is, Computer-Assisted Telephone Interviews – as it provided standardized, monitored interview conditions and sufficiently representative samples. We settled on sample sizes from each country that allowed for satisfactory precision in conventional statistical methods applied in the social sciences. Following a pilot study, the data were collected during November and December 2002. The target for these surveys was the population between 18 and 80 years of age in these six countries. Interviews lasted approximately 15–20 minutes, which is the generally agreed maximum for telephone interviews.

A questionnaire, translated into the six languages, was devised. Major emphasis was put on making the questionnaire concrete and specific in order to obtain a common context of meaning for respondents across all national settings and to avoid sources of misunderstandings of the questions. Words such as 'trust', 'confidence' and possible synonyms of these terms were avoided. We cannot preclude the possibility that some questions are interpreted differently across national and cultural settings, but believe that the thoroughness of our work and the specificity of the questionnaire reduce this problem to a minimum. Still, comparative data like this must be treated with great caution.[6]

Using a quota sample, sampling was based on databases of telephone numbers. The total number of completed interviews analysed was 8575. The source for all was a national pool consisting of thousands of telephone numbers. Respondents were drawn at random from this pool until the desired amount of interviews was completed. Gross response rates vary between countries, from 8 per cent in Portugal to 16 per cent in Norway. There is nothing alarming in these results; in fact, it is quite common with this type of sampling that only 10–15 per cent of a given gross sample actually agrees to do an interview. For a further discussion of sampling routines and the final sample, see Poppe and Kjaernes (2003).

Sample size was approximately 1000 in Norway, Denmark and Portugal. The Italian, German and British samples were larger, between 1806 and 2006, due to the ambition of looking at regional differences in these countries. For the purpose of country comparisons, national weights are employed to obtain representative sub-samples at that level. Our analyses are mostly based on the sub-samples, aiming at comparing national averages with one another rather than conducting individual-level analyses for the sample as a whole. An exception is made in Chapter 6, where analyses are made on data compiled for a whole sample. In that case, all country samples are given equal weight, irrespective of the original sample size or the size of the populations in question.

The questionnaire includes the following major items:

- measures of trust and concerns/worries;
- practices and strategies for consumers in the roles as shoppers, eaters and citizens, with a particular focus on practices related to eating and purchasing habits, but also expressions of dissatisfaction or protest, like complaining, boycotts, and mobilization;
- views on the distribution of responsibilities between consumers and various institutional actors with regards to key food issues, namely safety, quality, nutrition, value for money and ethics; and
- socio-demographic variables: information about age, gender, household type, educational level, employment status and place of residence in terms of urbanization, region and municipality, but not socio-economic status.

It should be remembered that seeing trust as basically relational, rather than individual and cognitive, has considerable implications in terms of the questions as well as for the analyses. The aphorism 'trust – in whom – with regards to what' provides the overall cue for these efforts. The resulting selection of measures of trust in food do not represent a comprehensive set of indicators. Key topic areas for questions tapping trust included the following:

- Trust in particular food items available in the marketplace.
- Confidence in food that is bought and taken home for consumption within the household unit.
- Trust in terms of evaluations of the long-term developments within the food sector.
- Trust in various institutionalized actors as information sources.

The methods of analysis used over the survey data are for the most part relatively simple and straightforward. The basic presentation of variables and results are made in the form of cross tabulations. The main analytical tool is regression, offering easy comparisons of mean differences between countries (linear and logistic regression analyses have been applied, depending on the nature of the dependent variable). In most cases, these are run in the background, so to speak, and not shown in the text here.[7]

3.4   Conclusion

The methodological challenge we faced was how to understand variations in public opinion as measured by the survey results, with an interpretation based on systematic qualitative analysis of institutional features of six European countries. In the first instance, the method of institutional comparison outlined above only makes much more explicit than usual the assumptions and frameworks that are quite typically brought to bear in order to understand survey data.

We can claim, however, to have gone at least a little further than merely being explicit about the interpretive framework. The process of deconstruction and reconstruction of societal configurations enabled us to exclude certain implausible explanations. It was possible to reveal that a given institutional variable – say, shopping in small familiar shops in a country whose retailing system was dominated by small shops – was or was not a plausible explanation for high levels of trust in food. Proceeding stepwise, it was, moreover, possible to see that clusters of institutional variables provided more or less plausible accounts of variations in the survey results. Finally, the method enabled us systematically to generate a comparison between our triangular configurations of societal relationships of trust: consumers of market actors; consumer trust of the state; and consumer trust of the relationship between the state and market actors. In this sense, the methodology served as a fruitful compromise between variable and case approaches – with the strong proviso that the most we can expect are *plausible* causal accounts.

4
Variations in Popular Trust

4.1 Public opinion on trust in food

Our study of consumer trust in food starts out with a representative survey of public opinion on food issues across six European countries. Considering all the turbulence around food, we ask in this chapter, what are the levels of popular trust in food in Europe? Is there a widespread distrust, as suggested by all the media attention and political concern? Moreover, are these levels of trust and distrust evenly spread out across various European countries? And if there are differences, where do we find the highest and the lowest levels of trust.

We are looking for systematic variations. Our interest is not in the psychological reasons for individuals reacting in the way they do. Instead, we seek macro-level variations that can be associated with the social and institutional context of peoples' lives. This chapter will concentrate on variations in opinion as such. The next chapter will explore in more depth how these opinions reflect different sources of trust, especially how trust is related to basic, cultural features or to more fluctuating factors related to the performance of institutions. We will use these questions as a basis for the analyses of social and institutional conditions for trust and distrust presented in later chapters. We will then be able to discuss not only how trust varies, but also why and with what implications.

Assuming, as we do, that trust in food will mostly be a tacit element of taken for granted, everyday routines, a telephone survey approach may seem somewhat paradoxical. Expressed opinions alone certainly cannot be taken as a sufficient reflection of public trust in food. Still, as will be demonstrated, differences between countries are quite consistent, and there are also systematic discriminations between various food items, institutional actors and key food issues, all of which suggest that the survey provides acceptable indicators or proxies of underlying dimensions of trust in food. Moreover, even though not necessarily linked directly to consumption patterns, public opinion as such has played an important role in the politics of consumer trust in food. We have stated earlier that much of the debate has been framed as a matter of 'consumer trust'. But apart from some shifts in demand, what has been recorded and discussed has been public opinion as reflected in media debates or, as in our case, through surveys. It is important to recognize that when people are questioned in surveys, they respond not only as buyers, but also as citizens, media users and carers.

The survey material reveals striking differences in opinion between the countries. Almost everybody everywhere seems to be concerned and worried when asked about specific food issues, like mad cow disease, food poisoning, healthy eating or animal welfare. But when enquiring about issues associated with trust, like optimism or pessimism regarding changes in the food sector or beliefs in the truth-telling of institutional actors, the answers are much more differentiated. While trust dominates in some countries, there is very widespread distrust in others. The national variations are also rather surprising. Dominant ideas about the quality of the food in various countries are not necessarily reflected in the patterns for trust and distrust. Nor are the number of food scandals in the press. Having experienced the very turbulent period of the BSE scandal and other food crises, the British generally turn out to be the most positive and optimistic. Food issues have been quite contentious even in Denmark, but trust is expressed at the same level as in Norway, where the situation has been much more uneventful. By contrast, people in Germany, another North European country, come out as much more worried and sceptical about the situation regarding food.[1] Considering the pan-European media emphasis on quality, provenance and the healthiness of a Mediterranean diet, Italians display a general distrust and pessimism that may seem surprising. Similar findings are found in Portugal.

4.2   Indicators of trust in food

The central focus of questioning in the survey is 'Who trusts whom in regard to what?' Survey questions tapped the various elements of this question. 'Who' refers primarily to consumers, where we may find variations between individuals, between social groups, and between citizens in different countries. Trust in 'whom' and in 'what' represent the key indicators of trust (that is, the dependent variables) in this analysis. Reference to 'whom' signifies the relational aspects of trust; which actors do people trust or distrust? 'In regard to what' refers to distinctions between food items, and to key food issues, such as safety, quality, and so on. Both the 'whom' and the 'what' can help us to understand how trust varies in terms of expectations and performance.

We used a number of standardized questions to tap various dimensions of public opinion regarding trust in food. None of our indices are very precise measures, and what is understood by each of them may be broader than experts' notions of terms like 'safety' or 'quality'. Also, individual opinions constitute only one limited source of data. Bolder statements can therefore be made when these data are later combined with other types of information on the countries.

Four different types of indicators of trust in food are presented. We begin with evaluations of trust in the safety of food items. The first question is a very simple one, about confidence in the safety of food bought by the respondent to be eaten at home. This is followed by assessments of the safety of specific food items. However, since safety is not the only food issue with relevance for trust, we asked respondents about their evaluations of long-term change regarding a range of key food issues – nutrition, quality, safety, ethics and value for money. National variations are substantial, but evaluations of the issues are differentiated. Finally, we examine answers to questions about the likelihood of eight different institutional actors telling the truth in a case of crisis. Even here we find distinct national patterns and different levels of trust in the various actors.

We concentrate on patterns across the six countries. Several of the trust indicators involve batteries of question, and we are interested in differentiation as it appears in the answers. But in order to get a better grasp of the overall picture, we also constructed aggregate measures for each of the trust indicators.[2]

Trust in the safety of foods

In the introduction to this book we stressed that trust is social. Nevertheless, trust issues are often posed in terms of particular foodstuffs. Food is a social product, both in terms of what has happened to the dishes before ending up on our plates and the meanings and classifications that we attach to the food. We therefore asked people about whether they trust the food that they buy. Thus, views on food items are seen as expressions of socially contingent norms and expectations. We focus initially on safety issues because they have been prominent on the public agenda.

Confidence in the safety of the food bought for one's household may depend directly on whether the marketplace is believed to have safe foods for sale. However, not everything on offer necessarily needs to be safe as long as the consumer in some way or the other is able to locate and buy items that are acceptable. Confidence may depend as much on how consumption is organized, the degrees of control, responsibility and discretion that the households have, and the social networks that they can rely on.

The first thing that comes to mind when looking at the results presented in Figure 4.1 is the rather widespread scepticism displayed across Europe when it comes to the safety of food. With the exception of Norwegians, half or more of the respondents have only some or a small degree of confidence that the food bought and brought home is not harmful. Next, people worry much more in some countries than in others. Norwegians are most confident, followed by the British and the Danes. At the lower end we find the Italians and the Portuguese, where very few display high confidence and almost one in three have low confidence with respect to foods in general. The Germans hold a middle position, but a considerable proportion have low confidence. This simple question indicates what will become a fairly consistent picture of

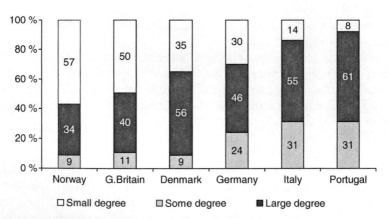

Figure 4.1 Confidence in own food: To what degree are you confident that the foods bought for your household are not harmful?

Note: Weighted results. N: Denmark 975, West Germany 988, East Germany 988, Great Britain 1528, Italy 1950, Portugal 989, Norway 995.

three relatively high-trust countries (Norway, Great Britain and Denmark) and three countries exhibiting a much greater degree of distrust (Italy, Portugal and Germany).

We also asked about trust in the safety of specified food items. The question was asked for 12 food items; eggs, chicken, pork, fresh fruits and vegetables, fresh tomatoes, canned tomatoes, beef, organic beef, sausages, burgers from a fast-food outlet, low-fat products, and restaurant meals.[3] Three options were used: 'very safe', which was meant to express a positive evaluation, 'rather safe' and 'not very safe'. Considering that the items included are ordinarily present in the diet all over Europe, we thought it unlikely that many people would say for example 'hazardous' or even 'unsafe', so we ended up using a milder term at the lower end of the scale.[4]

We cannot know for certain how respondents interpreted this question. There are no references to the household or what people themselves do. Food items are 'products' or 'goods' acquired by a household member to be transformed at home into dishes and meals. We expect the differentiations the respondents make to be based on broad and multi-dimensional classifications of the various items as well as more immediate experiences. As such, the answers may represent the state of affairs regarding what is generally offered to shoppers in the various countries. Food items represent distinct systems of provision, characterizing both assessments of performance and consumers' relations to the system. These systems will often differ between, for example, tomatoes and beef. But there will also be variations in what each item represents in the various countries. While Italians buy 'chicken' as fresh, unpackaged and unprepared meat, to Norwegians, 'chicken' will often represent a ready-to-eat barbequed fast-food sold at low prices in supermarkets.

Again, we find widespread scepticism as to the safety of particular food items among European consumers. But the results reveal clear differences between the various food items (Table 4.1). The pattern is relatively consistent across the various countries; fresh tomatoes in particular and fresh fruits and vegetables are most trusted for their safety, meats and particular types of meats typically take the medium positions, while sausages and burgers from fast-food outlets, along with restaurant meals, were ranked lowest. Differences seem to reflect three major distinctions.

The *first* is between vegetables and meats. People across all the countries are much more sceptical about the safety of meat products. They

Table 4.1 Safety of food items (percentage claiming that it is 'very safe' to eat ... in the various countries)

	Denmark	Norway	W. Germany	E. Germany	Great Britain	Italy	Portugal	Mean[1]
Fresh fruit/vegetable	57	51	39	40	79	37	65	53
Fresh tomatoes	58	51	31	33	78	37	63	51
Canned tomatoes	37	38	12	11	62	17	23	30
Beef	40	36	20	16	47	17	28	30
Organic beef	46	46	31	33	47	28	37	38
Pork	43	39	19	24	50	20	32	32
Chicken	30	18	15	24	50	20	24	27
Sausages	22	17	11	15	34	13	15	19
Burgers	10	4	5	4	18	2	2	7
Eggs	28	39	21	24	57	24	30	33
Low fat product	36	22	8	13	53	10	44	26
Restaurant meals	23	14	11	13	32	6	16	16

Note: 1. This is a mean calculated on the basis of arithmetic means for each of the country samples, so that all samples have the same weight.

Source: Weighted results. N: Denmark (1001), W. Germany (1594), E. Germany (407), Great Britain (1563), Italy (2006), Portugal (1001), Norway (1004). All 12 variables are dummies, coded 1 for 'very safe' and 0 otherwise ('rather safe', 'not very safe', 'don't know').

worry a little less about organic than conventional beef, but not very much. This is probably not surprising, as it is well recognized that meats are often more hazardous than vegetables with regard to food poisoning from bacterial contamination. Recent media attention and scares like those of BSE and salmonella, have also mostly referred to meats. There are potential safety issues even related to vegetables; for example, pesticide residues and genetic modification, but those issues seem to be perceived as less urgent. As can be seen from the table, these distinctions are very consistent across countries. However, the strength of the differentiation does vary. Most noticeably, a majority of the Portuguese view tomatoes and other vegetables as very safe, while compared to the other countries, they display relatively more worry about meats. Some food items seem to be more variable than others, as reflected in their relative ranking. This is particularly the case for eggs and chicken. Even though they cannot compete with vegetables, eggs cause little anxiety in most countries, but they are comparatively problematic in Denmark. Norwegians seem to be particularly sceptical towards chicken. So while we do find a lot of consistency regarding the ranking of food items across countries, people's opinions are also influenced by national agendas (like eggs in Denmark) and by how the item is prepared when for sale (like chicken in Norway when compared with Italy).

People's perceptions of food safety have been a key question in debates on trust in food. A number of studies of public opinion about food safety have compared these with expert evaluations, aiming at identifying the degrees of 'correctness' of lay rankings of risks and/or, less judgementally, of 'mismatches'. These results indicate a wider frame of reference than scientific evaluations and expert statements in mass media. This is further emphasized when looking closer at the evaluations in this study.

The *second* distinction is between fresh and processed foods. This is very evident when looking at the different assessments of fresh and canned tomatoes, and of beef (as steaks and roasts) and burgers. The same pattern is found for all unprocessed meat, on the one hand, and sausages or burgers, on the other. People are more sceptical towards processed than unprocessed varieties. But patterns are not exactly the same everywhere. Germans are particularly sceptical towards canned tomatoes, Italians and Portuguese towards burgers. We also included a question about a very different kind of food category, namely low-fat foods. This may indicate foods that are particularly nutritious and healthy, but also foods that are highly processed, including 'artificial' ingredients or removing 'natural' components. The results show a very mixed picture. While the British and the Portuguese, to some degree even the Danish, seem to think of these types of foods as healthy and safe, Germans and Italians, along with Norwegians, are highly sceptical. The degree of processing matters; Germans, or perhaps Italians, being the most sceptical. British respondents make the least definite distinctions between processed and unprocessed foods in terms of safety.

A Eurobarometer survey from 1998 (European Commission, 1998) asked a similar question about whether various food items were safe or not safe. The issue of fresh versus processed foods was emphasized in the list of items included. The same type of differentiation in trust assessments appears. Our study indicates an even clearer pattern, where British respondents have least problems with processed foods, while Italians make the sharpest distinction between fresh meats and vegetables, on the one hand, and canned foods and pre-prepared dishes on the other.

The *third* type of distinction revealed in Table 4.1 is between foods prepared in the household and foods served outside the home. When asking about food items, the underlying understanding is probably that these foods are bought and brought home for further preparation.

The exceptions in our list are burgers from fast-food outlets and restaurant meals. As we have already indicated, these are evaluated very negatively with regard to safety in all countries, again with the British and the Italians taking opposite positions.

In order to explore overall degrees of variations, we constructed an additive index for the 12 food items.[5] The index varies considerably between the countries. At the top, we find British respondents, whose index for all food items is 50.8 index points, followed by Denmark (35.8), Portugal (31.5) and Norway (31.2). At the bottom end, we find East and West Germany (20.7 and 18.8 index points, respectively) and Italy (19.4). The rank order of countries diverges somewhat from that found for the first question. The background for the more positive overall response to this question in Portugal is that they have few worries about the safety of fresh vegetables – as opposed to meats. The different position of the Norwegian opinions, on the other hand, may be due to a media scandal related to beef quality and safety occurring during the interviewing period, with people consequently taking a more sceptical view when meat was explicitly mentioned (see also Terragni, 2004).

Overall, if we consider trust to be influenced by the degree of control, then industrial processing, and even more so eating out, will reduce the direct control that people have over the final dishes. When buying food or a meal, one cannot usually rely on taste and smell to assess safety. The more processes and steps in the chain, the more problematic or complex this assessment becomes. The social scientific literature has seen this as central in understanding contemporary distrust in food. However, our data indicate that this is only one element behind the variations in trust. Even though the countries display many similarities with regard to the rank order of items, the overall levels are quite different. Because these national differences are so large and consistent they cast doubt on any general claim distrust emerges mainly from an increased rate of complexity in food processing.[6] Trust seems to depend on the characteristics of each food item, and their assessments at the household level, as well as the climate of trust in each country.

Multiple food issues

We will now move on to a more explicitly social framing of trust. Criticism and distrust in food does not always refer to particular cases, events or conflicts, but instead refers to more general questions about, for example, industrial processing and effects on food quality, profits as against concern for consumers' health, and whether consumers benefit economically from increased efficiency. We therefore asked for evaluations of long-term trends in the production, distribution and retailing of food regarding a range of key food issues. The evaluations can be taken as the respondents' assessments of overall institutional performance with regard to these issues, as very general indicators of whether expectations are being met. We asked the question 'Do you think that the conditions for prices, quality, farming methods, health and safety have improved, are more or less the same or have rather deteriorated over the last 20 years?'

This question allows us to escape one-sided attention to safety common in debates about trust in food. As indicated in Chapter 2, we contest theoretical arguments that link distrust primarily to safety and environmental hazards. Instead, seeing trust as an emergent property of institutionalized inter-relations means that a number of issues can arise, and problems can also be framed very differently in different contexts. A problem defined as a safety issue in one country may be defined as a matter of quality in another, and a question of ethics in a third. While the political agendas have focused on safety in recent years, leaving out classical consumer issues like value for money and quality as potential sources of distrust is dubious. Asking for optimistic or pessimistic views on long-term change is a relatively well-known type of question in studies of trust. The expression '20 years' does not necessarily refer to personal experiences over a very specific period of time, but indicates general impressions of trends over a long period. Hence, even young people would be able to answer the question, a point made explicit in the instructions to interviewers.

The proportions of those who think that conditions have improved (optimism) relative to those who think they have deteriorated (pessimism) gives an indication of overall opinion in each country. When adding these proportions for all five issues, we find very divided opinions and considerable national variation (Figure 4.2). Even though many people are sceptical, this is far from always reflected in a general pessimism towards what is happening in the food sector. The British generally express the strongest positive opinions, with more respondents talking about improvements than of deterioration for all the five issues. But there are still many who take the opposite, pessimistic view. The Danish and the Norwegians come out as positive or neutral on all issues. This considerably strengthens the impression of these three as high-trust countries. As for the first question we presented about confidence in food taken home, the Portuguese, together with the Italians, stand out as the most pessimistic. If we leave out food prices, both West and East Germany take a middle position, with views tending towards

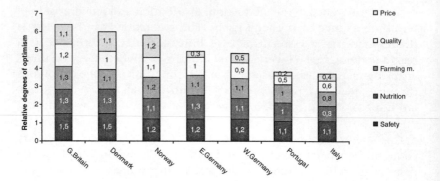

Figure 4.2   Key food issues, improvement or deterioration: Do you think that the conditions for (prices, quality, farming methods, health, safety) have improved, are more or less the same or have rather deteriorated over the last 20 years?

Note: Weighted results. N: Denmark 1001, W. Germany 1000, E. Germany 1000, Great Britain 1566, Italy 2006, Portugal 1000, Norway 1004. Scale: n improved/n become worse; >1 – net improvement, <1 – net deterioration for each issue. The y axis presents these relative proportions added together, the potential variation being 0–10, 5 representing a neutral position.

the positive. But opinions are relatively polarized and quite a few are sceptical about the overall changes in the food sector, especially in West Germany. The East Germans are actually more positive about long-term trends. The Portuguese and the Italians come out as clearly the most pessimistic. In Italy, only for safety is there a small majority saying that conditions have improved.

Yet, there are clear distinctions between the issues. When compared to other issues, we find that *food prices* cause most worry in four out of six countries. The proportions saying that conditions have become worse regarding food prices are considerably higher in the euro-zone countries and very few say they have improved – that is, Portugal (84 per cent say they have become worse), Italy (68 per cent) and the German regions (63 per cent, 75 per cent). The results therefore suggest a strong dissatisfaction with the price of food after the introduction of the euro. Pessimism over prices is lowest in Norway (23 per cent) where the value-added tax on food had been cut by half not very long before. Even though this question refers to long-term trends, the case of food prices suggests that trust in food can have strong elements of direct conditionality, referring to specific factors of performance.

Next among the food issues that cause scepticism and worry comes the *quality and taste* of food, which is considered to have deteriorated over the last 20 years by, overall, 40 per cent. Again the proportions are highest in Portugal (67 per cent) and Italy (60 per cent). Together with the West Germans, more respondents in these countries say that quality has deteriorated than say it has improved. It may seem as if the discourse on contemporary problems in the food sector has been framed primarily as a matter of price and quality. The British are, perhaps surprisingly, the most enthusiastic in this regard, whereas the other countries come out as relatively neutral. Many worry, but there are also considerable proportions who think conditions have improved and many do not take a position on either side.

Farming methods, an indicator of ethical issues, take a middle position in our list of questions. About as many people worry as there are people who think conditions have improved. Once again we find the same order of countries, with 48 per cent of Italians worried and 37 per cent in Portugal, while in Britain only 19 per cent think that conditions have become worse. The answers are somewhat more positive for n*utrition*, where there are relatively high proportions thinking that conditions have improved. The proportions of people worrying are highest in Italy (46 per cent) and lowest again in Britain (13 per cent). This is an issue where many think that conditions have not changed. Even though nutrition has emerged on the public agenda recently (obesity, school meals, etc.), this issue has not (yet) reached the attention of the mass public.

Safety – surprisingly – generates fewer worries and is the only issue where a majority in all the six countries thinks that conditions have improved. Yet opinions are polarized. Italian respondents are once more most negative (39 per cent) and the British least negative (12 per cent) when the focus is on long-term change.

This broader framing of trust produced results that must be interpreted with some caution. With the exception of food prices, they all represent wide and relatively vague issues. It is obvious that the framing of problems varies between the countries, reflecting different national agendas. But as a test[7] of the influence that these opinions on change have on trust, our index of food items gave some interesting results. These opinions explained very little of the variation in trust in food items in the high-trust regions – Denmark, Norway and Great Britain, but in the other countries they explained more. The questions on trust in food items focused on food safety. But worries over food quality make the most significant contributions to the explanations in Italy and Portugal – not worries over safety. This is less evident in Germany, where several of the issues, including safety, make some contribution. This test supports the view that trust (and distrust) can be framed very differently, and that an encompassing notion of food quality plays a central role in the two southernmost regions.

Nevertheless, there is considerable consistency in the answers when comparing across countries. The institutional studies to be presented in later chapters will lend more insight into varying national agendas and definitions, including the degrees and forms of conditionality involved in determining people's trust.

Truth-telling: An indicator of the relational elements of trust

We have insisted that trust is often 'trust in someone'. This someone can be persons, more or less specified institutional actors; an institutional order in, for example, a country; or even more diffuse 'systems'. In order to explore different types of roles and inter-relations, we focus on types of institutional actors. These various types of actors are expected to be subject to different evaluations, depending on structurally conditioned positions and responsibilities, and how they actually perform. Truth-telling is one aspect that can distinguish between various actors, indicating institutional transparency as well as integrity and responsibility. The respondents were asked the following question: 'Imagining that there is a food scandal concerning chicken production in your country, do you think that the following persons or institutions would tell you the whole truth, part of the truth, or would hold information back?' Actors from various arenas were included; press, television and radio; the processing industry, the supermarket chains; farmers; consumer organizations; politicians; public food authorities; and food experts.

With an additive index based on these questions, we identify general opinions about institutional actors in the various countries.[8] Similar to the trust in food items index, a first overall observation is that people tend to be quite distrustful. Norway occupies the top position with 35.8 index points, followed by Denmark with 32.3 points, Portugal with 26.0 and Britain with 25.9 points. At the bottom we find Italy (24.1) and East and West Germany (22.6 and 23.6 index points, respectively). We may take this index as an indicator of the overall trust that people have in institutional actors. As suggested in Chapter 2, we expect this to be important in understanding forms of trust. A lack of trust in institutionalization processes (including different types of actors) may make people more dependent on more personal and network-based exchange.

However, opinions about the various actors are so divided that we must look into this in much more detail. Figure 4.3 shows the proportions of those who think that the various actors would tell the whole truth. There is an identical ranking in each country, with consumer organizations and food experts at the top, food authorities and the media in the middle, and all market actors and politicians at the

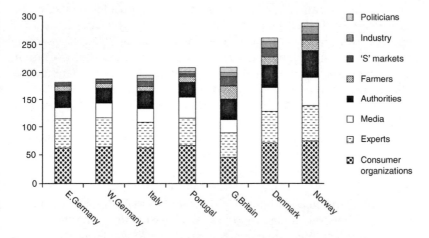

Figure 4.3 Telling the truth in a food scandal: Imagine a scandal with salmonella in chicken, would the following actors tell the whole truth, parts of the truth or rather withhold information? Percentage who would tell the whole truth, added for all actors

Note: Weighted results. N: Denmark 1000, W. Germany 1000, E. Germany 1000, Great Britain 1566, Italy 2006, Portugal 1000, Norway 1004.

bottom. This rank order seems consistently to reflect basically different roles, especially in relation to openness; that is, those of civil society actors, authorities and market actors. People believe all market actors will not tell the whole truth or will hold information back. This is in line with expectations that commercial, competitive actors will strategically protect their economic interests, also with regard to information. Economic organizations are typically rather closed entities. Public authorities, on the other hand, have a democratic duty to be open and transparent. But they may also be expected to act strategically for some political reason or to protect their reputation. A number of scandals in recent years have been related to food authorities lacking transparency and even misleading the public (as with BSE in Portugal and the United Kingdom). People's opinions here are typically rather ambivalent, even though noticeably and substantially different from the market actors.

At the top of this ranking of truth-telling, we find all the actors from civil society. Consumer organizations are met with large enthusiasm, even in the low-trust countries, almost the same as with food experts.[9] The high trust in food experts is a little surprising, as most studies of discontent and worry over food issues have tended to attribute this to scepticism towards science and expertise (see also Chapter 2). Moreover, as trust in the truth-telling of food experts is widespread across all countries, it seems to add little to the understanding of the characteristics of settings with low as opposed to high trust in food. Taking a middling position, the mass media are met with considerably more caution. Underlying this, people may make a distinction between different types of media, such as tabloid versus broadsheet newspapers.

Finally, politicians are met with the greatest scepticism. This may reflect a generally negative attitude towards what politicians say, but may also express the role that politicians have played in relation to recent food issues, where representatives from food authorities have generally been much more visible than politicians. Politicians select carefully which cases they become involved in. Food consumption conflicts may not align directly with party divisions in major political conflicts (except perhaps regarding support or resistance to European integration), and thus be less interesting to them. On the other hand, in several food scandals involving food authorities, ministers have in the end had to take the blame. This is a standard constitutional relationship between the government and its bureaucracy, but it may add to the understanding of why politicians and authorities are ranked so differently.

Yet, the various countries also exhibit distinctive features. British respondents seem to make the least clear division between public and private actors. Even though low in the rank order of actors, the British clearly have more trust in the truth-telling of their supermarket chains than people elsewhere. Trust in public authorities is relatively high, but they do not have the same confidence in civil society actors as their continental European counterparts. Norwegians and Danes make much sharper distinctions. Relatively high trust in public authorities is not matched by trust in supermarkets and industry, though both have a considerably higher trust in civil society actors. Germans, for their part, seem to lean on experts and consumer organizations, distrusting all others. The same tendencies are found in Portugal and Italy, altogether a shaky basis for trust.

The question used in our survey was a slight modification of a question used in a Eurobarometer survey carried out in 1998 (European Commission, 1998). With some caution, it is possible to compare the two and thus get an impression of changes in opinion. Figure 4.4 compares proportions saying supermarket chains, consumer organizations and authorities, respectively, would tell the whole truth. We find the same ranking of actors in both studies, as well as relatively consistent country variations. But the comparison indicates some significant changes over this four-year period. Most obvious, beliefs that food

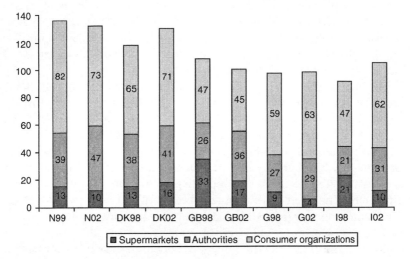

Figure 4.4 Comparing truth-telling over time: Would supermarket chains, food authorities and consumer organizations tell the whole truth in case of a food scandal? (Added percentages.)

Source: Comparing data from Eurobarometer 1998/Norwegian survey 1999 and Trustinfood survey 2002.

authorities would tell the whole truth have become more widespread in all countries, most noticeably so in Great Britain and Italy. Supermarkets, on the other hand, seem to have become somewhat less trusted in all countries but Denmark. For consumer organizations, the results are quite mixed, with no clear tendency. There are no simple interpretations of these changes. Direct evaluations of performance may certainly contribute, but opinions may also have been influenced by changing (or more clear) divisions of responsibilities.

In order to further explore these different roles and evaluations, we have analysed how trust in actors may impact on trust in food items.

Trust in institutional actors

Above, we found considerable national variations in the levels of trust in institutional actors. We also found that people across Europe seem to make similar distinctions regarding which types of actors are expected to tell the truth and which are not. But how does this differentiation affect trust in food? Which actors make most difference? Is it always a positive relationship, so that trust in particular actors is correlated with trust in food items? By combining this question with the trust in food index, we can learn more about 'who trusts whom in terms of what'. These questions seem straightforward, but the background is complex. Truth-telling is both a distinctive indicator of trust in itself and a form of confidence in institutions (as opposed to personal relations and networks) that may influence other dimensions of trust.

This section presents a regression analysis where trust in food items (the index) is examined as a function of truth-telling among institutional actors. A multivariate regression analysis is a test of the independent effects of various variables (here truth-telling of different actors) on a dependent variable (here the trust in food index), controlled for the effect of other variables included in the model. In this way, we can investigate the impact of people's evaluation of various actors' truth-telling on their assessment of the safety of food items. Identical regression models were used for each country individually (for a further explanation, see Poppe and Kjærnes, 2003).

The results are reported in Table 4.2. Looking at the test statistics for the model, two general features deserve to be underlined. First, the adjusted R^2 values indicate how much of the variation in the trust in food index is explained by all the truth-telling variables. The number 1 means that all the variation is explained, while 0 means that these independent variables do not explain any of the variation in the index. This latter option characterizes Denmark, meaning that varying views on truth-telling do not seem to impact on the assessment of food safety at all. By contrast, truth-telling matters to a substantial degree in many of the other national settings. For instance, in countries like East Germany, Italy and Portugal, the adjusted R^2 run as high as 8–10 per cent. Second, in all contexts but the Danish, evaluations of the truth-telling of several different actors have a statistically significant impact on trust in food items. Clearly, the two dimensions of trust considered here are related.

Table 4.2 provides information about the impact of each of the eight institutional actors. The results support our earlier comments about the rather marginal role of politicians. Believing that *'politicians'* are truth-tellers does not have any impact on assertions about trust in food items in any of the six countries.

Civil society actors are the most highly trusted to tell the truth. Believing that 'consumer organizations' *are* truth-tellers has a limited effect, making only a small difference in three national settings. As for 'food experts', belief in their probity raises the level of trust in foods strongly in Portugal and slightly in Britain. The third civil society actor, *the mass media*, has significant impact only in Italy, with more moderate impact in Norway and East Germany. This does not mean that civil

Table 4.2 Truth-telling and trust in food (Trust in Foods (Index) by Truth-Telling, weighted estimates, linear regression)

Truth-tellers	Denmark	Norway	W. Germany	E. Germany	Great Britain	Italy	Portugal
Constant	33.8***	23.9***	14.7***	15.4***	44.3***	15.0***	23.4***
Consumer organizations	−1.5	4.5*	1.0	2.8*	0.5	0.4	2.7°
Food experts	1.8	−1.4	1.6	0.06	3.7*	1.7	6.3***
Food authorities	0.8	1.5	5.7***	4.2**	5.1**	1.8	5.1**
Media	2.0	4.2*	−0.08	4.5**	1.7	2.3*	1.5
Farmers	1.0	3.6	4.5*	7.0***	5.0**	11.1***	9.0***
Supermarket chains	1.4	6.9*	6.6*	15.7***	7.0***	5.0**	−2.3
Politicians	3.4	3.0	3.0	0.6	−2.0	0.3	3.2
Processing industry	2.3	3.8	13.8**	23.2**	0.4	10.3***	5.7°
N	1,000	1,004	1,000	1,000	1,555	2,006	1,000
Adj. R^2	0.000	0.035	0.049	0.088	0.048	0.088	0.103
Index means	35.8	31.2	18.8	20.7	50.8	19.4	31.5
Cronbach's alpha	0.8830	0.8562	0.7413	0.7374	0.8410	0.7863	0.7568

Note: Levels of statistical significance: *** $p < 0.001$; ** $p < 0.01$; * $p < 0.05$.

society actors do not play an important role regarding food issues and public responses. They may, for example, provide a voice for distrust. And they may promote openness on food issues and procedures. But their performance as such does not seem to be very decisive for public trust in food.[10]

The results are quite different for 'food authorities', where we find statistically significant effects in four out of six countries. The exceptions are Denmark and Norway. One might assume that the role of public authorities is so widely accepted in these countries and trust in them is so widespread that it has no clearly differentiating effect on trust in food items. In the other countries, views on the role and performance of public food authorities are more divided – and trust in them does make a difference. As authorities responsible for enforcing regulations, they can influence the standard of the food directly. Varying assessments of their performance seem to have an impact and Chapter 8 examines whether this is reflected in differing regulatory arrangements and their relationships to consumers.

By far the strongest effects in Table 4.2 are associated with the market actors. Being confident that 'farmers', 'supermarket chains' and 'the processing industry' will tell the truth, has a statistically significant impact on consumers' trust in food items in most countries. Moreover, the coefficients associated with these variables are larger than those detected for other types of actors. For instance, having confidence in *'farmers'* is likely to increase trust in food items by 4.5 per cent in West Germany and 11 per cent in Italy. The variable is statistically insignificant only in the two Scandinavian countries. Also trust in 'supermarket chains' yields similar results in all countries but two: Portugal and Denmark. Third, the (few) Germans who believe that the 'processing industry' actors will tell the truth in case of a crisis, on average trust 14 per cent more food items in West Germany and 23 per cent more in East Germany than those who do not share this opinion. In absolute numbers this corresponds to nearly three food items. The effect is strong also in Italy. The effect of being confident in the food processing industry is a good illustration of what is actually happening. Typically, fewer than 10 per cent of respondents actually trust the manufacturers to tell the truth in case of a food scandal. Thus, we deal with a rather specific group of people with a particular perception of the food system environment. Believing in the industry means that hazards are by and large overlooked – at least in Italy, Portugal and the two German regions. Similar situations characterize the impact of the two other market actors variables: although the proportions of respondents involved are somewhat higher, they still represent quite particular segments of the population.

Market actors have more influence on the food that we buy, than do food authorities, That these types of actors have the biggest influence on trust does suggest that power and influence play a major role in popular assessments of trust in the safety of foods. This is something that we will investigate further in our institutional approach.

This analysis does not tell us very much about *how* various institutional actors influence public opinions of trust. The results point forward to the studies of structures, roles and performance of institutional actors and how these actors relate to ordinary people as consumers and citizens (see Chapters 7 and 8). Nevertheless, the survey analysis does say something about people's reasoning. Apart from the countries with the most widespread institutional trust, Denmark and Norway, there seems to be an association between people's assessment about food safety and their views about the trustworthiness of institutional actors. Trust depends on the social and institutional context. Importantly, it is generally the assessment of the actors most directly involved, market actors and public authorities, that matters most. The highly praised consumer organizations seem marginal. The actors which so far have received most attention in studies of trust in food, experts and the mass media, also seem not to matter very much (except in Portugal, perhaps as a response to other institutional actors being so distrusted).

Cross-country variation

In conclusion, we find considerable distrust in food across Europe. Many people are concerned not only about food safety, but even more so about other food issues, such as quality, nutrition and price. They are also sceptical towards institutional actors, especially market actors and politicians, while experts and consumer organizations are considered more trustworthy. Compared to some years ago, more people seem to assess food authorities as trustworthy. But opinion tends to be highly divided, and these divisions appear to a large degree as differences between countries. Considering together the various indicators that we have examined, distinct national profiles emerge:

Italy and Portugal on average exhibit low trust. But while Italy had low scores on practically all trust indicators, Portuguese respondents had greater trust in the safety of food items, where they also distinguished more strongly between different items. Considering widespread ideas about the status of food and culinary cultures (for example, Helstosky, 2004), these findings are highly surprising. Our findings are, however, in line with studies of trust, showing Italy to be a low-trust region especially in the southern parts (for example, Gambetta, 1988; Putnam, 1993). Can this be characterized as generalized distrust in institutionalized systems, or does it refer specifically to food provisioning and regulation? In terms of trust relations, is this balanced by alternative sources of trust, such as personal relations, networks and direct knowledge? These are open questions.

By contrast, *Denmark and Norway* generally score high on all trust indicators. Nor is this surprising, as these countries usually rank high in all matters of trust (Borre, 2000; King and Rothstein, 1994; Miller and Listhaug, 1998). Representing social democratic welfare states, they have many features in common, historically, culturally and politically. In terms of culinary cultures, however, they are quite different (Kjærnes, 2001). We also observe differences in trust. What social factors can give meaning to the findings that the Danish have considerably lower confidence in the food they bring home? And why is the ranking of concerns for various food issues so different? Does this suggest quite different references and conditions for trust in the two countries?

Germany and Great Britain exhibit very different levels of trust in food. These countries have some contemporary features in common (big and complex markets, food crises), but they are very different historically and politically. Our results indicate that while the British are quite enthusiastic about their food institutions, a majority is very sceptical in both parts of Germany. Considering the turbulence that both countries have experienced within the field of food, which were followed by major reforms in food policy institutions (see Chapter 8), this disparity forms a point of departure for further exploration. British consumers express a greater degree of trust compared to earlier studies (Berg, 2000a, b; Frewer, Howard and Shepherd, 1997). However, similar trends have been observed even in other studies (http://www.foodstandards.gov.uk/multimedia/pdfs/cas2002uk.pdf), thus giving support to our observation that changes have taken place.

A number of studies have revealed national and regional variations in social and political trust and used that as a point of departure for analysing the foundations and dynamics of trust. Patterns of trust in political institutions are relatively consistent. The Nordic countries, on the one hand, and Mediterranean and East European countries, on the other, generally represent the high and low extremes (Kaase, 1999). Similar patterns have been observed for inter-personal trust (Inglehart, 1997). Yet, if we look at changes over time and differences between various types of institutions, tendencies are very heterogeneous (Listhaug and Wiberg, 1995). This emphasizes a need to avoid stereotyping. If we move to consumer policy issues, a recent Eurobarometer survey of consumer protection showed a continuum from high-trust to low-trust societies, but there were also distinctive rank orders of countries in people's evaluations depending on the type of question or issue (European Opinion Research Group, 2003).

Our detailed analyses indicate that opinions are quite differentiated, not only between countries, but also between types of questions and types of issues. While we have shown that there is still considerable worry about food safety, this is the issue where more people think that conditions have improved. Other food issues cause more worry. Apart from reactions over food prices after the introduction of the euro, people seem to worry most over deteriorating food quality. We will discuss later how this framing of distrust, especially in Italy and Portugal, is associated with particular conditions in the food market and particular forms of trust.

People discriminate clearly with respect to where trust is placed; consumer organizations and food experts are most highly trusted in terms of truth-telling, public authorities are ranked in the middle, while market actors like farmers, supermarkets and manufacturers are expected to hold information back. The very parallel rank orders may point to a consensus of diverging roles that these actors play, with a clear and consistent distinction between third-party actors and market actors. But there are also differences. Scandinavians have limited confidence in private actors, compared with their high trust in food authorities. In Great Britain, on the other hand, people hold retailers in relatively higher esteem. In Germany and Southern Europe general distrust of food institutions and foods is more widespread.

Trust in various food items is also differentiated with respect to alternative modes of provision. People have generally higher trust in the safety of vegetables than in meats. They tend to think that fresh foods, like tomatoes and steaks, are safer than processed foods, like canned tomatoes and sausages. And foods bought for home preparation are seen as more safe than meals eaten away from home.

These various indices of trust in food correlate in all countries, but only moderately (Poppe and Kjaernes, 2003). An interpretation of this is that the indicators measure the same underlying phenomenon (that is, trust in food), but that they reflect distinctly different aspects or dimensions of the phenomenon. While the aggregate levels of trust in food, as expressed through the various measures applied in this study, vary considerably between countries, rank orders for trust in food items and for the evaluation of various food issues were quite similar, and were identical for trust in actors. This suggests some shared underlying criteria for evaluations of food items and actors, where the varying levels (between countries and over time) are indicators of differences in how the respondents see performance.

Taken together, this lends support to an interpretation of trust as relational, contextualized, and, at least to some degree, conditional upon performance. Next, we explore this further, applying more advanced statistical techniques to the survey data.

5
Culture and Performance: Trust in Meat

5.1 The politics of meat consumption

Salmonella, campylobacter, the hamburger bacteria, growth hormones, animal welfare conditions, the global use of grains for feed and for food – and BSE. The legitimacy of public authorities and the reputation of the meat industry have obviously been challenged, prestige and big money being at stake. Ministers have had to resign, public bodies have been reorganized, the meat industry has introduced wide-reaching and costly traceability programmes, labelling initiatives flourish, and alternative provisioning systems have emerged. Meat is an important and interesting subject to study. We have seen that trust can ebb and flow, but how is that related to assessments of changes in the food sector and the performance of institutional actors? And even if food items like meat may be judged according to the specific character of its provisioning, are there also general cultural influences on trust with other origins? In this chapter we will explore these questions, again relying on survey data.

Meat holds a special position in European everyday food practices and culinary customs. Meat is generally highly treasured. Across Europe, a large majority consume meat dishes as a central component of their diet. But the buying and eating of meat also arouses scepticism and protest. More people are beginning to refuse to eat meat or certain types of meats. Our survey showed, however, that omitting meat from the diet is quite rare in Scandinavia and in Portugal and Italy (2 per cent or less eat meat less frequently than monthly). It is different in Germany and Great Britain, where proportions are higher, around 9 per cent (Kjærnes, Poppe and Lavik, 2005). Still, many people who do eat meat are obviously concerned about it, for a number of reasons. At times, this concern has been reflected in significant drops in demand. For example, the demand for beef fell by 50 per cent in Portugal at the peak of the BSE crisis. Drop in demand was, however, limited only to some countries. The Danes saw a continued rise in beef consumption during this period. Now, previous levels of beef consumption have in most cases been restored (Kjørstad, 2005), while new issues, like avian flu, have affected the demand for poultry.

There seem to be intricate links between how meat is handled institutionally, public opinion and consumption practices. In some cases, trust is highly volatile and conditional, while the situation appears in other cases and contexts to be much more stable and indifferent. Many types of concerns and evaluations seem to be shared across the countries but, as we have seen, the effects on levels of trust are very variable. In Chapter 2, we distinguished cultural from performance-related explanations of variations in trust. Cultural explanations emphasize that deeply rooted social and cultural processes associated with inter-personal relationships and involvements in social networks are the basis for trust. These basic relations of trust or distrust form the foundation for the development of social institutions. Performance-oriented theories, on the other hand, suggest, first, that inter-personal trust and institutional trust have different sources and, second, that trust in institutions will depend on how well they perform in meeting expectations. We have suggested that rather than competing, these theories may be complementary. With its important role in the diet and its political contentiousness, trust in meat seems to form the right point of departure for exploration of the dynamics of trust. We will look for the influence of general, cultural elements reflecting trust in people and what the household can do, as opposed to conditional, relational elements referring to assessments of the food sector. Put simply, for example; to what degrees are the Danish optimistic views on beef safety based on positive evaluations of the good performance of their food institutions? And to what degrees are the Italian much more negative responses based on general scepticism and pessimism towards other people and prevailing social relations?

After an introduction to the stepwise regression model and its various elements, the chapter will proceed by presenting the influence on trust in meat by each of the elements and steps included in the model. Finally, a discussion of the overall patterns that appear from the analysis shows that most of the questions introduced do have an impact on trust in meat, but that the effects are very variable in the different countries. As important, while these indicators of cultural and performance related opinions contribute significantly to explain variation in trust in meat in some countries, the overall model appears to be much less relevant in others.

5.2   The analysis of dimensions of trust in meat

Realizing that trust in food will often be specific to particular systems of provision, we have selected the area of meat as a focus. Trust in meat safety is taken as a dependent variable in an analysis of cultural and performance-related explanations because its evaluations are so varied, even within countries. In Chapter 4 it was indicated that 'safety' may be understood very broadly, and, especially in some countries, linked to an encompassing assessment of other conditions regarding food quality, nutrition, as well as farming methods. Table 5.1 gives the proportions of respondents who believe that various types of meat are very safe to eat. We see a clear ranking of the meat items, with organic beef at the top and sausages and burgers (specified as coming from a fast-food outlet) at the bottom. This picture is almost identical in all countries, but the proportions are highly diverse. For example, while 50 per cent of the British respondents think chicken very safe to eat, only 18 per cent of people do so in West Germany. Something similar holds for all meat items. As discussed in Chapter 4, meat is particularly contested. While almost everybody thinks that vegetables are safe to eat, hardly anybody thinks the same about restaurant meals or burgers.

From the six meat items we have again constructed an additive index, 'Trust in Meat'.[1] The countries clearly divide into a high-trust and a low-trust groups with respect to meat products, in a similar way to the more general indicators discussed in Chapter 4. Table 5.2 shows that the

Table 5.1   Trust in safety of meat (percentage claiming that it is 'very safe' to eat different types of meat in the various countries)

	Denmark	Norway	W. Germany	E. Germany	Great Britain	Italy	Portugal	Mean
Organic beef	46	46	31	33	47	28	37	38
Beef	40	36	20	16	47	17	28	30
Pork	43	39	19	24	50	20	32	32
Chicken	30	18	15	24	50	20	24	27
Sausage	22	17	11	15	34	13	15	19
Burgers	10	4	5	4	18	2	2	7

Note: Weighted results. N: Denmark (1001), W. Germany (1594), E. Germany (407), Great Britain (1563), Italy (2006), Portugal (1001), Norway (1004).

Table 5.2 Indices of trust: An overview of the frequency distributions for the variables included in the stepwise regression model

	Denmark	Norway	W. Germany	E. Germany	Great Britain	Italy	Portugal
Trust in meat index (mean scores)	32	27	17	19	41	17	23
Trust in people (% yes)	64	57	29	23	34	20	14
Confidence in food (% high)	35	57	31	30	50	14	8
Truth-telling index (% high)	33	36	24	23	26	24	26
Evaluation of change (% negative)	25	25	32	34	20	53	53

Note: Weighted results. N: Denmark (1001), W. Germany (1594), E. Germany (407), Great Britain (1563), Italy (2006), Portugal (1001), Norway (1004).

highest mean scores are found in Great Britain, Denmark and Norway. The lowest averages are found in Italy and West Germany, but East Germany and Portugal also belong to the low-trust group.

The question is to what degree can cultural factors and institutional performance in the food sector contribute to explain variations in trust in meat? The method used to explore different dimensions of trust is ordinary least squares regression, where the dependent variable in the analysis is the trust in meat index. We proceed in two steps. In the *first*, we analyse how trust in meat is influenced by questions with cultural references, whereas, in the *second*, we also include indicators of opinions about institutional performance. An important feature of the procedure is that identical models are successively implemented within all seven national sub-samples. Hence, possible interaction effects between the various countries and any of the independent variables are automatically accounted for. In each step we include two indicators of each underlying dimension. The reasoning behind the model as well as the statistical procedures are explained in more detail in Poppe and Kjærnes (2003).

The cultural dimension is constructed from two variables: whether or not the respondent trusts most other people, and whether or not there is confidence that the food bought and taken home is safe to eat. The former, 'Inter-personal trust', is a well-established general indicator of trust taken from the World Value Survey (Inglehart, 1997). The rationale is that, from early childhood onwards, we learn to trust and distrust through interaction with other people whom we meet. It is a disposition established in primary socialization and developed throughout secondary socialization processes. From this emerges a generalized understanding of trust that, at least to some extent, 'spills over' into organizational and social life. Consequently, the question is commonly interpreted as an indicator of a basic type of trust which is relatively resistant to rapid changes at the social and institutional levels. Our results for this question are generally in line with what have been found in other studies (Freitag, 2003; Kaase, 1999). Differences across European countries seem to be very stable. We find that Denmark and Norway rank highest, followed by Great Britain and West and East Germany (Table 5.2). The most mistrustful respondents are found in Italy and Portugal.

By contrast, 'Confidence in own food' is more specifically related to food practices and the household. The framing is different from the questions on trust in meat and other food items, where we found major distinctions being made according to provisioning characteristics. The idea is that safe foods are, at least in part, obtained by utilizing one's knowledge, skills and social networks. It follows that adequate food procuring strategies may generate a feeling of safety with respect to the meat one actually buys, even in institutionally hazardous environments. We found similar distinctions between high- and low-trust regions, but, according to Table 5.2, proportions confident in their own food do not display exactly the same patterns revealed in the general question about trust in other people. While Norwegians clearly had the largest degree of confidence in their own food, the Portuguese rank last, with a third having little confidence. The Germans, on the other hand, have moderate confidence in their own food within an environment of widespread distrust.

The institutional performance dimension is also covered by two indices: 'Evaluations of change' and 'Truth-Telling'. Both of these refer explicitly to conditions in the food sector, the first asking for assessments of change regarding five key food issues, the second dealing with how people see the truth-telling of various institutional actors. In contrast to the two 'cultural' questions, these two indices are both complex, based on a battery of questions. Frequencies of answers to these two sets of questions are presented in Figures 4.2 and 4.3, respectively. For the purpose of this regression analysis, these sets of questions each had to be reduced into simple but continuous variables (Table 5.2).[2] When combined to form an additive index, the 'Evaluation of change' index may be interpreted as assessments of long-term institutional developments within the food area. Likewise, the 'truth-telling' index reflects how many of the eight institutional actors one feels will tell the whole truth in case of a food scandal about salmonella in chicken, a situation assumed to be relatively familiar in all the countries.

5.3 Cultural influences on trust in meat

Step I in the regression analysis reflects how the two 'cultural' indicators affect trust in meat. Generally speaking, the results from Step I indicate that interpersonal trust and confidence in own food affect trust in meat products in all countries (Table 5.3). However, they do so with varying magnitude and degrees. For instance, variations in trust in meat explained by the two questions are as low as 1.7 per cent in Britain and 2.6 per cent in West Germany (as indicated by R^2). People who trust that the meat is safe are in these countries not very different from those who do not when it comes to trusting other people or the food in the household. By contrast, explained variances are relatively high in countries like Norway, East Germany and Denmark. Turning to the effects of each of the two questions separately, Portugal is the only place where having confidence in one's own food does not contribute to trust in meat products. In five countries, trusting in other people increases confidence in the safety of meats. However, underlying analyses show that 'trust in other people' is mostly less influential than confidence in own food. The mean difference between a generally trustful and a non-trusting respondent is estimated as equivalent to declaring one extra meat product to be safe. This, of course, does not mean that trust in other people is without theoretical significance. Indeed, when generalized, such trust may still act as a lubricant in many social contexts. This means that trust in other people may form an important basis for confidence in food within the household context. Precisely because of its general – not to say diffuse – character, it is well worth noticing the significant spillover impact that inter-personal trust has on specific and socially distinct topics such as assertions about food safety. Moreover, the fact that the effects are robust even when we continue to include more variables in Step II suggests that we might be facing an important underlying mechanism in the construction of trust perceptions.

One of most striking results from Step II is the high impact of inter-personal trust in Portugal and Norway. These effects appear even more remarkable when they are compared with the outcomes for the countries that culturally, historically and institutionally resemble them the most, Italy and Denmark, respectively. The effects of inter-personal

Table 5.3   Modelling trust in meat

Model	Variables	Denmark	Norway	W. Germany	E. Germany	Great Britain	Italy	Portugal
Step I:	Constant	24.0***	14.2***	14.1***	14.6***	36.8***	13.7***	20.8***
	Trust in other people	3.5	8.1***	2.3	5.9***	5.8***	4.5***	13.6***
	Conf. in own food	15.2***	13.5***	7.0***	10.6***	5.8***	15.2***	2.3
	Adj. R^2	0.057	0.089	0.026	0.072	0.017	0.069	0.042
Step II:	Constant	24.4***	11.9***	17.6***	15.8***	35.3***	12.6***	22.2***
	Trust in other people	3.3	7.3***	1.0	3.9*	4.7**	2.5*	9.6***
	Conf. in own food	14.7***	11.3***	5.9***	8.8***	4.4**	13.6***	1.4
	Evaluation of change index	−0.04	−0.07*	−0.2***	−0.1***	−0.1***	−0.07***	−0.2***
	Truth-telling index	0.03	0.2***	0.1**	0.2***	0.2***	0.2***	0.3***
	Adj. R^2	0.057	0.108	0.074	0.123	0.053	0.125	0.148
Index means		31.9	31.2	17.1	19.2	41.2	16.9	23.0
Cronbach's alpha		0.8092	0.8562	0.6276	0.6047	0.7633	0.6599	0.5697

Notes: Linear regression (OLS). Unstandardized coefficients. N = 932 (Denmark), 948 (Norway), 969 (W. Germany), 965 (E. Germany), 1437 (Great Britain), 1910 (Italy) and 973 (Portugal).
Levels of statistical significance: *** $p < 0.001$; ** $p < 0.01$; * $p < 0.05$.

trust are considerably less there and, in the Danish case, statistically insignificant. Given the large differences in institutional conditions in the four countries, the explanations are likely to be different, too. Substantively, the Norwegians' high trust in meat has a strong basis in the widespread trust that they have in people in general, but these two phenomena are not so closely linked in Denmark. This implies a very stable situation of trust in Norway, which is what we see even within the area of food. A parallel, but opposite, situation is observed in Portugal, where the few who trust meat share a high inter-personal trust. Italy scores low on both indicators, too, but without this clear association. This is actually surprising, as Italy has represented a typical case where trust is reserved for closed family networks, while strangers as well as societal institutions are strongly mistrusted, by some characterized as 'amoral familism' (Banfield, 1958).

It might also be noticed that the effect of interpersonal trust on trust in meat is clearly significant in East Germany, while it is insignificant in the Western part of the country. This may indicate that even though the two German parts show similar levels of trust in food in most respects, the underlying dynamics may differ. A lack of interpersonal trust has been observed in several East European countries and has been analysed as indicating a culture of low trust in social institutions in those countries (Seligman, 1997; Inglehart, 1997).

Looking across the countries, we find that general cultural factors do matter – but more in some contexts than in others. Trust in other people has an effect on trust in meat in both high- and low-trust situations, but in both situations we find cases where there is a separate effect and where there is not. However, more detailed explanations should be sought for in systems of cultural norms as well as in nation specific characteristics of food institutions.

Regarding the second cultural variable, 'confidence in own food', we anticipate that people who are confident that their own food is safe to eat are likely to be more trustful of meat products. Most of one's food is typically purchased in the market economy. It follows that in as much as one feels good in one's generalized assessment of the market situation, the 'trust in meat' index is likely to be influenced in a positive direction. However, there is no logical contradiction involved in making the opposite assertion. A feeling of safe eating resulting from adequate household strategies may of course take place in reasonably safe as well as in hazardous market environments – at least in the countries making up the actual dataset. Strategic behaviour may avoid the dangers that loom large in a basically distrusted market environment. The figures in Table 5.3 show, however, that confidence in own food predominantly tends to have a positive effect on trust in meat. The exception is Portugal, where the effect is statistically insignificant. In the six remaining contexts, the mean difference between confident and non-confident respondents ranges from 5.8 index points in Great Britain to 15.2 points in Italy. All these effects are controlled for the impact of 'trust in people'. It is therefore an additional effect that refers particularly to the food sector. Several mechanisms may account for this. In particular, since none of the countries have been subjected to anything approaching a collapse in food supply, 'confidence in own food' is primarily about adaptations to fluctuations within a system that, after all, offers a comfortable range of alternatives to the consumer.[3] Thus, in as much as one feels content about the output of one's own food-procurement practices, there are likely to be some spill-over effects onto overall assessments about the system as such. The direction of the effect may, of course, be the opposite; in that trust in meat products may lead to a more general confidence in the food brought home.

The link between 'confidence' and 'trust in meat' may not be as straightforward as it seems. The impact of cultural features and national-specific systems of action is at least suggested by the fact that the coefficients vary inconsistently with the observed variations in proportions of confident respondents in the six countries. Consider, for instance, the cases of Italy and Portugal. In both countries, the percentages of confident people are modest: 14 per cent and 8 per cent, respectively (Table 5.2). Still, the impact of having 'confidence in one's own food' is very different: statistically and substantively significant in the former, insignificant in the latter, when controlled for trust in other people. In Italy, then, a minority of confident respondents trust their own food as well as meat products in general, clearly distinguished in these respects from a majority of sceptics. For the majority of the Italian respondents trusts neither their own food nor other people, and on average they only find 13.7 per cent of the meat products – or about one out of six items – 'very safe' to eat.[4] In Portugal, on the other hand, an equally small group of confident respondents is not distinguished from the majority with respect to trust in meat when controlled for the effect of interpersonal trust. Tendencies in Portugal are similar to those in Italy, with a majority distrusting meat and lacking confidence in own food. But as we see from the constant in the model, the average trust level among these basically distrustful consumers is still markedly higher. Similar differences are found between countries where the groups of confident and non-confident respondents are both large. The substantial effect recorded for the Norwegian sub-sample, and the much lower coefficient associated with British respondents, illustrate the point.

These conflicting tendencies imply a need to investigate the nature of food-related practices in each country if we are to explain the observed impact of 'confidence in own food'. Is it what people in some countries do in their capacity as a consumer and household member that makes their confidence about their own food more stable and resistant to fluctuations in the food provisioning system? We are talking here not so much about each respondent's strategic considerations, but rather about different ways in which food consumption is institutionalized. These findings indicate the need to explore consumption practices, and the role and influence of consumers in the various countries.

5.4   The effects of institutional performance

So far, we have directed attention towards consumers and their reference to households and social networks. But our overall analysis seeks also to investigate how food institutions influence trust. The aim of Step II of the regression analysis is to identify influences from aggregate level mechanisms by retaining within the model the two 'cultural' indicators and adding two indicators of institutional performance: 'Evaluation of change in the food sector' and 'Truth-telling of institutional actors'. These additional variables represent different ways of assessing institutional performance. By referring explicitly to the institutional context, we might better understand how and to what degree trust in meat is affected by people's experiences with, and views on, food institutions. A number of studies have shown that risk perception and evaluation of information are influenced by trust in the information source, the sender (Löfstedt, 2004; Slovic, 1999). Others suggest that rather than being a determinant, trust is an expression or indicator of worry, for example for GM food (Poortinga and Pidgeon, 2005). We would like to get behind a rather tautological observation that trusting attitudes depend on evaluations of trustworthiness. We will later in this book take a closer look at what institutional actors do and whether there are identifiable patterns that distinguish low- from high-trust settings. But first we examine opinions about institutions and actions. For example, how do people handle situations of distrust in food institutions? Do personal relations constitute an alternative to trust in institutions? And what are the roles of different types of actors in establishing trust? Bringing evaluations of institutional performance into the survey analyses of variations in trust in meat is one step in that direction.

The measure of *'Evaluation of change'*, indicates an overall assessment by the population of the direction of long-term developments within the food sector, and whether performance is declining over the years. The *'truth-telling'* variable, indicates the degree of trust that the respondents have in the truth-telling of institutional actors within the food sector, the kind of trust measured here perhaps being best described as honesty and openness. The overall assessment will then refer to how people judge institutional actors, as opposed to familiar inter-relations in personal networks.

Results from Step II of the regression analysis, presented in Table 5.3, show that both evaluations of change and a belief that institutional actors tell the truth, affect trust in meat. Adding these two variables is significant even when controlled for trust in other people and confidence in own food (Step I). The exception is Denmark, where institutional performance does not seem to matter at all. Also, in all countries except Denmark, much more of the variation in trust in meat is explained by these two 'institutional' variables than by the 'cultural' variables. In other words, evaluations of institutional performance matter more for trust in meat than indicators of culturally founded trust in other people or confidence in own food. The effects of institutional performance are particularly strong in West Germany, Britain and Portugal, where the R^2 values are doubled or even tripled, when compared to Step I.

On the other hand, the significance of cultural factors seems in most cases to be retained even when adding indicators of institutional performance. This means that the effects of these variables are mostly direct and independent of the institutional indicators. In East Germany and Italy, however, the effect of trust in other people seems to be more indirect, as the magnitudes of the effect and the corresponding levels of significance are reduced considerably when adding indicators of institutional performance. In other words, high distrust in other people, which is prevalent in these countries, has an indirect effect on scepticism towards institutional actors. It is also noticeable that the effects of 'confidence in own food' on trust in meat seem direct and independent of how the respondents evaluate institutional performance. This supports our interpretation that how food is handled by the household plays a relatively independent role in relation to the evaluation of food institutions. Regarding our understanding of trust in food as emerging from a societal configuration of institutionalized relationships ('triangular affairs'), this is an important observation that will be taken further in later sections of this book.

Taking all four variables together, these indicators best explain variations in trust in meat in Portugal, Italy, East Germany and Norway, where 10.8–14.8 per cent of the variance is explained.[5] These are also the countries where both cultural mechanisms and institutional performance have substantial effects on trust formation. In West Germany and Great Britain, the impact of cultural factors is obviously very modest, while institutional performance has significant effects. In Denmark it is the other way around, cultural mechanisms (specific to food) are the only ones that seem to impact trust formation.

The discussion suggests that trust in meat is highly sensitive to institutional performance. Starting out with 'Evaluation of change in the food sector', it distinguishes itself from 'trust in most people' and 'confidence in own food' by the fact that it is not a dichotomous but a continuous variable, taking on values between 0 and 100. It follows that the seemingly small coefficients imply potentials for large effects. To illustrate, even in Italy and the Scandinavian countries where the impact of 'Evaluation of change' is at its lowest, the maximum difference between those who are not pessimistic about a single issue and those who believe that all five of them are negative, could be as high as 7 index points or half a meat item on average – other things being equal.[6] In West Germany and Portugal the corresponding maximum difference is 20 index points. In absolute and substantive terms, the most pessimistic West German consumers trust 1.2 (out of 6) meat items less than do their non-pessimistic counterparts. In other words, there is a much stronger effect of evaluation of change on trust in meat in West Germany and Portugal, when controlled for the other three questions. The effects are also relatively substantive in East Germany and Great Britain.

The 'truth-telling' index is also a continuous variable which may take on a similar range of values. Except from Denmark, where institutional performance is unimportant for explaining trust in meat, and West Germany, where the effect of 'Evaluation of change' is larger than the impact of 'truth-telling', the coefficients for the remaining five contexts vary between 0.2 and 0.3. This means that in countries or regions like Britain and East Germany, the difference between those who think that all eight institutional actors are truth-tellers and those who judge none of them believable is about 20 index points or 1.2 meat items. In Portugal the predicted difference is even larger. So, overall, views on the truth-telling of institutional actors have substantial effects on trust in meat.

The most noteworthy observation produced by including the two institutional performance indicators into the model is the significant increase in the level of explanation (R^2) for West Germany and Britain, suggesting that the low and high levels of trust in meat, respectively, are a product of institutional rather than cultural features. The results indicate high sensitivity to institutional performance in these two settings. At least, the coefficients for the two variables imply substantive shifts in predicted values on the dependent variable across observed levels of evaluation of change or truth-telling assertions. This situation is reversed in Denmark, partly even in Norway, where cultural features matter much more than institutional performance.

Any possible combination of values from the four independent variables represents a particular social group with a mean level of trust with respect to foods. Thus, according to Step II where all four questions are included, trusting respondents are characterized by having trust in people, confidence in own food, few negative evaluations about food issues, and belief in many actors as truth-tellers. But the estimated scores for comparable groups across national settings may of course vary considerably. To arrive at good explanations for such variations, an in-depth inspection of national-specific institutional conditions is paramount.

5.5 Concluding remarks

Trust in food is a complex and dynamic phenomenon, where systematic variations between countries exist. Put simply, people can start out by being more or less sceptical towards meat and food institutions and they can be more or less responsive to, or perturbed by, events and experience. This chapter has explored the role of cultural as opposed to performance-related factors in order to explain variations in how people trust the safety of meat. As is often the case, the analyses cannot give a single, unambiguous answer. Influences seem to be multifaceted and also diverse across the countries. What is clear, however, is that the questions that we have included in the analytical model are of relevance for trust in meat. The stepwise model indicates that each of the elements have a different role to play. This will be developed in the institutional analyses in Chapters 7–9.

Interpersonal trust, explored in a number of previous studies, does seem to have an impact in most of the countries. When more specific questions are introduced, the effect disappears or is reduced in some countries, but not in others. So, the presumption that this general, cultural influence forms an important background for trust in institutions gets some support.

If we first turn to *East Germany* and *Italy*, they exhibit widespread distrust, both in general and with particular references to the food sector. It is therefore not very surprising that interpersonal trust is important even in the field of food. But food-specific confidence is even more important. These are long-term trends. Yet, in Italy as well as in East Germany, institutional factors add considerably to the explanation of variations in trust in meat. People seem to share a general scepticism towards other people as well as institutions, but it does matter how particular institutions perform as well. It will therefore be of interest to see how institutions affect public distrust in these contexts.

Portugal is similar. It is the context where our model works best, where the overall explanation is highest. Particularly in Portugal, trust in other people matters a lot, but not the food-specific confidence (in direct contrast to Denmark). The two performance-related questions are also very important, thus suggesting that both generalized and conditional factors are important to explain levels of trust.

We have characterized all these three as places of low trust. By way of contrast, *Norway* scores high on most trust-related questions. Our model seems to indicate that there are strong underlying cultural forces behind this high trust, especially referring to general, inter-personal trust, but even to food-specific confidence. Like Denmark, evaluations of trends in the food sector are not very important, while truth-telling is. As to this latter question, it must be noted that a food scandal was taking place in Norway just during the period of our interviewing. The scandal was about a big supermarket chain that had sold frozen, long-stored beef as fresh beef, thus touching issues of quality and safety as well as truth-telling. This example shows that even in a context like Norway, where deep and stable cultural factors seem to sustain a high level of trust, it is still conditional on institutional performance. High trust may even here be supported by good institutional performance and people do react when something happens.

In *Denmark* and *West Germany* trust in meat does not seem to be strongly affected by general inter-personal trust, neither directly nor indirectly. In Denmark, it is only confidence in own food that matters. As the more directly performance-related questions do not add to the explanation, one might suggest that the confidence question in the Danish case reflects that trust in meats is based on influences specific to the food sector, but in a less contingent form than in the other countries. The opposite seems to be the case in West Germany, where both evaluations of changes in the food sector and views on the truth-telling of institutional actors matter, both indicating a higher degree of conditionality in trust formation, while the factors not referring to institutional conditions have little effect.

Finally, *Great Britain* appears to be the most performance-oriented with regard to trust in meat. As we have seen in Chapter 4, views on meat safety here are highly polarized. Many are very confident, while a considerable proportion is still strongly sceptical. Cultural factors do not seem to have an independent, direct effect – or any strong indirect effect – while performance-related questions do. So, as in Western Germany, this seems to be a context where trust is highly conditional. From these analyses, we can also observe that while levels of trust in food are quite similar in the two parts of Germany, the dynamics behind differ in some respects.

Table 5.4 Cultural- and performance-related factors for trust in meat

Explanatory factors	Country levels of trust	
	High trust in meat	Low trust in meat
Cultural factors most important	Denmark (confidence in own food, less explained variation)	
Performance most important	Great Britain (less explained variation)	West Germany (mainly evaluation of change)
Both cultural factors and performance important	Norway (performance: only truth-telling)	East Germany (all factors important) Italy (all factors important) Portugal (confidence in own food not important)

The overall patterns found in the various countries are summarized in Table 5.4. Both in high- and low-trust regions we find cases where general and/or specific cultural factors matter a lot, together with institutional performance. Denmark is the only country where this is not the case. But for high as well as low trust contexts, we also find examples of high contingency with reference to institutional performance, without clear influences of general cultural factors. This is a first step towards our institutional account of different configurations of trust.

A number of questions emerge from this analysis. For example, why are the patterns so different in the three high-trust settings? Is this reflected in varying institutional conditions that produce trust? Actually, the low-trust regions seem somewhat less varied. Can we then identify some common features in what produces distrust? Before moving on to an analysis of the major institutional elements, the provisioning systems and regulatory arrangements, we will first take a closer look at the construction of the consumer and consumer practices.

6
Mobilizations of the Consumer

6.1 Introduction

What might people do to assure themselves that they can trust the food that they eat? Chapter 5 showed that, to a large degree, trust refers to institutional performance. However, we also found that trust may emerge from within the household and how the household copes with food issues. In principle, if uncertain about the safety, quality or value of their food, people may, as individuals, take various courses of action to establish, restore or enhance their trust. We place the activities they reported in the survey in the context of understandings of the contemporary consumer. The dominant notion sees 'the consumer' as an individual who freely chooses in a market situation that which they most prefer. However, 'the consumer' is increasingly viewed as a powerful and active agent whose powers extend beyond the point of purchase. Most accounts of the courses of action available to consumers fall into two types; one economic, the other political. Very broadly, 'consumers' may do one of two things. They may mobilize their economic resources, individually or collectively, to put pressure on producers and distributors to offer cheaper or better products. Alternatively, they might exercise their political powers, exerting their rights of citizenship, to try to persuade the state to intervene in relations of market exchange. This simple distinction between economic and political action is a useful orientation towards understanding movement for change in the realm of consumption, but it is far from perfect. It posits the existence of distinct types of action, but ultimately the alternatives are increasingly hard to distinguish clearly. After considering some analytic issues, we examine in turn economic and political actions reported in the survey which might be expected to condition levels of trust. We look first at strategies of household food purchasing and then at forms of political or quasi-political engagement. In the final section we offer the results of a statistical analysis which shows that the economic and political actions of individuals are associated with their perceptions of changing food quality, but that most of the variance in trust still remains attributable to features captured about their country of residence rather than individual characteristics.

6.2   Locating the consumer

One of the most highly distinctive features of modern capitalism is the separation between the economy and the polity. In almost every other type of society, economic activity has been tightly circumscribed and constrained by political or moral considerations. Conceiving of the economy as a separate and autonomous sphere, subject to a special logic of atomistic, individual and self-regarding economic action, became common, if still controversial, in the nineteenth century. The most influential version of the idea was formalized in neoclassical economics from which our current dominant notion of the consumer derives (Gagnier, 2000; Winch, 2006). The implication of this conception is that the consumer thought of as a buyer can secure his or her economic interests most effectively through markets. Because only the consumer personally can determine what he or she wants most, then transactions are best left to individual negotiation. Political intervention can be expected only to hamper the operation of markets whose aggregate effect, it is argued, is to ensure that in general supply will adapt to consumers preferences.

However, classical political economy did not divorce economic from political action in this manner (Gagnier, 2000, 19–40). The economy was politically constituted. The proper relationship between the political and the economic spheres has remained controversial, however. For much of the period from the Great Depression to the mid-1970s, the key political problem of Western parliamentary democracies was how the state could tame and regulate, in the name of the public good, the potentially anarchic, competitive and inegalitarian tendencies of the capitalist market system. Socialism, social democracy, corporatism and European conservatism alike pursued policies which required widespread state intervention in economic processes. The intellectual framework and presuppositions might be considered continuous with the idea of classical political economy, acknowledging that the political and the economic cannot, or should not, be torn asunder. Though they were interested in consumption in aggregate, they had little place for the idea of an individual consumer. If the post-war European welfare state functioned through extensive political intervention to control the economy and redistribute (somewhat) more equitably the proceeds of national economic growth, the neo-liberal New Right threw the levers into reverse.

The primary principle of the political programme of the New Right was to reduce the role of the state in economic life. What was distinctive was the vehemence with which neo-liberalism insisted that the state should play a minimal role in managing economic activity. All that could be left to market transactions, should be. A revived and militant doctrine of the free market has percolated from the United States, through world economic institutions like the WTO and the World Bank, increasingly into the European Union and, though in different degrees, down to the governments of individual European states. Such a doctrine emphasized the difference between the political realm and the economy, reasserting that they were separate entities with distinctive logics. Unsurprisingly, the consumer became much more important as a political figure in the wake of the diffusion of neo-liberal economic doctrines of the New Right. The more the market is extolled, the more its alleged beneficiary, the consumer, is drawn into the limelight of public debate.

The language of both markets and politics came to be suffused with references to the consumer. This has provided a major impetus to a notion that consumers are increasingly active and powerful. At the end of the twentieth century many different powerful actors increasingly appealed to 'the consumer'. Organizations hoping to sell food to customers invest significant time and resource into trying to understand the desires and constraints facing households so that they might target their products accordingly. The complex of product innovation, market research, advertising and sales strategies indicates that commercial enterprises take people as consumers very seriously. In modern marketing the sovereign consumer of economic theory is deferred to, his or her power to withdraw custom or to pursue novelty being embraced as a disciplinary force. Effort devoted to keeping customers happy, loyal and trusting has never been more sophisticated. This is prompted by the need to secure a sufficient share of the market, though corporate strategies attempt to conceal the more brutal aspects of economic exchange. Since markets always are arenas where trust is shallow and conditional, the imperative to sell at a profit is masked by promises of serving the consumer, meeting needs, responding to concerns, and offering choice and a competitive price.

The idea of individual choice, the most beguiling of the promises of contemporary marketing, has been conspicuously incorporated into political discourse. The privatization of public services and the introduction of quasi-market mechanisms within state-managed organizations delivering services are advocated frequently in terms of extending choice. The impact of the free market doctrine has been to stress that the principal virtue of the market mechanism is that it allows people to choose what suits them best. No longer allocation, instead choice.

The figure of the consumer has been transposed into the field of politics, a key instance of a trend to represent individuals as autonomous, self-regarding, calculating and utilitarian in all dimensions of their lives. The dispositions appropriate to market exchange are interpreted as pervading all spheres including personal relationships (Becker, 1977) and aesthetic judgment (see Gagnier, 2000, on the way that the reasoning of neoclassical marginalist micro-economics was transposed into an aesthetics of personal preference). Increasingly the public is conceptualized and represented in terms of the disposition of consumers, and all the major actors, the EU, national authorities, retailers, farmers, and of course consumer organizations, claim to respect the rights and expectations of 'the consumer' – although they do not necessarily have the same consumer in mind. In competing discourses the consumer turns out to be a figure with many separate characteristics and dispositions. To the extent that the consumer comes to be represented as a political actor, the boundaries between the economy and the polity, and between economic and political action, become blurred.

Recently, historians have been making a major contribution to the understanding of the construction of the consumer by placing contemporary notions in a longer temporal context (for a review, see Trentmann, 2004; see also Bevir and Trentmann , 2004; Daunton and Hilton, 2000; Strasser, McGovern and Judt, 1998; Trentmann, 2006). They remind us of neglected traditions of consumer politics, of times when political projects to organize consumption with altruistic ends in mind were commonplace (see Cohen, 2000, 2003; Daunton and Hilton, 2000; Hilton, 2003, 2004). Cohen (2000) captures the difference when making her effective, if rather ungainly distinction between the citizen-consumer and the customer-consumer. The former are 'consumers who take on the political responsibility we usually associate with citizens to consider the general good of the nation through their consumption, and the latter being consumers who seek primarily to maximize their personal economic interests in the market place' (ibid., p. 204).[1] She shows how that distinction played out in US development, with the former orientations being fairly prominent in the first half of the twentieth century but largely disappearing thereafter. A labour and consumer alliance which emerged as part of the New Deal, with its Keynesian objectives to maintain demand and deal with poverty in the Depression, and which had its apotheosis in collective restraint during the Second World War, was replaced by a quite different politics in the subsequent period of abundance. This changed discourse, agenda and policies. For Cohen, the move (from the mid-1980s onwards) to consumer choice in public service delivery is the last, or latest, stage in the shift from consumption away from being a citizenship issue.[2] The United States, Cohen claims, has become a 'consumers' republic':

> As the market relationship became the template for the citizen's connection to government, the watchdog, public-spirited consumers of the 1930s and 1940s increasingly were replaced by the self-interested government customers of the 1990s, who were encouraged to bring a consumer mentality to their relations with government, judging public services and tax assessments much like other purchased goods, by the personal benefits they derived from them. (2003, 397)

However, conceptualizing change in terms of this simple shift is problematic. It implies that economic action is the self-interested individual pursuit of economic benefits and that political action is oriented to the public good. At the extremes there is little ambiguity. On one side, consumers may always 'exit' a market relationship if dissatisfied, turning to another supplier or an alternative product. On the other, citizens may form a political organization, say a Cooperative Party, to exert influence through representative democratic channels. But other acts are less easily classified. Political mobilization around consumer issues is not always altruistic, and economic acts are not necessarily self-regarding. For instance, political organization in pursuit of free trade is often instrumentally calculating, while refusal to buy South African goods was for a period directed towards the political overthrow of the apartheid regime. Moreover, the economic model of the consumer tends to assume independent individual action. Yet most effective economic pressure on the part of the consumer occurs collectively through the informal mobilization of a boycott or the setting up of formal organizations like consumer associations. The latter have often dissociated themselves from political objectives, engaging instead in product testing and legal redress for their members. Yet they almost inevitably get drawn into political terrain, thereby contributing to the political agenda of consumption. Other groups, meanwhile, begin with political objectives, for instance the Fair Trade movement, but by virtue of their tactics have their impact on the operation of markets. The political and the economic are thus deeply and intricately entangled. While the consumer of neoclassical economics is considered to act essentially independently of political considerations, the reality of contemporary societies is that the economic and political dimensions of consumption are intricately inter-woven. So are individual and collective actions. In the end, the separation proves problematic for understanding actions associated with consumers. The boundary between acting as a customer and acting as a citizen becomes difficult to draw. Ultimately the distinction between citizen and customer is a limited analytic device for an adequate understanding of the action of individuals and groups engaged in the management of their consumption.

Lacking suitable concepts to deal with this entanglement, we pragmatically examine in turn different types of action. The first is the exercise of care and attention in deciding where and what to purchase, avoiding that which is considered harmful or inadequate. Avoidance, or 'exit', has the effect, on aggregate, of penalizing those producers and retailers who fail to satisfy a customer's requirements. In such a case consumers might be said to exercise power by virtue of their purchasing practices, cornerstone of the ideology of consumer sovereignty. The second is to seek through political or quasi-political means to extract guarantees that food is safe, wholesome and of promised quality. Effectiveness generally requires that others also act in a similar fashion, through informal or organized political mobilization. The attention paid recently to the powers and rights of the consumer has made both types of action more visible. However, the efficacy of such acts has always been questioned, primarily because it usually requires many customers, or alliances of customers, to offset the greater power of producers. It is for this reason that consumers have sought collective representation through more formal organizations, in consumer associations and cooperative parties. Recent, more informal equivalents, social movements whose objectives are to change consumption behaviour, currently attract much attention as new collective vehicles for reintroducing consideration of the public good (Sassatelli, 2006). With this in mind we turn again to the survey which gives us some evidence about activities through which people might actively ensure that the food they purchase is acceptable.

In the next section (6.3) we examine briefly activities surrounding shopping and purchasing. We have seen in Chapter 5 something about practices associated with the politics of meat consumption. We develop this further by looking briefly at how individual or household strategies for the purchasing of beef and tomatoes vary, and consider how these might affect trust from country to country. We see that shopping matters to some degree; but that the way in which households make their purchases is not much help in understanding their trust in food, the food system and other actors. We reserve most of our discussion of consumption patterns to the next chapter, where we insist that it is less a matter of individual purchasing behaviour, and more the nature of the institutionalization of the consumption process as a whole which makes it possible to explain the different emergent national patterns of trust. In the subsequent section (6.4) we consider variation in political and quasi-political activity, located in the context of the contemporary political construction of 'the consumer'.

6.3 Shopping strategies

Acts of food purchasing ultimately represent the key to a relational understanding of trust in food. We anticipate that routines and experiences associated with food purchases will make the reference points for trust different for shoppers than for those who rarely or never shop for food by themselves. We might also assume that various systems of distribution and retailing entail different types of relations and thus also different conditions for trust. Modern large supermarket chains represent a very different, impersonal, standardized and contract-based form of relation, compared to small-scale, specialized outlets like butchers, fruit and vegetable shops and food markets, which rely much more on personal relations. Survey material on how households organize their purchasing gives a preliminary grasp of the everyday and practical basis of their trust in food.

We saw in Chapter 4 that people discriminate between food items in their assessments of trust. Interpreting these distinctions as socially and relationally founded, we asked a few questions about shopping habits with specific reference to tomatoes and beef. We asked where and how often these items were bought. We also asked whether a personalized connection to the retailer mattered, whether the national origin of the product was of concern, and how important cheapness was. We were thus able to explore whether alternative courses of action had any effect on whether the product was considered safe. In each instance we imagined that these might reveal ways in which people take precautions to ensure that their food was safe and wholesome.

Table 6.1   Shopping habits and strategies, by country (percentage)

	Norway	Denmark	Great Britain	W. Germany	E. Germany	Italy	Portugal
Usually buy tomatoes in supermarkets*	93	81	80	64	66	49	59
Usually buy beef in supermarkets*	86	74	64	31	43	39	20
Important that shop is accessible (beef)**	72	68	74	51	58	63	61
Important know origin of beef**	54	59	66	70	65	88	83
Often pay more for good taste***	41	55	53	48	32	48	51

Notes: * Alternatives: supermarket, fruit and vegetable shop/butcher, another small shop, a food market, another way; ** Alternatives: Important, matters a bit, unimportant, don't know; *** Alternatives: Often, sometimes, seldom, don't know.

There were of course considerable differences in the practices of the populations of the countries; for example in where people normally buy beef and tomatoes. Table 6.1 shows that supermarket dominance is strongest in Norway and Denmark. A large majority of Danes buy their beef and tomatoes in a supermarket, but there is also a certain proportion of respondents who usually buy beef in a butcher shop and tomatoes in a fruit and vegetable shop. In Norway, alternatives hardly exist. If we turn to Great Britain, tomatoes and beef are mostly purchased in a supermarket, but quite a few buys beef in a butcher shop and tomatoes in a vegetable shop. Patterns are more heterogeneous in Germany, where people buy tomatoes in fruit and vegetable shops, on food markets and in supermarkets, as well as in other places, and a majority of the respondents buy beef at the butchers or in other places, rather than supermarkets. The balance is even more towards small shops in the Southern countries. Many Italians buy tomatoes in specialised shops and on food markets and the majority buy beef in a butcher shop. This suggests a predominance of contexts where personal relations are more important. However, we should not overlook the high proportions of supermarket shopping in Italy, which is nearly 50 per cent for tomatoes and nearly 40 per cent for beef. While a little more than half of the Portuguese respondents buy fresh tomatoes in supermarkets, only one-fifth buy beef there. Most people in Portugal buy beef from a butcher (77 per cent), the highest proportion among our cases. There is thus some general sense in which the populations of high-trust countries are more likely to be purchasing food in supermarkets and, as we will see below, there is some indication that this is also true of individuals, at least with respect to issues of food safety.

However, there was very little direct association at the individual level between such shopping practices and estimates of the safety of produce (Kjærnes, Poppe and Lavik, 2005). The results of the analysis exploring this connection were largely negative, especially in respect of tomatoes. Most people considered tomatoes safe and there was scarcely any statistical relationship between judgements about safety and procurement strategies. Tomatoes, as we anticipated at the beginning of the study, were unlikely to be controversial and we would have been surprised if special measures were thought to be necessary by shoppers to protect themselves or their households from harm. The case for beef, however, might potentially be expected to be different. It is considered a less safe product everywhere and among the reasons for that are precisely the publicity associated with BSE and other crises. It is thus not unreasonable to hypothesize that there would be some association between household practices and perception of the safety of beef. For example, one might expect people who thought it unsafe to be less likely to buy it and for people generally to take greater care when shopping for a more risky product.

To investigate this question we conducted a multi-nomial regression analysis, which is reported in detail elsewhere (Kjaernes, Poppe and Lavik, 2005). The question posed was did respondents think beef was 'very safe', 'rather safe' or 'not very safe'.[3] In a nutshell, analysis showed that there was some association between our measures of practice and perceptions of the safety of beef within countries, though the effects were not very strong and were very uneven across countries. It was everywhere the case that people who never ate beef, and who never purchased beef, were more likely to pronounce it 'not very safe'; and conversely, those who ate beef regularly were more likely to pronounce it 'very safe', though the effect was statistically significant only in West Germany and Italy. It may seem as if this drastic form of 'exit', declining to buy and eat a foodstuff like beef, is a strategy that people employ when they distrust, but only in some circumstances. Most other effects of shopping practice – as estimated by a procedure where the effects of other characteristics, activities and attitudes were controlled (see note 3) – were marginal. Danes who bought beef in supermarkets were more likely to think it 'very safe', as were Britons; but Britons who purchased elsewhere than in supermarkets were no more likely to deem their beef 'not very safe'. There were no effects in other countries. In Denmark and Germany, those who thought it important to know the shop or the staff where they bought beef were more likely to think it safe, whereas the opposite was the case in the United Kingdom. In the other countries the desire for familiarity with the retail outlet had no significant effect. In sum, people who used different purchasing strategies did in some instances exhibit different degrees of trust, but the effects were not great or consistent across countries. Emphasis on familiarity, that is, knowing the staff and the shop, seems to distinguish between countries more than between individuals.

By contrast, there was some greater effect on estimations of trust from answers to the question whether people were confident that the food they took home was not harmful. Having interpreted the answer to this question as indicating that whatever they might think about food in general, the respondents might adopt various strategies to ensure that the food that they themselves bought was safe, then this is a question which suggests the taking of care over procurement. When included in the same multi-nomial analysis, this proved a better predictor of perceptions of the safety of beef. In Norway, Denmark, Britain and Italy, those who had confidence in their own food were statistically more likely to consider beef 'very safe'. Conversely, in West Germany, Britain and Denmark,[4] those who had confidence in their own food tended to deny that beef was 'not very safe', while this was statistically insignificant in Italy, Portugal, Norway and East Germany.

In general, then, we found no strong direct relationship between shopping practices and trust, even in the case of beef where it might have been imagined that people would be prone to taking special precautions. Practices vary, within and across countries, but their association with perceptions of trust are not much apparent at the level of the individual.

6.4 Mobilizations of the consumer

Wherever market exchange has prevailed, people have been mobilized on occasion as consumers (Greenberg, 2004), and as consumers of food. However, political attention to 'the consumer' and to issues of consumption increased towards the end of the twentieth century (Brobeck, Mayer and Herrmann, 1998; Brown, 1998; Gabriel and Lang, 1995; Theien and Lange, 2004). More people were mobilized, around more issues, than earlier. Mobilization was in part effected by, and certainly reflected in, the spread and influence of organizations set up to speak for and act on behalf of consumers. Other key actors who are typically identified as having interests contrary to those of the consumer – corporations and the state – have also dipped deeply into the discourse of the consumer. Corporations describe their strategies and orient their organizational culture towards satisfying customers on a growing range of issues. Politicians increasingly appeal to potential voters by promising to promote and protect them in their role as consumers, thereby encouraging a consumer orientation within politics. Burgess (2001), for instance, makes a good case that governments are increasingly speaking as the representative of 'the consumer' – rather than the nation, or social classes – a tendency which addresses citizens as individuals who make personal choices rather than as custodians of the public good or as members of social groups and categories. The figure of the consumer presents as a prominent political actor.

In the last decade consumer policies have become a separate and distinct policy area, having been constructed discursively as a major policy concern in a number of countries and at European level (Bergeaud-Blackler, 2004; Ilmonen and Stø, 1997; Jensen, 1984; Kjærnes, 1997). The EU itself turned from an overriding concern with the creation of a single market to explicit consideration and obeisance to the consumer. Consumer politics now have a high profile. In such circumstances, parties appeal to quasi-economic orientations, self-interest and, most especially, individual consumer choice rather than the common good and collective determination. But at the same time, establishing the internal market has required new collective political arrangements for protecting consumers and their welfare. Over the same period, public debates have accorded individual consumers increasing power and influence in relation to political problems. In some quarters increasingly much is expected of consumer activism (Sassatelli, 2006). This re-politicization is most often focused on the responsibilities and duties that people should assume when purchasing with a view to achieving environmental sustainability (Uusitalo, 2005), but it has also occurred in relation to food issues (Halkier, 1999; Micheletti, Follesdal and Stolle, 2003). Consumers have come to be attributed agency on the stage of public affairs, agents who are accorded a presence, interests and capacity for action. The idea of the active consumer reflects a growing sense of empowerment to respond positively to dissatisfactions regarding the operation and regulation of markets. How much this is purely rhetoric, how much a mark of a real shift in power, is debatable. One means to explore this issue is to review some of the forms of mobilization revealed in our survey. We consider also how mobilization affects levels and types of trust.

6.5   Consumer organizations

One type of agent playing a significant role in forming popular attitudes to food provision is the consumer organization. The survey revealed that consumer associations are the most trusted of institutional actors in terms of truth-telling in all countries. There are active consumer associations in all the countries and at the EU-level, and all the countries except Norway have associations of which consumers are direct members. The degree of membership is roughly the same in all of these countries – below 10 per cent of the population.

However, when looking at the institutional position of consumer associations, and at individuals' views of consumer associations, some differences emerge. As Theien indicates (Theien and Lange, 2004, 1), there have been collective organizations acting to regulate food consumption since the mid-nineteenth century. Cooperative movements for communal purchasing were followed by associations promoting ethical consumption for social ends, and then by organizations devoted to supplying consumers with reliable information about products and producers. All are ways of defining and serving the consumer interest. Each type of organization continues to exist in all the countries in our study, though with different degrees of presence and importance in each.

We find organizations particularly devoted to voicing consumer interests in all six countries. Great Britain has five large independent consumer associations of different ages and purposes, the oldest one being The Vegetarian Society, and the newest, The National Consumer Federation, being an umbrella organization for different local consumer groups. These two associations are the only ones with active membership rights for ordinary consumers. In the other countries, the number of consumer associations and their roles vary considerably. Norway has one main consumer association, the Consumer Council, which is financed by the state and has a long history of close cooperation with actors of food regulation and provision. Denmark has two organizations, one partly financed by the state and with a long history of close cooperation, like in Norway, and one new organization, which promotes more radical political action. In addition, environmental organizations play a role, for example in relation to GM and functional foods, where consumers are attributed more agency. Germany has many consumer associations, partly due to its federal political system, though there is an umbrella organization for all of these with, for example, a website containing consumer information. But in Germany food issues are as likely to be raised by environmental groups as consumer organizations. Italy also has a large number of consumer associations, which are connected as members in a national council of consumers and they are active in relation to food ethics. Furthermore, Italy also spawned the Slow Food Movement, with a focus on quality, which, though not solely a consumer organization, has gradually diffused to other countries. Portugal has three main consumer associations, all relatively new compared to the consumer associations in the other countries, and prioritizing safety and quality.

Public perceptions of the efficacy of consumer associations vary. The survey included a question on whether consumer organizations are very important, quite important or not important in monitoring the safety and quality of food. While the majority thought that these organizations are very important in most of the countries (the mean was 65 per cent), somewhat fewer Norwegians and British thought so (50 per cent and 57 per cent, respectively). It does not seem surprising that British consumers regard their associations as unimportant, since these associations are thought to be somewhat less trustworthy and powerful, compared to the other countries. But the Norwegian case must have a different explanation; the public food authority is considered by far the most important caretaker of safety and quality, which renders all other actors largely irrelevant. More surprising, Italians rank highest, with 75 per cent. Perhaps because Italian public authorities are neither trusted nor regarded as powerful, independent actors like consumer organizations (and food experts) are attributed an important role, despite their lack of power. Overall, there are few generalizations to be made about consumer organizations except that they are popularly well regarded – even though they are not very powerful.

6.6 Consumer activism and perceptions of responsibility

Whether or not people have confidence in consumer associations to represent them collectively, they may also engage, on a personal basis, in forms of consumer politics and quasi-politics. We asked a range of questions about people's perceptions of their role as consumers, and about whether they had taken any form of personal or political action in the last year with respect to influencing the food supply. The results indicate some aspects of the way in which the consumer is institutionalized in the different countries.

We asked a number of questions to gauge people's opinions about who they considered was, or should be, responsible for ensuring standards in particular areas. These were mostly posed in relative terms, as, for instance, whether people thought that the consumer had more responsibility for safety of food than the government (see Table 6.2). On that question there was not much variance between countries. There was more variation with respect to the question whether consumers were more responsible than manufacturers for nutrition, where Italy stands out because it accords the consumer much more responsibility than do others. Asking whether consumers had more responsibility than farmers for ensuring animal welfare revealed that many Germans feel that, as consumers, they can (and should) improve animal welfare. The Germans generally also do not feel that consumers have much power, except on the issue of animal welfare. Britons felt empowered as consumers generally, whereas Danes and Norwegians were beneath the mean for all questions indicating consumer responsibility. In some ways, in the two countries where a model of a 'modernized' consumer circulates more freely (that is, Britain and Denmark), people expect the state to do less. Danes think very strongly that farmers have more responsibility than the public authorities for the proper treatment of animals, whereas Norwegians sit at the opposite extreme. On the now contentious question about what should be done to encourage healthy

Table 6.2 Perceptions of consumer responsibilities (percentages who 'fully agree')

	Norway	Denmark	W. Germany	Great Britain	Portugal	Italy
Consumer more responsible than government for safety*	13	27	25	34	30	35
Consumer more responsible than manufacturers for nutrition*	39	35	31	39	46	61
Consumer more responsible than farmers for improving animal welfare*	5	11	24	19	10	16
Promotion of healthy diet *should* be public responsibility*	63	34	46	53	62	70
Consumer association very important to monitor safety and quality**	43	66	48	61	60	72

Notes: * Percentage of those who 'fully agree' (rather than 'partly agree' or 'disagree') with the statement; ** Percentage of those who consider this 'very important' (rather than 'quite important' or 'not important').

eating, Danes, Britons and Germans thought that this was not particularly a matter for the state, whereas the state was accorded responsibility in Italy, Portugal and, again, Norway. These questions of who is or should be responsible indicate expectations of how state and markets do, or might, operate and reveal different perceptions of the consumer role in different countries.

6.7. Active individuals

Table 6.3 indicates the propensity of populations to engage in various market-oriented and quasi-political activities directed to influencing the operation of the food supply. Individual activity is more common than engagement in collective protest.

The most common type of action is complaining in the shop. However, almost as many people have consciously directed their purchases, by refusing to buy, or actively buying, in support of a cause. For all of these actions, almost a third of the respondents gave positive answers. More organized, collective action is much lower, generally below 10 per cent for the practices we asked about. This applies to

Table 6.3 Consumers' individual and collective participation (percentages; values at or above mean are in bold type)

Involvement during the last 12 months	Great Britain	Denmark	Norway	W. Germany	E. Germany	Portugal	Italy	Mean
Complained to retailer about food quality	29	21	**34**	31	24	22	**44**	32
Refuse to buy food types or brands to express opinion about a political or social issue	**33**	**35**	21	**43**	30	24	22	30
Bought particular foods to support their sale	**37**	**39**	**32**	**33**	**46**	14	19	30
Participated in organized consumer boycott	**12**	5	4	**9**	4	7	**12**	8
Member of organization that works for the improvement of food	**7**	6	5	**9**	4	5	4	6
Taken part in other kinds of public or political action to improve the food we buy	**7**	3	5	**12**	6	6	**7**	7

actions like contacting a politician, signing a petition, supporting a campaign with money, distributing leaflets, or participating in demonstrations, as well as membership in organizations. There are, however, large variations between the countries, both in terms of the levels of participation and the types of actions.

Portuguese consumers are the least active; in all activities they score below the mean. At the other end, German consumers are the most active, scoring above the mean on all activities except complaining to the retailer; there are, however, noticeable differences in the kinds of activities occurring in the Western and the Eastern parts. British consumers follow the (West) Germans closely in being active in individual strategies as well as collective strategies. But Britons do not complain to retailers very often. The Danish consumers tend mostly to take individual action, refusing to buy food items in order to express an opinion and by positively buying food items in order to support particular solutions to food issues. Italian consumers complained more than average to the retailer – they display the highest frequency of all the countries in this respect – and they also score above mean on participating in an organized boycott and undertaking some 'voice' activities. Norwegian consumers tend to take little action themselves, but they do complain to retailers and buy in light of political purposes.

We also included in the survey some questions about alternative forms of shopping, like using farmers' markets, box schemes, buying directly from the farm, and so on, and about buying organic food as a general shopping strategy. Alternative shopping strategies were generally most popular among the Germans. Systematic purchase of organic food was most common in Denmark and Great Britain. There is a sharp distinction between the Danes, for whom such strategies are relatively common, and the Norwegians, who were least involved in all these practices.

6.8   The voice of individuals

Figure 6.1 shows the degrees to which respondents in the various countries think that their voice as a consumer matters. Here we have asked people to think of themselves explicitly as 'consumers'. In Norway, Denmark and Germany, their voice matters little. This is in accordance with answers to the questions about responsibility. Norwegian consumers express consistently that they as consumers have little responsibility for the key food issues in question (safety, nutrition and ethics) and Danish consumers tend to agree, except that they tend to be less convinced that

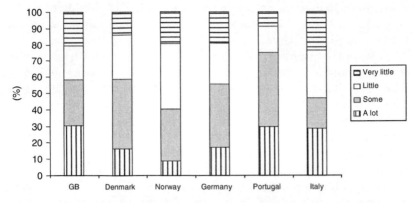

Figure 6.1 Importance of consumer voice: To what degree do you think that your voice as a consumer matters?

promotion of a healthy diet must be a public responsibility. German consumers only see themselves as more responsible than other actors for issues of food ethics (here operationalized as animal welfare).

In Italy, Portugal and Great Britain, more consumers think their voice matters a lot. Few among the Portuguese respondents regard their voice as unimportant, but in Italy, the most polarized country, a considerable proportion also thinks that their voice matters very little. Italian consumers think of themselves as personally more responsible than other actors for everything except nutrition, where they strongly favour public responsibility. Portuguese consumers see themselves as more responsible for safety than public authorities and more responsible for nutrition than manufacturers. British consumers see themselves as more responsible for safety than their government, just like their co-consumers in Italy and Portugal. Otherwise, British consumers ascribe more responsibility to themselves than other actors only on the issue of ethics.

Consumers' views of their own role make analytical sense when seen in conjunction with patterns of collective action. In Norway, for example, consumers neither see their own individual voice, nor the voice of their consumer associations as important, and they are not very active individually. Norwegians rely on the state to take care of food issues, a state which also finances the main consumer association. Perhaps it is difficult for the individual Norwegian consumer to disentangle their consumer association from the state. Furthermore, alternative forms of food provisioning play a minimal part in provisioning, although

Norwegians have informal ways of getting what is considered to be
'natural' and 'pure' food, because of a strong tradition for hunting,
fishing and picking berries.

In contrast, consumers in Great Britain see their own individual voice
as very important and they are active in individual strategies, so it may
therefore make sense that they do not ascribe great importance to their
consumer associations. British consumers seem to have more readily
taken on responsibility and assumed a high degree of agency, though
mainly in relation to the mainstream food provisioning system.
Alternatives, such as box schemes and farmers' markets, are limited.

Patterns in other countries need more institutional context to make
sense. Danish consumers, like the Norwegians, do not consider their
own voice as consumers to matter much, but they see their consumer
associations as important watchdogs and are personally active in exit
strategies. Danish consumers also have access to a widespread network
of box schemes, where you can subscribe to a box of organic food, delivered to your doorstep. The most successful, called 'Aarstiderne' (Seasons),
has 35,000 subscribers. Maybe the Danish consumers are content with a
perceived 'division of labour', whereby the consumer associations, the
state and the farmers are expected to live up to certain institutional
responsibilities. Under such favourable circumstances occasional recourse
to exit strategies may be all that is required to maintain confidence.

German consumers seem highly ambivalent, being very active
individually in all strategies, but only ascribing more responsibility to
themselves in one issue and not judging their own voice as important.
Alternative food provisioning systems are not widespread or widely used.[5]
Maybe German consumers find it necessary to be active themselves
because there seems to be little consensus and clarity about responsibilities among other societal actors, especially for safety. But, on the other
hand, German consumers do not find consumers' individual responsibility to be an acceptable solution. In this sense, one of the differences
between the Danish and the German consumers may be that Danes have
positive experiences of some sort of empowerment in taking on individual responsibility as consumers, whereas Germans have more negative
experiences of taking on personal responsibility because no other actor
appears to offer protection. As we will see later, German consumers are
also more poorly represented and considered in decision-making fora.

Both Italian and Portuguese consumers consider their own individual
voice important. But where the Italians are active as individuals in some
strategies, the Portuguese are not active at all. In both contexts,
consumer associations are not very influential, there is not an efficient

public regulation of, for example, safety, and the food provisioning system is still dominated by small shops. The Portuguese paradox of consumers not being active and, at the same time, believing their own voice to be important, may be explained by the particular structure of food distribution. As shown above, a relatively large proportion of purchases are made in small shops. The Portuguese also more often buy fresh rather than processed foods. This means that direct interaction associated with food purchases are quite particular to Portugal, with more possibilities for personal exchange. Voice may for many Portuguese and some Italians refer to this possibility for direct personal feedback, rather than influencing the decisions of big institutional actors (whom they generally distrust). Individual and collective activism may also be less relevant within this context.

Taken together, these differences produce an interesting but heterogeneous pattern. Among the high-trust countries, Britons are broadly active, through individual and collective, political and economic action. Danes act mainly via economic strategies of exit, while Norwegians exhibit a general loyalty by doing almost nothing. And among the low-trust countries, the differences are just as great. The West Germans are politically active by all measures, Italians act mainly as customers but with some *ad hoc* political activities, the East Germans are very like the Norwegians, and the Portuguese also do almost nothing. We might conclude that low levels of expressed trust do not necessarily generate active dissent and activism does not necessarily indicate a situation of widespread distrust.

6.9 Eating, purchasing and protesting: The limits of consumer power

We have seen very great differences in the ways that consumers are positioned and act across the countries. However, differences in the behaviour of individual consumers do not explain much variation in levels of trust. Once again, individual consumers do not make enough difference. This can be briefly demonstrated by considering how social characteristics, shopping patterns and political mobilization jointly affected individuals' perceptions of change in the qualities of the food that they ate. Without dwelling too long on the regression analysis involved, we describe a series of models which set out to examine why some people thought that quality, safety, prices and nutritional standards had improved over the last 20 years.[6]

We look at four types of explanatory variable besides country of residence: socio-demographic characteristics, shopping habits, engagement in political activity around food, and general measures of a civic ethos. The main features we explore are as follows:

- Whether people's opinion regarding the improvement or deterioration in standards of quality, price and safety can be explained by each of these types of explanatory variable.
- Which variables have the strongest association with those opinions.
- How the statistical associations vary between different key food issues.

We examine the similarities and differences between the four key food issues, comparing full regression models for each issue. We entered five different types of independent variables in three stages.[7] Analysis was stepwise. The first step inserted country (Model 1). The second stage added socio-demographic characteristics of respondents (age, sex, etc.), then some variables to capture shopping strategies, and then reported political activities (Model 2). Finally, we entered measures (as reported in Chapters 4 and 5) of cultural circumstances – confidence in food taken home and trust in people (Model 3). Models gave rather similar results for the four key food issues examined (see Table 6.4).

Many of the independent variables included in the models are statistically significant, a function of the large sample size of over 5000 in each instance. Table 6.4 indicates the strength of coefficients, a 'z' measure which is the ratio of the size of the coefficient and its standard error, and 'p', a measure of significance. It can be seen that in most cases the same independent variables are significant, in quite similar strengths, across all four of the key food issues examined. This suggests that sources of opinion associated with trust are little different across issues and brings into question whether, especially in the case of opinions about safety and nutrition, respondents distinguish clearly between these attributes of food. Notably, all five types of explanatory variable contribute something to an explanation of opinion. Among the socio-demographic characteristics, sex and age, and usually geographical location, matter. The effects are not very strong, but there are similar patterns across all four issues.

Shopping habits, however operationalized, matter on occasion, but not to any great degree. Interestingly, the indicator identifying retail outlets that people normally use is statistically significant in one case, the case of safety, where the more people concentrate their shopping in supermarkets the more they are optimistic that safety has improved. There is no strong effect for the other key issues. More powerful is the sense that those who do not ever shop tend to be more pessimistic than

Table 6.4 Modelling perceptions of the improvement of food

N	Taste		Prices		Safety		Nutrition	
	Coef.	p > !z!	Coef.	p > !z!	Coef.	p > !z!	Coef.	p > !z!
Model 1								
Germany = base case								
Denmark	−0.24	*	1.86	***	0.68	***		
United Kingdom	0.49	***	2.00	***	1.04	***	0.71	***
Italy	−1.06	***					−1.03	***
Portugal	−1.60	***	−0.85	***	−0.35	**	−0.97	***
Norway			2.48	***	−0.63	***	−0.82	***
Likelihood ratio, Model 1	768.6		1,654.5		474.4		644.8	
Model 2								
Female	−0.23	***	−0.57	***	−0.31	***	−0.23	***
Age	−0.01	***					0.00	*
City 100k+	−0.18	*			−0.20	**	−0.16	*
Town 10k+	−0.21	**						
Never buy food			−0.49	**	−0.64	***	−0.38	**
Occasionally buy food	[0.18]							
Never buy beef or tomatoes			−0.22	*	−0.60	***	−0.18	*
Eat out monthly or less			−0.20	*				
Never eat out			−0.43	**	−0.34	**	−0.25	*
Buy mostly in supermarket					0.22	**		
Consumer has little influence	−0.32	***	−0.24	***	−0.25	***	−0.34	***
Refused to buy product	−0.24	**			−0.21	**	−0.30	***
Supported a product								
Joined boycott					[−0.20]			
Likelihood ratio, Model 2	909.8		1,822.6		761.4		780.0	
Model 3								
Large degree confidence in own food	0.69	***	0.27	*	0.70	***	0.68	***
Some degree confidence in own food	0.35	***	[0.19]		0.51	***	0.42	***

Continued

114   *Trust in Food*

Table 6.4   Continued

N	Taste		Prices		Safety		Nutrition	
	Coef.	p > !z!	Coef.	p > !z!	Coef.	p > !z!	Coef.	p > !z!
People can be trusted	0.19	**	0.39	***	0.34	***		
Index of actors truth telling	0.11	***	0.09	***	0.13	***	0.13	***
Constant			−2.00	***	0.57	***	0.41	*
Pseudo R2	0.14		0.25		0.12		0.12	
Likelihood ratio, Model 3	1,045.3		1,889.8		953.2		919.4	
Model 2–Model 1	141.1**		168.1**		287.0**		135.7**	
Model 3–Model 2	135.5**		67.3**		191.8**		138.9**	

Notes: Factors associated with holding opinion that quality, price, safety and nutritional value of food has improved, rather than deteriorated, over the last two decades (binary regression coefficients and p > !z! as measure of significance).
1. p > !z!: *** <0.001; ** <0.01; * <0.05; [ ] <0.10.
2. There is no agreed general measure of the amount of variance explained by a binary logistic regression model. A pseudo-R² statistic can be computed to give some rough indication of the relative power of the model. In this regard comparatively little variance is explained, especially considering that country of residence is included in the model. We can explain most variance with respect to price, least with respect to safety, though least only by a tiny amount when compared with the variance explained with respect to improvement in nutrition. A more adequate measure is to examine the significance of the Likelihood Ratio calculated for each model and to examine the difference between each model. In this regard, all our models for each key food issue proved robust. Each was also significant according to a Bayesian Information Criterion (BIC) test. Each step in each model proved to make an improvement in the explanation.
3. Likelihood ratio: ** p < 0.01; * p < 0.5.

those who do. Never buying food and never eating out probably indicate a lack of responsibility for, and lack of interest in, food or the properties of food. It might be imagined that for people in this situation their information, the sources of their opinions about food, come less from experience and more from media sources, with the hypothetical implication that they are inclined to take a relatively pessimistic view of trends as a feature of the news to which they are exposed. With less responsibility and experience, they may also be less in control of the situation.

Political orientations towards consumer issues also add something to the explanation. Those who feel that the consumer has little or no influence always tend to pessimism. Occasionally refusing to purchase particular products, or buying others to support them, affects opinion. But generally, variables identifying political activism are weak and add only a little to an explanation of variation.

As in our earlier analyses, general measures of civic and consumer ethos – having confidence in food taken home, trusting other people and believing that strategic actors tell the truth – almost always add substantially to the power of the explanation. This is true of each of them with respect to every issue, with the exception of improvement in nutritional quality, where trust in other people was not a significant predictor. These measures add quite significantly to the explanation of variance in the sample and seem to be orientations which differentiate populations within countries with respect to their attitudes to food.

The other set of variables, for country of residence (Model 1), is perhaps most interesting of all. The fact that key characteristics of individuals add so little to the explanation over and above a country effect is itself important. It suggests that there are many other aspects of national institutions and context that affect opinions which we have not been able to measure in our survey. Location by country is more important than the socio-demographic characteristics of individuals, their personal shopping habits, their political engagement or their general civic attachment. This might suggest that it is a taken-for-granted, shared, probably tacit, understanding – derived from primary socialization, commercial and social routines and mass-media messages – that underpins attitudes towards the food supply. Nonetheless, the way the differences occur between countries is significant. For each issue, the base case for the country indicators is Germany. The extent to which the balance of opinion, issue by issue, differs from that in Germany is indicated by the coefficients and their degree of significance. Clearly, perceptions of change differ from country to country and across the key issues. So, for example, with all other variables controlled, opinions on safety and price are not significantly different in Italy and Germany, but they do differ on taste and nutrition. On taste and quality, though, Germans are indistinguishable from the Norwegians, while on nutrition there is no difference between Germans and the Danes. This is evidence for there being features in common among the countries. At the same time we can also see significant differences, the result of varied institutional history and systems of regulation.

6.10 Conclusion

The consumer is everywhere deferred to as powerful, her opinion deemed important. Although it is a commonplace of contemporary cultural analysis that the consumer is assuming more authority, becoming more active, more able and willing personally to act in order to manage their own lives through the process of consumption, evidence of this effect was not very pronounced in our data. Consumers, and their representatives, seem to have comparatively little capacity to control the quality of the food that they receive. Yet, because it has been so frequently announced that the consumer is important, ordinary individuals have probably been emboldened to reassess their expectations and rights of proper and fair dealing by business and the state. They are particularly prominent figures in discourse, and they may have had considerable indirect influence because of the lip-service paid to them by other powerful actors even if their reputation for power is far from matched by their efficacy in the determination of economic and political outcomes.

When expressing opinions on food issues, people are rather more likely to be involved in economically oriented action than in political protest, though we have seen that the distinction between these two is rather problematic. At least when asked directly, a large majority of people express concern about a great many issues related to the safety and quality of food. Yet only a minority take action in response. This suggests a situation where potential discontent is largely submerged, possibly as a result of people attributing to other institutional actors of responsibility for worrisome issues and feeling rather powerless themselves, or, more likely, the effect of the adoption and routinization of locally conventional practices surrounding food preparation and consumption. In the course of normal daily life food is managed without too much reflection upon its negative aspects. The story is more one of routinized consumption than active consumers or citizens.

People differ in the ways that they think about their roles as consumers and they exhibit a differential propensity for engagement in strategies for actively changing the conditions in which they consume. The history of consumer associations, modes of political conflict resolution and perceptions of the appropriate role for 'the consumer' has influenced collective activity around food. Nonetheless, there are no apparent strong direct connections between individual and collective activism and generalized trust. As might be anticipated, consumer activism is highest where a need for reassurance is most prevalent; that is, where there is no longer primacy of personalized familiarity, on the one hand, and no generalized system confidence, on the other. So confidence persists in Denmark and Norway; familiar assurance is still primary in Portugal and seems to be moderately effective. But neither Germany nor Italy has a centralized system in which the population has confidence. There is a high level of suspicion of both market actors and state. This induces popular activism. But, as yet, channels for a satisfactory response to discontent (that is, a responsive institutionalization of distrust) have not transpired. In the United Kingdom, by contrast, a new system based upon institutionalized distrust emerged, with appropriate institutional arrangements generating reassurance, at least with respect to matters of safety.

Confirming the findings of Chapters 4 and 5, we see that, despite some internal differentiation in trust-related beliefs and actions (for example women being less trusting than men in most countries), national differences are more significant. Not only is this true around the issue of safety, but also around other key food issues. This was made clear in the final section of this chapter which demonstrated that, with respect to perceptions of change, personal and household characteristics, shopping patterns and political engagement all make a difference. Yet, even when considered together they explain much less of the measured variance in opinion than does country of residence. Nor do they directly explain the more general patterns of difference in national levels of trust. This suggests that we need to look in addition at other aspects of the institutionalization of food delivery – at the organization of markets and regimes of regulation.

Overall, we see that the ways in which people act on consumption issues vary significantly from country to country, and that when it comes to explaining their views of change in the realm of food, much of the variation seems to be a result less of their own practices – of purchasing or mobilization – than of their country of residence. This, we believe, is one reason why analysis of the changing nature of trust should be focused less on individuals, their personal characteristics or action, and more on the institutional context in which they are located. It is not sufficient to look at individual consumers to understand consumption! In this regard we suggest that the enormous political and academic attention paid to 'the consumer' is often misleading because it ignores the sense in which consumption is itself highly institutionalized. The actions of consumers are less a matter of personal choice, and more constrained by the institutional arrangements of household and retail system in the different countries. In the next chapter we therefore look more closely at the societal patterns of consumption which constitute the foundations upon which consumers meet providers in the relationship of market exchange. Understanding the interdependence of institutionalization of consumption and the organization of provision offers a further step forward in explaining consumer trust in context.

7
Buying into Food

In this and the following chapter, we progressively develop the institutional and relational foundations for variations in trust in food. The survey demonstrated major variations between countries in levels of trust for safety, but also for many other trust dimensions of truth-telling, value for money, quality of food, nutrition and ethics of food provisioning. In the last chapter, it was shown how the figure of the consumer has been constructed, with particular focus on the articulation between consumer and citizen.

Given that trust is a question of 'who trusts whom about what', there are three connected relationships that are key to understanding trust in food: between consumers and provisioners; between consumers and the state, especially the regulatory bodies; and between the state and the provisioners. This means that we are looking at a triad of relationships, which we call 'triangular affairs' of trust. Although our focus is on consumer trust, however, it is worth emphasizing the distinction made between trust as an emergent property of relationships and the relationships themselves. The significance of this distinction lies in the fact that, for example, between supermarkets and consumers *relationships* must be reciprocal and asymmetric (both depend on each other, but the one sells, the other buys); but *trust* is non-reciprocal. Few people question whether supermarkets trust consumers, and it is unclear what they would mean if they did. This presents a strong contrast with inter-personal or inter-business trust relationships, where trust may well depend on reciprocity even where relationships are asymmetric. So from the outset, *consumer* trust raises different questions to other kinds of trust, as an emergent property of the consumer–provisioner relationship. A parallel but not identical line of reasoning applies to relationships and trust between consumers and state authorities, where a crisis of legitimacy generally refers to a distrust of consumers towards authorities, not the other way round.[1]

The argument over the next two chapters develops stepwise. Each pole of the triad of relationships has its own internal organization. Consumers of food, for example, are organized in households in ways that vary between countries. Provisioning systems, including the way retail shops sell food to consumers, differ greatly. And finally, state regulatory and political systems are strongly contrasted between countries. So, each of the poles of the triad are explored in terms of variations in their internal organization. But differences in the organization of the poles internally are only developed in interdependency with the other poles of the relational complex. Having characterized the poles, therefore, the complex of relationships within the triad is built up, until we arrive at our triangular affairs.

In this chapter, we start the process by looking at the first relationship of the triad, that between consumers and provisioners (Figure 7.1).

A core trust relationship for food is shaped by who *buys* what from whom, and how. It is almost inescapable: consumers must buy what they eat. This constitutes the relationship between consumers and provisioners, mediated by the activity of shopping. An enormous societal variety exists across Europe in how this relationship is instituted. Consumers may have very different habits and practices within a country but, short of emigrating and outside delimited cultural 'pockets', it is impossible to buy into food in a fully Italian mode in England, or behave like a Norwegian shopper in Portugal.

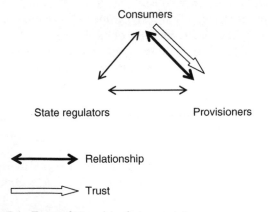

Figure 7.1 Trust relationships between actors

Each of the two poles to this relationship is open to substantial variation. At one pole there are the different ways consumer behaviour is organized – the societal norms and routines involve the 'institutional-ization of consumption'. This concept is a key to the difference between the approach developed here, and those methodological individualist approaches to the consumer described earlier. There are describable structured norms and routines of consumption that mark differences between countries, differences at the societal level. This is not to say that there are not also significant differences within societies, but the aim here is to match the level of explanation to the evident societal differences in levels of trust discernable from the survey.

At the other pole, there is what we call the food provisioning system. These also differ at the societal level in terms of the organization of retailing outlets, farming, processing and logistics – resulting in huge contrasts in the presentation, range and quality of foods available to consumers in different countries.

But, and this will be an important part of our argument, it is possible for changes in one or both poles of the relationship to result in provisioning systems and societal modes of consumption becoming out of kilter with each other. Broad cultural changes in consumer lifestyles, on the one hand, can occur independently of food consumption, yet nonetheless impact on it – the growth of home entertainment or sporting activities are examples. It is equally possible for changes on the provisioning side to produce conflicts and disruptions in previously accepted norms of quality, consistency, reliability, value for money, safety or ethics of food. The conflicts or crises, whether on the provi-sioning side (BSE, salmonellas, dioxin) or on the consumer side (slow food, animal welfare, environmentalism), are only the more highly visible manifestations of changes that can disrupt the core relationship.

So in this chapter we test out what kind of explanation will emerge from looking exclusively at this market relationship between con-sumers and providers. In broad terms, from the survey it is already clear that consumers in countries most characterized by shopping in super-markets have higher levels of trust. In countries where more familiar, personalized and traditional relationships continue to predominate, trust in food is not only lower, but there is a general perception across issues of price, quality and nutrition that things are getting worse. How much and what can be explained by looking at the institutionalization of consumers and differences in provisioning systems in each of the countries?

7.1 Variation in the institutionalization of consumption

One pole of variation between countries centrally concerns the 'institutionalization of consumption'. By this is meant different societal patterns of behaviour related to food in household-provisioning and consumption, and here we isolate some of the key societal parameters of interest. Food provisioning does not end, necessarily, at the shop door. To sustain end-market exchanges between consumers and retailers, a whole range of organized consumer practices is assumed, which cannot be derived directly from supply-side characteristics. The household as a primary institution for food consumption is not simply an effect of the products bought and consumed within it. Coordinated acts of purchase, food preparation and eating within households are critical to the asymmetry of power between sellers and buyers of food, and equally to trust considered as a relationship between them. Thus, for example, whatever the balance of products available in retail outlets, the purchases and preparations by consumers complete a process of food provisioning that affects nutrition, health, quality, economy and ethics. There is a division of labour and responsibility, and hence of who trusts whom over what, that is constructed through this relationship: a ready-meal heated in a microwave entails quite different possible trust relationships between retailers/manufacturers and consumers than food bought as raw/fresh ingredients to be prepared in the household. Labour market participation can also be expected to affect not only the gendering of consumer-side food provisioning, but also the extent to which food preparation is undertaken in households or on the supply side. Meal structure and cuisine can be expected to be at least partially shaped by the interdependency between household and commodity-producing market economies, and differences between countries in these terms.

A further aspect of the institutionalization of consumers with profound impacts on the nature of food end-markets relates to what is eaten, when and how. National and regional cultures of food consumption, themselves historical and changing constructs, shape patterns of food purchasing, and have been argued to be constitutive of national identity. A nation is (in part) what it eats (Appadurai, 1988; Hogan, 1997; Mintz, 1996). The structure of meal-times, the balance in significance between meals at different eating times, as well as the content of meals, has complex interactions with working time, and the way that has historically evolved. The place of the meal in the household as part of its social fabric is changing not only within the internal dynamics of its social organization, but in relation to leisure activities, and competing social relations. The eating and design of food is a changing cultural and social institution that is structured and organized in the sphere of consumption beyond, but in interaction with, the market.

Summarizing these parameters for variation in institutionalization of the consumer, the following seven indicators can be seen as pointing to significant societal variation:

- Variations in cuisine
- The proportion of expenditure on food within the household budget as an indicator of the significance of food
- The extent of reliance on prepared food, including ownership of microwave ovens. The pattern of eating, in terms of how many main meals in the home per day, when, and how frequently eating out occurs
- Patterns of shopping behaviour
- The level of gender gap in paid employment, as an indicator of women's role in household provisioning
- Differences in household composition

Eating is a complex practice which requires a great deal of organization, at societal, household and personal levels. How to eat is governed by conventions of cuisine, or food culture. Food items have varying cultural significance, some prized, others shunned. Different ways of cooking convey different symbolic meanings. Particular dishes convey ritual, collective and emotional resonances. Meals, the basic form of the social ordering of food consumption, are constituted by a set of conventions which govern when they occur, what should be eaten, where and with whom. The preparation of food to source meals is also subject to complex social arrangements, involving societal and domestic divisions of labour. Food items emerge from distinct supply chains, technologies, expert knowledge, regulatory regimes and public discourses – which will influence expectations, experiences and trust relations. Foodstuffs are, then, 'products' or 'goods' acquired by a household member to be transformed at home into dishes and meals. Items playing a central role in the everyday diet may imply higher sensitivity towards trust issues. But the opposite may also hold, in that frequent use is associated with a taken-for-granted trust, more marginal foods being met with more reflection and perhaps stronger scepticism. Both might mean a correlation between the frequency of eating and trust, but in different directions.

We asked a very simple question about the frequency of eating various food items and find very varying patterns across the countries (Table 7.1).

Table 7.1 Frequency of eating various food items: 'Daily' or 'weekly' (percentage)*

	Norway	Denmark	W. Germany	E. Germany	Great Britain	Italy	Portugal
Vegetables	97	95	95	98	97	94	95
Fresh tomatoes	74	78	72	75	86	80	78
Canned tomatoes	44	39	14	11	51	52	27
Fish	80	58	56	65	71	75	96
Meat	94	97	85	92	86	93	96
Beef (roasts/steaks)	31	63	42	39	56	63	57
Minced beef, products and dishes from that	73	79	48	52	51	55	23
Cooked meal outside the home (restaurant, canteen, etc.)	20	26	31	31	39	30	42
N	1,004	1,000	1,000	1,000	1,566	2,006	1,000

* 'Don't know' has been excluded.

While broad food categories like meat and vegetables are represented in most people's diets all over Europe, we found large variations for more specific food items, and, in particular, for more processed varieties. The frequency of eating foods like canned tomatoes, fish, beef and minced beef vary significantly between the countries. We see variations in the prominence of our two food cases, beef and tomatoes. Moreover, while patterns are quite homogeneous within some countries, there is much more variation and polarization in others. We will comment on these patterns in relation to the distinctions identified for trust in food items.

Vegetables and meat have very different roles as elements of diets and meals. Both are in Europe usually part of 'cooked meals', but the structure of such meals as well as the daily rhythms may be quite diverse. While Danes and Norwegians eat only one cooked meal a day, two cooked meals is a more widespread norm in the rest of Europe. That means, for example, that food items and dishes, which represent alternatives on the daily menu in Denmark and Norway, may very well both appear daily in the other countries. Moreover, while a contemporary cooked meal in Northern Europe is very often 'a plateful' (staple *plus* meat/fish *plus* salad or cooked vegetable), several serial dishes are more common in the South. Fresh tomatoes seem to be part of the ordinary menu in all the six countries, most so in Great Britain, least in Germany and Norway. Eating beef is much more varied, this time with Italians and Danes ranking highest, while again we find Germans and Norwegians at the bottom of the list.

At this very general level of recording national eating patterns and their potential links to trust, there do not seem to be any clear patterns. This is hardly surprising. The figures show that food items like beef and tomatoes are important parts of the ordinary diet all over Europe and are thus not easily swapped for other types of food. While tomatoes have remained uncontested with regard to food safety, there has been much more turbulence around beef. Logistic regression analyses indicate that there are links between eating tomatoes and beef and trust in them, respectively, even when controlled for various socio-demographic background variables (Kjærnes, Poppe and Lavik, 2005). So not eating may constitute an exit strategy for people who are very sceptical about the safety of a food item. Aggregate effects of that were demonstrated when demand fell sharply as an immediate response to (domestic) cases of BSE (and the publication of its effects on humans). But this sudden response was short-lived. Demand – and eating patterns – was gradually normalized (Kjørstad, 2005). Moreover, this drop did not happen to the same degree everywhere. Denmark has experienced a long-term increasing trend in beef consumption during the whole period, despite a couple of incidents of BSE. Norway, with no cases of BSE at all, has had a stable, slightly upward trend. Vegetarianism may, in part, be interpreted as an expression of distrust. But there are no clear national patterns in the proportions not eating meat as related to trust in the safety of meats. The proportions are highest in Great Britain and West Germany, while remaining very small in all the other countries. Declining to eat certain items often seems short-lived, habits representing a strong force. But, in some cases, habits have changed. The occurrence of such responses seems to depend on the institutional context, rather than being linked to individual habits as such or to, for example, household resources.

In global terms, there are considerable differences, not explicable in terms of overall disposable income, between allocation of household budget to food in the six countries (Table 7.2). It would be rash to take this as any precise estimation of the cultural importance of food in a given county. Not the least, the proportions are influenced by the overall levels of income. Nonetheless, it is clear the two Nordic countries dedicate much lower percentage of household expenditure on food than the two Southern countries, with Germany and the United Kingdom falling in between. This is in spite of the notoriously high relative price of food in Norway.

As a token of the extent of food preparation in the home – or rather the lack of it – there is also considerable variation in the extent of microwave ownership, one that shows quite different trends from ownership of other electrical goods, such as Hi-Fi or mobile phones, for example. The United Kingdom stands out for its high levels of ownership of microwaves, and we know that the level of ownership is closely shadowed by the growth in the market for ready-made meals that has doubled from 1994 to 2004 (Mintel, 2005d; Pira Market Report,

Table 7.2 Percentage of household expenditure on food and ownership of microwave ovens

	Household budget, % expenditure on food	Ownership of microwaves
Italy	19	25
Portugal	18	33
United Kingdom	16	83
Germany	16	56
Norway	10	66
Denmark	6	58

Source: From National Reports, www.Trustinfood.org.

2005a, b). Conversely, Italy followed by Portugal, have significantly lower ownership, and viewed overall, these countries have a low consumption of ready-meals, chilled or fresh. The United Kingdom dominates Europe in the extent of its consumption of chilled ready-meals (Pira Market Report, 2005a, b) with 49 per cent of the total market, followed, interestingly, by France. Summarizing these two parameters, it is worth emphasizing that household expenditure is highest where most work is done in the home, and that purchasing ready-meals and relying on microwaves does not imply a shift to spending proportionately more on food in order to lessen the time and effort spent in household provisioning.

Following this first indication of the importance of household provisioning in the overall food provisioning system, we now turn to the variation in the organization of the household, first in terms of household composition, and then in terms of labour market participation. The distribution of tasks within households has been changing in most countries, as a function not only of pressure from feminist politics about fairness, but as a result of changing rates of participation in paid work by women and changing family and household structure. This too influences meal content and plays back upon typical eating patterns.

Much of food provision and consumption still occurs in the home. But the home is not the same sort of place for everyone. Indeed, household composition and domestic organization are currently subject to considerable transformation. The results of examining the association between household structure and food consumption indicate that the status of the household matters everywhere, both for eating and purchasing, to some degree even for trust. In particular, single people tend to eat and buy less beef, in some places even tomatoes. We must here remember that the household structure is very diverse across the countries. In particular, the 'single' category is smaller in Italy and Portugal, with few young (or not so young) people who have not yet established their own family, divorcees and so on, while the proportion of widows is larger. There are also more families with more than two adults, for example a grandmother or a grown-up son. This is a reflection of the family institution as such being stronger in Italy, and food consumption patterns vary in association (Barbagli and Saraceno, 1997; Lewis, 1997). Similar patterns are observed in Portugal. The relatively larger proportions of large families show distinct patterns, especially reflected in more use of beef. Also, especially in Portugal, eating out means something different, representing a daily alternative to home eating as opposed to, for example, Britain, where eating out is more a treat. A very noticeable characteristic of food purchasing in these family-oriented countries is the considerably larger division of labour between the genders.

The character of the household has an impact on consumption patterns in the other countries too. The point is that the family structure is different, in particular with higher proportions of singles, and the overall picture of the institutionalization of food consumption therefore becomes different. Norway and Denmark barely differ from one another. Controlled for other background variables, gender is significant for eating as well as trust in these two countries, but is not reflected in purchasing practices and the division of labour within the household. Germany seems to be quite similar, but perhaps with somewhat larger differences in consumption practices between the different household types. Britain is distinctive, in that gender matters less, while distinctions according to education are more pronounced.

This gendered aspect of household organization is critically related to labour market participation (see Table 7.3) and, as a negative mirror image, the extent to which women engage full time in unpaid work in the household.

As is well known, Nordic countries have high levels of women's participation in labour markets, whereas, particularly in full-time employment, the gender gap is highest in Italy and Germany, lowest in Denmark, Norway and the United Kingdom. It can be assumed that full-time employment gender gaps are the strongest indicator of constraints on time for women to be engaged in household provisioning of food. As observed below, the household mid-day meal is less an option for households with men and women working full time, and more characteristic of those countries with women more fully engaged in the household.

Shopping patterns likewise are an integral part of the household provisioning activity, also linked to the scheduling of time and participation

Table 7.3 The gender gap* between male and female employment (percentages)

	Denmark	W. Germany	United Kingdom	Italy	Portugal	Norway
Gender gap employment rate	8.3	13.1	12.7	27.1	17.3	6.1
Gender gap part time	−10.8	−18.7	−7.9	−8.1	−5.1	−17.2
Gender gap full time	19.1	31.8	20.6	35.2	22.4	23.3

* The 'gap' is calculated as the difference between the proportion of adult males and females of working age who are economically active.

Source: European Labour Force Survey, 2002.

Table 7.4 Where customers shop for tomatoes and beef

	Norway		Denmark		United Kingdom		Germany		Italy		Portugal	
	Toms	Beef	Toms	Beef	Toms	Beef	Toms	Beef	Toms	Beef	Toms	Beef
Supermarket	93	86	81	74	80	64	65	34	49	39	54	20
F&V/butcher	6	11	11	19	12	30	12	52	26	57	11	77
Small shop	0	0	2	1	4	3	4	2	2	1	8	0
Food market	1	3	3	1	3	2	12	1	18	1	21	1
Other way	1	0	3	6	2	1	8	11	5	3	6	2

in the labour market. This is one aspect of the institutionalization of consumption, the role of the consumer as shopper. Shopping also directly involves interaction with the provisioning system and the exchange relation itself: where consumers buy into food and from whom they buy food. Taking the two food items, tomatoes and beef, there are considerable differences across the six countries. Reading from left to right, Table 7.4 below presents countries most dominated by consumers that shop in supermarkets to those that are most represented by consumers buying from small shops and food markets. It is perhaps surprising that Norway is by a margin the most supermarket-dependent, and that the United Kingdom only ranks third. As will be discussed later, this perhaps demonstrates clearly that there is no straightforward relationship between patterns of consumer behaviour and supermarket-retailer dominance within the provisioning system. It is possible for consumers to shop more in supermarkets even where supermarket retailers themselves are not the dominant players in the provisioning system.

Conversely, Italy and above all Portugal demonstrate how much shopping is undertaken in food markets for tomatoes and butchers for beef, even though supermarkets have become significant sources for both food items. Germany falls quite distinctively betwixt and between the two major groupings of supermarket-dominated shoppers and food market/small dedicated retailer shopping consumers. It is similar to Italy and Portugal when buying beef, but in between when it comes to buying tomatoes.

From the survey (see Table 7.4, see also Table 6.1), it also appears that the practice of shopping is closely related to the nature of the social relationships involved. Very broadly, in the high supermarket-shopping countries, most consumers do not consider personally knowing the retailing staff matters very much (how could it?), whereas knowing the shop from previous experience matters to many more consumers, and in the case of the United Kingdom, by a large majority. Conversely, in the countries where people frequent small shops and food markets, Italy and Portugal, knowing both the staff and the shop matters a lot to most consumers (Table 7.5).

It is perhaps significant that two countries at opposite ends of the spectrum in terms of shopping behaviours, the United Kingdom and Portugal, are those that often enjoy their shopping (33 per cent and 62 per cent, respectively), whereas Norwegians stand out in their displeasure of the activity (only 9 per cent frequently enjoying the experience). Supermarket shopping is not one and the same thing everywhere.

Finally, only Germany and Italy retain the mid-day meal at home on a general basis, most countries having decisively shifted to a main meal in the evening. Portugal is characterized by two cooked meals, one at the place of work. This is also reflected in their high frequency of people eating out daily. Italy, too, retains the two cooked meals routine, but both are eaten in the household.

In terms of the concept of 'institutionalization of consumption', there is clearly a sense that each of these parameters hang together, and that there are distinctive ways of organizing food provisioning. Eating, cuisine, organization of meals, food significance, provisioning and food preparation, household organization for food, and food purchasing

Table 7.5 Familiarity and shopping (proportion of consumers considering knowing the staff personally and/or the shop from previous experience when purchasing beef to be important)

	Norway	Denmark	Great Britain	W. Germany	E. Germany	Italy	Portugal
Important to know staff	12	21	38	39	35	63	65
Important to know shop	37	55	73	61	55	79	70

constitute an ensemble, and it is as an ensemble that we see social variation. In this sense, the concept expresses more than a bundling together of otherwise completely independent consumer practices. A food lifestyle and organization, a scheduling of activities (Southerton, 2003), a division of labour, entails an interdependence and coherence between the practices, and not an infinite number of possible combinations. Together, these dimensions generate a picture of how much responsibility consumers assume for food provisioning, and the importance of eating at home in the social life of the household. In one sense, this could suggest a way of determining the level of commodification of the food provisioning system, and thereby the extent to which food trust relationships between consumers and provisioners have become commercialized, shifting the locus of responsibility away from consumers. Low gender differentiation in labour market participation can contribute to this variation of levels of commodification, and reliance on commercialization of provisioning in terms of time spent shopping, preparing, and cooking.

There is significant and systemic variation in the institutionalization of the ensemble of consumer behaviour in household provisioning and consumption across the six countries. Picking on some striking contrasts, in Norway expenditure on food is relatively low, time spent on food preparation and cooking is relatively low, and there is a single main daily meal, in the evening. Italy and Portugal provide the contrary cases of high expenditure on food as a proportion of the household budget, and considerable home provisioning, preparation and cooking, especially considering that many households enjoy two main meals at home.

Exploring these contrasts, however, the picture is certainly not a simple commodified versus non-commodified, commercialized versus personal familiar household provisioning and consumption pattern. In Portugal, nearly a quarter of consumers appear to eat one main meal out on a daily basis, and this contrasts with Italy as much as with West Germany. Amongst the high supermarket-shopping countries, both Denmark and Norway contrast with the other main high supermarket-shopping country in terms of the budgetary significance of food purchasing in the household budget. It appears that the wider price and variety range of United Kingdom supermarkets is matched by consumption of more elaborate, if often pre-prepared food. Yet a further nuance is suggested by Germany, especially West Germany, where strong gendered division of labour and relatively low levels of women's participation in paid employment does not result in high levels of food preparation from raw ingredients that is found in the two Southern European countries. Indeed, reliance on frozen ready-made food in Germany is high, constituting the largest European market for this type of food (Pira Market Report, 2005a). The modest level of household expenditure on food appears to match the discounting strategy of supermarket provisioners, but patterns of shopping, as already noted, are far more mixed in Germany between extremes of low-price quality-insensitive food, and high-price, traditional quality foods.

So, overall, there is substantial variation within the two most contrasting groups of countries, Norway, Denmark and the United Kingdom, on the one hand, and Italy and Portugal, on the other. Germany is a quite distinctive third main example, and should not simply be viewed as falling in the middle of a single continuum from the commercialized to the non-commercialized household provisioning and consumption patterns.

Nonetheless, the selected dimensions of institutionalization of food consumption and household provisioning can be seen to underpin the nature of the exchange between provisioners and consumers. There are different modes of 'buying into food', involving different divisions of responsibilities between these two actors, as a consequence of patterns of consumer behaviour considered in their own right.

7.2   Variation in provisioning systems

Working outwards from the end-market exchange between consumers and retailers towards the provisioning system, there is a large and changing cast of classes of economic agents involved in interdependent exchanges: different types of retail outlet, food processors (branded and supermarket own-label), distributors, logistics, packaging, marketing, seed manufacture, farmers, agricultural services, biotechnology, and so on. For sake of systematic comparison, however, we have chosen to consider principally three major classes of economic agent: retailers, food processors and farmers. Institutional bases of trust are fundamentally altered by the nature of the relationships between these classes of actors in the provisioning system. Each of these interdependent markets is characterized by its own specific asymmetries of power and mutual dependency, and how these successive markets are articulated with each other has a critical impact on the nature of exchanges in the end-market (Harvey, Quilley and Beynon, 2003), and hence on consumer trust.

Four dimensions of variation in the relationship between the three main provisioning agents are of major importance:

- The quality of asymmetric power exercised by different actors in relation to each other.
- The relative concentration within each class of economic agent.

- The integrative or serial interdependency between and across multiple markets.

- The *relativity* of geographic scale of exchange relations between trading classes – of economic agent (for example, global–global, global–national, national–local, local–local).

Consumers may have limited knowledge of what lies behind the purchase of food on the provisioning side. Nonetheless, between our three main provisioning actors, farmers, manufacturers and retailers, it matters a great deal where the power lies, and there may be no uniform pattern within a given national provisioning system – never mind the role of major global international food producers. Retailers are at the direct interface with consumers. If they exercise strategic power over the food provisioning system, they are capable of rapidly responding to and transmitting consumer shopping patterns back to farmers and manufacturers. Retailers however, control only the access of food to market. Producers, whether manufacturers or farmers, exercise quite a different kind of power, over what and how food is produced and how it is advertised. If they hold strategic power, their impact on consumers is quite different, through global brands or through claims to authenticity of a regional produce or speciality, such as Champagne or Parmesan cheese.

Closely connected to the question of which of the three types of actor hold strategic power, there is the question of the relative concentration or monopoly in each part of the provisioning system. When shopping in the United Kingdom or Norway, for example, consumers effectively only have a handful of possible retailers from whom to purchase their food. In the one case, however, the UK retailers have strategic control over the provisioning system, whereas in Norway, producer organizations still maintain considerable ownership and control over retailers. In Norway, unlike the United Kingdom, the manufacturer brands of instant coffee, yoghurt or breakfast cereal are either predominantly global from Nestlé and Unilever or from powerful domestic producers: milk from Tine and minced beef from Gilde. The balance of power and the concentration of power is critical in assessing who trusts whom about what: a farmer's authentic produce, a manufacturer and a branded product, or retailers and their own range of services and products.

A third dimension of a provisioning system that can have significant impacts on the consumer concerns the extent to which there is integration and coordination from farm to fork. Much of the current language concerning provisioning of many consumer goods, as well as food, speaks of integrated supply chains. But the picture across Europe is much patchier, as we shall see. There are often significant breaks in the chain. Where wholesale markets still exist, the consumer is a remote and quite insignificant figure to the primary producer: all that matters is getting a good price for the produce, and selling as much as possible of the crop or catch. At the opposite extreme, farm-gate sales, and direct producer street markets, eliminate all but the first and last link of a chain. Integration can involve just one aspect of food, whether it is organic or not, for example. In some countries, one authority dominates certification and standardization of what is organic, while in others competing actors with conflicting standards can generate significant confusion and uncertainty.

Finally, the geographic scale of the different actors, and more particularly, their scale relative to each other, has a major influence on how and what presents itself for purchase to the consumer. As one of our chosen foods illustrates well, it is one thing to buy a tomato in Italy, quite another in Norway or Germany. Importing and exporting food is a critical aspect of provisioning. For some primary produce there are global and highly concentrated wholesale distributors (wheat, bananas, pineapples) (Davis, 2001; Morgan, 1979). In some countries, predominantly national producers deliver goods to predominantly national-scale retailers. And in yet others, local produce is sold through local shops and markets. In recent years, there has been strong advocacy of a return to Short Food Supply Chains (SFSCs) seen as a counter-tendency to globalization and standardization (Green, Harvey and McMeekin, 2003; Murdoch and Miele, 1999; Ward and Almås, 1997), and claims are made for a counter-valent concept of quality in their end-markets. But it is clear that different scale relativities between interdependent markets are constantly being reshaped. The reinvention and branding of localized small-scale production of many food products by globalizing retailers is but one of many examples that illustrate the point.

From the survey, consumers demonstrate quite divergent evaluations of the importance of where the food they buy comes from. Table 7.6 below shows the percentage of respondents in each country that considered it important that their beef or tomatoes were home-country produced.[2]

Table 7.6 Percentage of consumers deeming it important for food to be produced in their home-country

	Denmark	W. Germany	E. Germany	United Kingdom	Italy	Portugal	Norway
Beef	66	76	76	62	84	86	63
Tomatoes	68	51	62	57	84	78	55

Italy and Portugal are by a margin the most nationalistic, the United Kingdom and Norway the least – in spite of, or possibly even because of, the latter's highly protected quota system limiting considerably the availability of non-national food. Germany is quite schizophrenic, being strongly nationalistic for beef, but more realistically less so in regard to tomatoes, the overwhelming majority of which are imported.

Based on this framework for analysing provisioning systems, and using the qualitative empirical material from the institutional research, the main contrasting features of provisioning systems in the six countries can be systematically compared.

The United Kingdom has perhaps the most developed retailer domination of the food provisioning system. Three national supermarket chains, with Tesco their significant leader, dominate the share of the grocery market. As an economic indicator of this power, there is the highest level of supermarket own-label produce in Europe. But perhaps even more conclusive, even major global branded manufacturers are constrained to produce goods under a Tesco or Sainsbury own label. Moreover, a style of product quality and price differentiation has become a nationally dominant one, and neither Wal-Mart's purchase of Asda nor continental European discount, price-oriented retailer strategies have made significant inroads. It is in this sense that we can talk of a hegemonic model of national retailing in the United Kingdom for a price–quality differentiated market. This concentration of power has enabled supermarkets to develop integrated supply chains, from farm to fork, under the prescriptive orchestration of the retailers. Moreover, this provisioning supply is global and competitive, not only in terms of counter-seasonal produce, but in terms of general food items. The range and variety of food has been thoroughly transformed.

Norway is if anything characterized by even greater supermarket retail concentration with the top four players accounting for 90 per cent of the market (Mintel, 2003b). But, in contrast to the United Kingdom, they do not exercise equivalent power over the provisioning system. The largest is Norgesgruppen, a company based on franchising, the next two are ICA (Ahold) and the consumer cooperative (Co-op Norge). Related to this, although beginning to change, is the relatively low level of supermarket own-labels: branded manufacturers are the primary identity for packaged food, fresh or processed. Wholesale markets – especially for fish – are still significant, and in general there is only partial integration of supply chains. But perhaps the most conspicuous feature when shopping in Norwegian supermarkets is the predominance of Norwegian food products. Strict quotas and tariffs prevent or restrict the entry of foreign food in competition with Norwegian food, especially within the meat and dairy sectors. In this protected market, prices are high although quality is standardized at the lower level, preventing the price–quality differentiation evident in other markets. Agricultural production is relatively fragmented, but there is a well-organized constituency of primary producers capable of exerting strong political influence. Farmers also exert considerable power via the very dominant manufacturers owned by producer cooperatives. Overall, one can say that Norway substantially remains a producer-oriented provisioning system. In these circumstances, there is a market consensus around safety and national origin of food, but other food dimensions are either contentious or below the radar.

Denmark in many ways resembles Norway with the important difference that agriculture is much more export oriented, and non-protectionist. As with Norway, supermarket dominance in retailing is not combined with supermarket power over the provisioning system, the main power, economically and politically residing firmly with producers. The two dominant retailers – Coop Danmark and Dansk Supermarked – represent contrasting models, the first a consumer-owned and franchising retailer, the second a retail multiple. So behind the façade, extensive franchising covers a multitude of small retail-store owners. There is a strong and growing presence of German discount retailing (Aldi), but also alternative suppliers and niche marketing for quality foods. Legislation passed in 1997 has strongly restricted the growth of large out-of-town hypermarkets. Food producers have become much more concentrated over the past 30 years, with the number of farms reducing by two-thirds, but remaining relatively fragmented. Manufacturers are no longer producer-owned and some (like Arla and Tulip) have grown to become major global players. Nonetheless, under the Agricultural Council, farmers are highly organized and maintain considerable political influence (Nielsen and Møhl, 2004). Safety and price form the core of any consensus between market provisioners.

Germany provides a striking contrast, with a highly divided food provisioning system, and conflicting food strategies, even food-value systems. Agricultural production is, in general, quite fragmented with cooperatives dominating in the old East Germany, and family farms in the West. There is a strong organization of smallholders, the German Farmers Association (DBV), closely linked with the Christian Democratic Union (Lenz, 2003). The retail sector is split between some dominant hard-discount retailers focusing mainly on non-fresh food produce and a multitude of small, specialist and traditionalist retailers.

Aldi and Lidl account for nearly 30 per cent of food market share, with Edeka and Rewe, both voluntary groupings of franchisees rather than multiples, providing a supermarket alternative to discounting (Mintel, 2005c). In this context, the provisioning system overall has no generalized supply chain integration, but rather parallel and disparate patterns of organizing supply from farm to fork. This is compounded by a relatively high level of regionalization, mirroring federal political structures. In a way, this only emphasizes the contrast in organization and values between the nationally scaled hard-discounters and the food cultures of the rest of the provisioning system.

Turning to Italy, again one finds a new range of contrasts, demonstrating the extent of the diversity of provisioning systems even within Europe and its 'single market' embraced by a Common Agricultural Policy. Moreover, within Italy there are profound differences – as with many other aspects of Italian life – between the north and south. Overall, compared with most of Northern Europe, there is a very high level of smallholdings and family farms, often with very low hectarage/acreage, northern Italy has much greater presence of agribusiness than the south. The same pattern is reflected in food manufacturing, although there is often a heavy but localistic concentration of specialist food production (Barilla for pasta, Parma ham, etc.). Fragmentation elsewhere in Italy, both of primary and manufactured food provisioning, is such that any supply chain integration is effectively precluded (Ferritti and Magaudda, 2004). The power of large retail chains is the lowest in Europe, with only one retailer, Coop-Italia, reaching 10 per cent of the market (Mintel, 2005a). However, Italy, especially in the North, has been open to an increasing presence of large foreign retail chains, with the French Carrefour a significant player, followed by Auchan (having recently acquired Gruppo Rinascente), threatening Coop-Italia's market leadership. Otherwise, retailing is characterized overwhelmingly by small independent traders and local enterprises. If supermarketization is growing, therefore, it is significantly from outside Italy, so confirming the contrast between a traditionalist, localistic and fragmented provisioning system and a modernizing, national or international provisioning system. If both Germany and Italy can be seen as heterogeneous, the dimensions of contrast are quite different, and the concomitant food cultures and values also.

Finally, Portugal displays some of the same characteristics as Italy but with food production, distribution and retailing being overall less developed, it is perhaps unsurprising to find that all of the top five retailers are wholly or partially owned by foreign companies (Ahold, Carrefour, Auchan and Intermarché). The top two, Modelo Continente and Jerónimo Martins, however, have a higher share of the provisioning market than Coop-Italia, and together achieve nearly 30 per cent of the market (Mintel, 2003c). This externally led modernization of retailing, which has resulted now in hypermarkets and supermarkets accounting for over 75 per cent of the urban market, is in sharp contrast to developments in agriculture and manufacture. Prior to Portugal joining the EU in 1986, agriculture was highly protected, and traditional small-farming predominated, with the highest level of agricultural population (23 per cent) scattered in farms whose average size was only five hectares. Even after 15 years, and a reduction to one-third in the number of farms, the average size remains at ten hectares, and family farms represent 90 per cent of all agricultural enterprises (Domingues, Graça and de Almeida, 2004). The contrast here is within the provisioning system, with a modernizing retailing system grafted onto an agriculture still deeply marked by its history of protectionism.

From this comparison, it is clear that there are major systemic differences in food provisioning in our six countries. Where the power lies, how far it is concentrated or dispersed between and within the three classes of provisioning actors, varies considerably. Two countries, Norway and the United Kingdom, both with high levels of supermarket concentration, are nonetheless starkly contrasted with respect to the power of the supermarkets, the development of integrated supply chains, and the reliance on, and even elevation of, national sourcing of food. Fish is much more central to the Norwegian cuisine, and as a consequence the wholesale market characteristic of both countries (the unfarmed sea-fishing industry being generally the least amenable to supply chain management) becomes a much more salient feature in the Norwegian context. Other countries, such as Italy and Portugal, rely much more heavily on local sourcing and much small-scale farming, no doubt partly sustained by the Common Agricultural Policy. Another dimension of contrast is that in some countries food provisioning is nationally organized, even if there may be some regional variation in consumption patterns. In other countries, there is a high level of regional or even local provisioning. So it is possible to see some countries as having nationally integrated provisioning systems (the United Kingdom, Denmark and Norway), whereas others do not (Italy, Portugal), and in Germany there is a mixture of strong national and regional provisioning.

The reasons why these variations matter for trust relations becomes obvious through making the contrasts. For example, strongly national sourcing by largely national actors creates a basis in Norway for trusting

Norwegian food, but not necessarily either enjoying buying it, or caring where it comes from. The food is 'protected'. In Italy, there can be much more regional rivalry, but also the actors to be trusted are regional or local, so the trust relationship is unlikely to be a generalized national one. Nonetheless, food must be from somewhere in Italy, not outside. In the United Kingdom, the actors to be trusted are certainly national, but commercial-national, and are the actors that are central to the consumer's purchase of food: their trust is trust in Asda, Sainsbury or Tesco. One of the most interesting findings of the United Kingdom Competition Commission's (2000) investigation of supermarkets was the strongly habitual pattern of shopping in the same store, week in, week out, even where competitor stores existed in close proximity.[3] The problem was not that supermarkets were displaying uncompetitive behaviour, but that consumers were not behaving as market actors should! Combining these dimensions with the distribution of power, it clearly matters whether the actors with whom consumers have the most direct contact, the retailers, have power over the provisioning system or not. Trusting an actor with the power to make a difference is quite distinct from trusting one with whom the consumer might have a much more equal power relation. In countries where branded-food manufacturers have a strong power position, the trust relationship is indirect.

At another level, provisioning systems can be analysed in terms of their integration and the presence or absence of an hegemony or consensus over the five key food issues of safety, quality, value for money and ethics. The question is whether the market actors are competing and/or cooperating with each other on the same playing field, or playing quite different games, even disputing the worth of the values promoted by their rivals. Here a different kind of trust issue arises. In Norway, there is a high level of consensus, without market hegemony, over the overriding significance of safety in food, which combines with the relative protectionist, solidaristic virtues of national sourcing. In the United Kingdom, there is also a high level of consensus, but combined with market hegemony of the main food actors, around a broader range of values related to the five key food issues: largely the main supermarkets compete on the same terrain of quality and price differentiation, value for money, global sourcing of globalized cuisine, and promotion of organics as a strong niche. Organic ideals are not generally articulated by actors opposing the supermarket hegemony, but have been absorbed within it. Germany, by contrast, exhibits quite a high level of conflict, lack of market integration, and absence of consensus amongst food provisioners. There are, on the one hand, powerful national discount retailers, where price is the supreme virtue, and on the other, various traditional, or organic, or local, values and virtues that are promoted frequently in antagonism to the price-discounting mode of cheap food. Finally, and this is probably a more general phenomenon, Italy and Portugal, to different degrees, reflect the emergence of more powerful national retailers and manufacturers, and a decline of a previously hegemonic traditional and local provisioning system. But the rise of one set of values, and the decline of another, has created a dislocation concerning the 'what' is trusted as well as the 'who' in the trust relationship, especially in relation to how provisioners ensure quality standards. In circumstances of confusion, dissension and conflict *amongst the provisioning actors* over what matters most about food, and how it can be delivered, trust relationships become more complex than where there is hegemony and consensus.

7.3   Putting the relationship back together

At the beginning of the chapter, we argued that the central relationship 'who trusts whom about what' concerning food was between provisioners and consumers. Although we argue that trust is inherently relational, it has been necessary to discuss the two main parties to the relationship separately, before putting them back in touch again. There are two issues at stake here. First, once in a relationship, it is sometimes difficult to disentangle what each party distinctively brings to it. Thus, consumers buy most of their food from supermarkets (small shops, food markets), because most food is sold in supermarkets (small shops, food markets) or vice versa. This raises the old sore of supply versus demand (Harvey, 2002), but on the bigger scale of what kind of shops consumers demand (as opposed to individual food goods). Do supermarkets exist in response to consumer demand, or do consumers buy food from supermarkets because that is how retailers most profitably sell food? By separating out the institutional characteristics of provisioning and consumption, it becomes possible to understand the different contributions that each party brings to the relationship. Second, and by the same token, in many cases and through the very sustainability of relationships, there appears to be an almost natural matching between the parties. But, by pulling the relationship apart, it becomes possible to explore the potential for, and even the presence of, mismatches. The pace and nature of change of provisioning systems may throw them out of kilter with the practices, norms and expectations of consumers – or vice versa.

In a stylized way we can present the key relationship of buying into food for each of the six countries, here emphasizing their distinctiveness, rather than the many characteristics they may share (Figure 7.2).

These six, highly schematized and societal caricatures display very contrasting relational foundations for trust between consumers and provisioners. At first glance, the implications for trust as an emergent property of these relationships might seem quite straightforward. Where

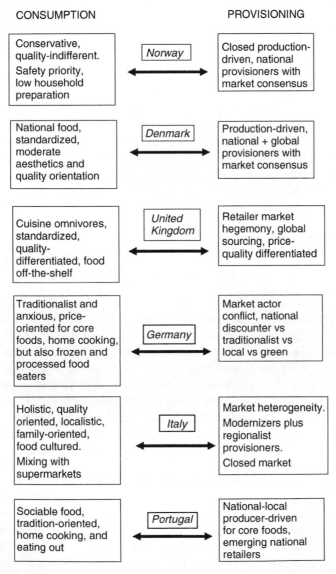

Figure 7.2 Market exchange relationships between consumers and provisioners

supermarkets have modernized food provisioning systems, and consumers have organized their lives around minimizing the time and family sociability around food, their trust in food, and a general sense of improvement, has developed. This could be a consumer *and* market modernization thesis: consumers have organized their lives around modern urban cultural norms, downgraded the social centrality of home food consumption in concert with changes in provisioning systems that have developed the means of delivering mass standardized products to an acceptable safety, certainly, and in some cases with quality, value and ethics too. By contrast, the countries with most unsettled consumers in relation to conflictual or heterogeneous market provisioners, Germany, and above all Italy, are countries that display considerable levels of distrust. In the next chapter, we will see that Germany in some respects distrusts market actors more than any other country, even if its distrust of food safety, and other key food issues, is not as acute as in Italy. So these countries could appear to present a picture of disrupted relationships on the road to modernization of both consumption and food provisioning.

However, even restricting the analysis to the consumer–market relationship, this dualism of modernizers versus unsettled traditionalists appears far too simplistic. It can readily be seen that the potential nature of trust differs sharply even between countries characterized either by the high salience of supermarkets for both provisioners and consumers, or by those countries with much localized or regionalized provisioning systems and traditional, quality-oriented consumers. If there is market consensus amongst most provisioning actors in Norway and Denmark, there is nothing equivalent to the market hegemony exercised by the main retail chains in the United Kingdom. Very different societal consumer orientations and practices towards these supermarkets means that there is a different kind of matching of norms and expectations in these countries. Norway, in particular, displays power still residing heavily in food producers – supermarket own-label production and retailer orchestration of the supply chain are only encroaching at the margins. Rather, Norway has almost the most closed and protected traditional consumer–market relationship of all – even more so, perhaps, than Portugal.

Germany provides an interesting case of multiple consumer values and conflicting market provisioning strategies, which could generate high levels of consumer discrimination and diversity of practices. The result could be as much a multiplicity of different relationships around different matching norms and expectations as destabilized or disrupted relationships.

Both Italy and Portugal display some of the same characteristics – in some ways not that different from Norway – with a conservative traditionalism[4] still very much in evidence. However, in both those countries, but especially in Italy, disruption of old relationships, and conflicts between embattled consumer norms and expectations and newly emergent modernizing provisioning systems and shopping habits provide examples of conflict and mismatches in consumer–provisioner relationships. Italy can be partially characterized by modernizing consumers in conflict with norms of familial, home-oriented provisioning systems, based on tradition. Corruption scandals of major food manufacturers in Italy lend a distinctive edge to these disrupted consumer–provisioner relationships, not found in countries more affected by directly food-related crises, such as BSE (Ferriti and Magaudda, 2004). Standa, one of the main supermarket chains in competition with Coop-Italia, for example, fell under the shadow of Berlusconi, owned (1988) and then sold (1998) by his multifarious finance company, Fininvest (Lane, 2005).

This chapter has focused on trust as an emergent property of changing relationships between institutionalized consumers and provisioning systems. But the issue of trust cannot be reduced to an exclusively market relationship. It is already implicitly clear that markets themselves are regulated differently (for example Norwegian protectionism), and that consumers have different voice and organizational presence in different countries. The explanation so far, moreover, has almost passed over food crises and scandals to look at longer-term and underlying shifts. Governmental responses to these crises – both at national and European levels – are clearly critical. So although, as everyone knows, dyadic relationships are complicated enough, we have to expand our analysis into triangular affairs by bringing the state fully into the account.

8
The State and Triangular Affairs of Trust

8.1 Introduction

Viewed from the perspective of the market relationship between consumers and food provisioners, the thesis that high consumer trust is related to their successful mutual adaptation in a process of modernization, supermarketization and globalization, and that low trust is an outcome of disrupted traditional and familiar relationships, was tested and found useful, but insufficient. In this chapter, the relational institutional underpinnings of trust are further explored by adding the third major pole to the triad of relationship that makes up our 'triangular affairs': the state. The role of the state in regulating food has a long history (e.g., Burnett, 1989; Burnett and Oddy, 1994; Lyon, 1998), partly driven by crises. Since the end of the nineteenth century the state has assumed a major responsibility for food safety, pricing and quality, and increasingly other issues of nutrition and ethics. By virtue of the varied and progressive assumption of that responsibility, consumer trust in food immediately becomes one that involves the state as well as market actors. The ways in which different states regulate and monitor food provisioning, and indeed consumption habits, become a matter of trust in the state: its effectiveness, complicity of interests, performance, truthfulness and democratic accountability become engaged. Food scandals rapidly become issues of trust in governmental responses as much as in food provisioners, together with their responses.

In building our triangular affairs of trust, therefore, we now look at two more relationships, and how they might form the institutional basis for emergent properties of trust. Once again, there is an important distinction to be made between the relations themselves and the emergent trust, as demonstrated in Figure 8.1.

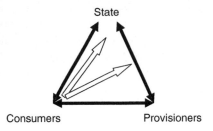

Figure 8.1   Relationships between consumers, the state and provisioning

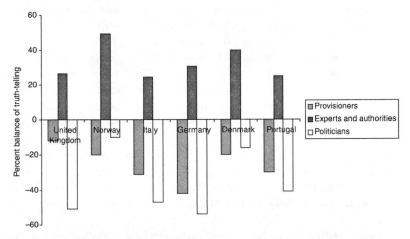

Figure 8.2   The balance of trust in truth-telling of state and market actors in the event of a food scandal

In this complex of reciprocal but asymmetric relationships (solid black arrows), trust or distrust is non-reciprocal (white arrows): the question is whether consumers trust *both* the state *and* the state's regulatory relationship with provisioners. If there is an issue of trust of consumers by the state, it is hardly comparable and the state's trust of consumers' relationship with provisioners does not arise as an issue.

Revisiting the survey results on how much consumers would trust different actors in the event of a food scandal concerning chicken, the central importance of state regulation in the triad of relationships becomes clear. In Figure 8.2, trust in truth-telling by state authorities (experts and authorities) and market actors (farmers, retailers, manufacturers) is compared. Politicians are treated as a separate category. The graph presents a 'balance of trust': the percentage of consumers believing that actors withhold the whole truth is deducted from that of consumers believing actors tell the whole truth. In the case of state authorities, for all countries the balance is positive: more consumers trust state authorities than distrust them. The opposite is the case for market actors: more consumers distrust market actors than trust them. Politicians, with the two notable exceptions of Norway and Denmark, are significantly more widely distrusted than market actors, a point we will return to later.

But there is another way of looking at this balance. As a first interpretation, it is interesting to observe that the extent to which more consumers trust state authorities outweighs the extent to which more consumers distrust market actors in each of the high food-trust countries (the United Kingdom +27 per cent versus −12 per cent; Norway +50 per cent versus −20 per cent; Denmark +40 per cent versus −20 per cent). The lower-trust countries by contrast are all in negative balance: the extent to which more consumers trust state authorities never compensates for the extent to which more consumers distrust market authorities (Germany +31 per cent vs −42 per cent; Italy +25 per cent vs −31 per cent; Portugal +25 per cent vs −30 per cent). Clearly, the interpretation of these numbers cannot be stretched to suggest that there is any simple causal balancing process, but it nonetheless points to the need to think of trust in food in at least a triadic context, beyond either trust in the state or trust in market actors in isolation.

To address this question, the analysis moves on to explore the two relations involving the state in Figure 8.1. In particular, focus will be sharpened on two significant aspects: the shifting alignment of state regulation with market actor controls in relation to the food chain (the state–market relation), and the shifting institutional roles *within* state regulatory structures of the consumer and producer interests (the state–consumer relation). Having explored these two further relationships, the second part of this chapter will then reconstruct the triangular affairs as a whole.

8.2   Variations in state regulatory relationships

As with the characterization of the systems of provisioning and institutionalization of consumers, in order to facilitate comparison of different national regulatory institutions some key dimensions have been selected. But in considering these, the European Union context is also of primary importance, adding a further layer of policy initiatives and institutional arrangements. The fabric of European regulatory institutions has been deeply conditioned by the project of creating a unified internal market, and hence, by an appropriate regulatory framework for the free circulation and exchange of food products. There has been a continuous process of development of these frameworks, with influences going from national to community levels, and back down again. The Common Agricultural Policy (note, agricultural, not food) has underpinned this construction of markets, much as the early history of the European Union reflected the *political* as well as economic importance of primary producers, iron, steel and coal. So, in making comparisons, we will be concerned about variations in the way in which European and national levels interacted in the formation of national regulatory systems.

Moreover, to present a complete picture, it is necessary to consider these regulatory arrangements in relation to each of the five key food issues, and in many cases they are inextricably interconnected. There have been quality crises, resulting in changes in regulation, at both national and European levels, over what counts as chocolate, labelling of food ingredients, and most notably claims for the origin and differentiation of food quality,[1] reflected in rules for Parma ham, champagne, or cheeses with geographical appellations. The institutionalization of a peculiarly European concept of quality has been a continuing source of conflict and tension, seen as protecting European agriculture against external competitive pressures in World Trade Organization rounds, including the most recent Doha round. But also within Europe, it has involved the construction of a distinctly European-level institution of quality, although one that reinforces some national conceptions. In the strongest case, Products of Designated Origin (PDO), these quality designations protect the use of the name against any producer outside the designated geographical location, in respect to all stages of production. It rolls together traceability, quality, product specification, typicality and tradition, and the agricultural producers with their local know-how, in one package. The most recent and disputed case, initiated in 1994 and finally resolved in 2005, is feta cheese, which now cannot be produced under that name outside Greece.

Divergences in conception of quality are reflected in national institutions, with mainly Southern/Latin European countries adopting and regulating these forms of traditional quality, as against Northern European countries that have either focused narrowly on safety or relied on market branding to establish marques of quality (Barjolle and Sylvander, 2000; Bergeaud-Blackler, 2003).[2] In 2000, of the total of 518 PDO/PGI (Protected Geographical Indications) protected products, 406 came from Spain, Italy, France, Greece and Portugal; only 41 came from the combined provisioning systems of Belgium, Denmark, Finland, Luxemburg, the Netherlands, the United Kingdom and Sweden. Interestingly, for our argument, Germany falls between the high and low users of this institutionalization of quality, with 60 protected products (Barjolle and Sylvander, 2000; see also European Commission, 2004). These divergences persist, it can be argued, because of differences both in national regulatory systems and provisioning systems, as analysed in the previous chapter.[3]

Competition and trade law, import and export quotas, the Common Agricultural Policy likewise affect the openness and closure of markets, and, indirectly value for money. We have already seen that currency reform, the introduction of the euro, may well underlie the high levels of pessimism and growing distrust in relation to value for money across the eurozone. Animal welfare, regulations over claims for free range, or for the transport and rearing of livestock, also have been a concern of regulation at national and European levels. The directive defining a European standard of 'organic' was issued at the same time as those promoting PDO and PGI, instituting a 'quality turn' (Allaire, 2004; Bergeaud-Blackler, 2003) at the European level, with a stated aim of enhancing consumer confidence.[4] Closely related to quality issues, the growing obesity crisis in some European countries has raised the nutrition issue to the top of the regulatory agenda, resulting in new conflicts between provisioners and state regulators (and between consumers and regulators).

Nonetheless, it is clear from our institutional research that the major transformations of institutions that have occurred, if unevenly, across Europe, have been primarily in response to crises in safety, and especially the BSE outbreak. There was something qualitatively different about the BSE crises from more locally or nationally contained crises. Not only was it a crisis that brought to the forefront of public consciousness some of the processes of industrialized farming, in which both science and regulation were complicit, it was also an immediately European and rapidly global crisis through trade in meat products and cattle, in a competitive context of the generalization of meat production technologies using recycled and possibly prion-contaminated meat protein.

This can only be seen in part, however, a consequence of the severity and reach of the crisis, including the risk to human life. Even before this crisis, and irrespective of the long history of such crises, safety of food related to the risk to human life has been seen to be a fundamental state responsibility, in much the same vein as safety on the rail or roads. Safety of food could not be left to provisioners and consumers alone, as a 'private affair'. The state had to assume a general public responsibility over questions of public welfare and social order. At the same time, however, in modern democratic societies political parties seek seats in constituencies where farming interests are strong, and where they therefore promote the economic welfare of farmers. Different countries, partly as a consequence of different patterns of urbanization and structure of the economy, have different types of rural interests, from small family producers to large agricultural businesses (see Chapter 7). This has been reflected in the structures of the state. A major conflict of interest came to the forefront in the BSE crisis between state authorities traditionally oriented towards producers – the departments of agriculture – and responsibility for the protection of consumer safety. It was a conflict of interest that, to varying degrees, shook the foundations of post-war state institutions.

The state responsibility for other key food issues, although widely recognized, is often more contested and varies more between countries, as noted above. This is therefore an important dimension for comparison in its own right. Indeed, state divisions of responsibility, reflected in institutional architectures that may have endured for decades, underpin a societal construction of food. If one department of state relates to farmers and primary food producers and another to health, and another to market competition and trading, this is a societal way of dividing up dimensions of food. If the division of responsibilities for these issues are so separated as to be compartmentalized, then issues or crises – such as obesity – that cross boundaries, challenge a society's established institutional divisions of responsibility for food. The European 'crisis of confidence' and the regulatory responses of our six nations and the European regulatory bodies thus provides a lens for understanding the role of the state in our triadic complex of relations. We primarily focus on three main dimensions of the role of the state in the wake of this crisis (ramified by the many others in recent history).

First, we consider the internal organization of the state itself, and how this might affect consumer trust. The key issue here is one of state 'performance' (Hardin, 2001; Inglehart, 1997; Putnam, 1993; Uslaner, 1999), and there are several contributing issues of importance here. There is the extent to which the state is centralized or decentralized, and how well different geographic levels of responsibility are coordinated.

How the state responsibilities for different key food issues are coordinated *or not* by the organization of governmental ministries responsible for agriculture, health, and consumer affairs is also critical.

Second, we consider how the division of responsibility and alignment between the state regulatory institutions and the market actors is established in different countries. In all countries, control over key food issues is shared in some way or other between state and market actors, if only because of a necessity for continuous and detailed monitoring of production and distribution processes beyond the capacity of any state. An issue therefore arises as to coordination between state and market controls, and hence between the respective organization and objectives of these controls. At the European level, the 'farm to fork' approach, on the one hand, and the traditional quality (PDO, PGI) concept on the other, are potentially in tension as alternative modes of organization and objectives of regulation. There are also potential tensions between the traditional 'policing' role of the state according to fixed rules and standards, and a more mediating role, focusing on collaboration and negotiation. These are key to the consumer trust in the relationship between the state and market actors.

Third, we consider the extent to which consumer interests are institutionally represented within the state regulatory bodies. A number of alternative institutional responses are possible, and will be explored below, from labelling strategies requiring the state to provide better information, to organized consumer representation within the state's regulatory institutions. This reflects the state–consumer relationship, and involves how accountability, transparency and consumer influence is reflected in state institutions.

Clearly, this is by no means an exhaustive list of dimensions by which to characterize and compare different state regulatory systems. These dimensions cut the cake in a particular way, and there are other models for doing so differently. They are, however, significant for an explanation for the institutional basis for trust, and variations in the nature of trust under different societal arrangements. It matters whether the state regulatory system is centralized or not, inasmuch as trust is much more widely diffused, and less 'all-or-nothing', in state regulatory systems that are characterized by high levels of decentralization and devolution of powers. But clearly that also depends on whether there is coherence and articulation between different regulatory bodies, or between the different geographic levels of a decentralized system. Conflicts over respective responsibilities, or over performance, can be endemic to state regulation, and this can impact strongly both on whether the state itself is trusted to meet norms and expectations, or whether market provisioners are effectively regulated. Likewise, trust and distrust can vary, depending on whether the state is bureaucratically efficient and if state officials effectively administer regulations, irrespective of whether the regulatory system is centralized or decentralized, coherent or conflictual.

The dimension referring to the degree of alignment between regulatory systems and the powers and procedures of control exercised by market provisioners requires some explanation. The public bodies established to take care of food safety were initially (i.e., nineteenth and early twentieth century) often established under health – or even police – authorities, in many cases under a very decentralized system. In the post-Second World War period and before, it was common across Europe for there to be governmental departments responsible for agriculture and primary food producers, often driven by the experience of war and the need to secure national food sufficiency. In many cases, this primary producer-oriented institutional architecture was duplicated in regulatory responsibilities for food safety, subordinated to these agricultural state departments. This resulted in multiple systems and responsibilities, across governmental departments and administrative levels. Two quite different developments have occurred to an uneven extent in different European countries to undermine that alignment between regulation and market provisioning at the national (and EU) level. First, as discussed in the previous chapter, provisioning systems have been transformed in many countries, the balance of power having shifted from primary producers and manufacturers to retailers. In some cases, this has developed into integrated supply chains managed and controlled by retailers. To a certain extent, governmental institutions were slow if not positively resistant to reflect such a change, retaining a regulatory orientation to primary producers. As discussed before, changes in one party to a relationship can throw the other party out of kilter.

But second, European market integration and the major food crises have brought to the fore the political necessity for control systems to be able to detect and manage risk at all stages from farm to fork. Following the BSE crisis, the European Commission White Paper, 2000, set out to 're-establish public confidence in its food supply, its food science, its food law and its food controls' (European Commission, 2000, 7). The subsequent European Food Regulation (EC/178/2002) attempted to stimulate national regulatory systems to develop the farm to fork approach. So, from the other side of the relationship, changes in regulatory systems could also become more or less out of step with national provisioning systems, where integrated supply-chain management simply does not exist. It is one thing for there to be governmental failure to institute and implement a new regulatory order, quite another for the realities of provisioning systems to resist such forms of regulation. So this dimension relates to quite fundamental changes in the relationship between regulation and provisioning systems. It is also clearly linked to the dimension of the relative power of departments of state over regulation of food issues where different departments of state reflect producer, population or consumer interests.

Finally, in terms of the state-consumer relationship we attempt to capture the important shifts that have occurred over recent years with the rise to prominence of the citizen-consumer, and political representation of distinctly consumer – rather than worker or employer – interests. Thus, following the crises, there have been calls for much greater transparency and accountability towards consumers, and this may be reflected in governmental institutions, as well as the consultation processes between departments of state and consumer organizations. Beyond and above enhancing informational performance, however, there have also been examples of major institutional changes, notably that initiated by the UK Food Standards Agency, but then reflected at the European level by the European Food Standards Agency, and other countries emulating these models. These institutional changes have involved, at least to some degree, institutional separation from *any* department of state, and official consumer representation within the Agencies. This dimension therefore seeks to compare countries according to the extent to which there is a consumer presence in the institutional architecture of regulation. The significance of this for consumer trust in food is not difficult to appreciate: if consumer organizations are accorded an institutional role responsible for regulation by the state, even at arm's length from the state, then the state effectively shifts or at least shares responsibility with those consumer organizations. Incorporating consumer interests within the regulatory apparatus, distinct and independent from politicians and governments, can become a device both for enhancing trust and for deflecting distrust towards organizations with some claim to represent consumers.

These three dimensions for variation and comparison in response to the European crisis of confidence in food are constructed with the purpose of examining societal institutional bases for trust in food in the six countries. A useful starting point for drawing out some of the main points of comparison is the story of the emergence of the Food Standards Agency (FSA) in the United Kingdom. Its significance lies partly in the scale and impact of the BSE crisis itself, from its country of origin across Europe; and partly in that the institutional model in response to it also spread upwards to the EU level of governance and across Europe to influence reform of national regulatory institutions. At a fundamental level, it altered the traditional, producer-oriented models of state regulation that typified many European nations' relation to food provisioning systems. A point of comparison, therefore, is the varied extent to which the shift occurred in our six countries.

8.3 Regulatory reforms

Before the BSE crisis, the mode of regulation in the United Kingdom was a typical one with divided and compartmentalized responsibilities: a producer-oriented Ministry for Agriculture Food and Fisheries (MAFF) on the one hand, and the Ministry of Health on the other. Even under the Food Safety Act of 1990, only six years before the crisis and in the context of lesser scandals, there had been no place given for consumer representation (Schofield and Shaoul, 2000: 540–1). The BSE crisis fundamentally challenged this entrenched regime of regulation, most of all, it could be argued, because the emergence of the problem of trust also reflected the much broader emergence of the consumer as a complex of constituencies, accountable in their own right. Consumers, and their propensity to consume, could no longer be taken for granted. Slow to fully emerge into the public domain, as soon as the crisis broke in March 1996, the first governmental responses typified a path-dependent institutional response: within the perspectives of existing ministries, it was perceived as a safety crisis by MAFF and a health crisis by the Department of Health. Measures were developed piecemeal to eliminate perceived safety risks, as a technical solution to a technical problem, in conditions of considerable scientific uncertainty as to what might constitute a technical solution to a still little understood threat to health. The industry actors immediately saw the issue quite differently, and responded differently. Whether in the retailing industry, closest to consumers, or in the agricultural industry directly concerned with production, the consumer trust issue was considered the key dimension, in order to eventually restore the market.

From the point of view of our analysis of 'triangular affairs', it was thus very soon clear that the crisis was much more than one of trust in food safety as such or even in food provisioning systems, but rapidly spread to engulf the government and regulation, as well as the independence and reputation of food scientists. At the same time, it critically resonated with the much broader political shift towards the consumer, and the need for political systems to explicitly recognize and institutionally enshrine diverse consumer interests. The possible conflicts of interest between producer-oriented governmental departments, the food industry and consumer interests were explicitly recognized. As a senior official of the FSA expressed it in interview:

> Because the remit of the Food Standards Agency is about consumer protection, we would always take the stance that consumer protection and public health protection should come first and if that is damaging to the industry, then so be it.

Two years after its initial establishment, the consumer presence in the FSA was further reinforced by the addition of a Consumer Committee with powers to influence and monitor policy, a committee that included representation from the major consumer organizations as well as consumer experts in food provisioning, nutrition, and health.

The FSA was not only a radical institutional innovation for 'putting the consumer first'. It was radically disconnected from the producer-oriented departments of state, and also independent of *any* department of state. The objective was to reinstitute the autonomy of judgement from possible narrow political interests, and to re-establish the autonomy of the food scientists within it so guarding against any possible conflict of interest that might arise from being 'government scientists'. And finally, it established procedures for 'deliberative democratic accountability' and transparency in its own conduct of business, uncharacteristic of departments of state.

However, in some respects the development of the FSA also brought about an alignment with modes of control already anticipated by the market actors in food provisioning. To an extent, the old governmental structures lagged behind developments that had taken place within the provisioning systems. Measures such as beef labelling, or the EU Regulation 820/97 on traceability had been foreshadowed by supermarket retailers' own systems of Hazards Analysis and Critical Control Points, already in place across the industry from 1993, before the BSE outbreak (Wales, 2004). Retailer control of an integrated supply chain from the consumer-front end meant that the regulatory responsibility involved in 'due diligence' placed responsibility in market actors that already did exercise effective, even increasing, control on the ground, all the way up the supply chain. This issue of alignment in state regulation and market actor control is important because no system of state regulation can assume responsibility for the continuous monitoring and control involved in production and logistics at every phase from farm to fork. The implication is that different alignments are involved for different provisioning systems.

Across Europe, there were similar institutional reforms in the wake of the crisis, and in response to developments at the EU level that to an extent mirrored changes in the United Kingdom. In 2002, the EU established the European Food Standards Authority, and placed issues of food safety and consumer protection under the newly formed General Directorate for Health and Consumer Protection (DG Sanco) in which European consumer organizations were represented. But no country went as far as the United Kingdom in separating producer from consumer interests, or a government department from an independent food agency. In Denmark one of the two dimensions of the shift was achieved in 2004 by the unanticipated creation of a new Ministry of Family and Consumer Affairs, following a high-profile presence of consumer interests in food policy-making. Transparency and accountability were notably manifest in the introduction of the 'Smiley system' in 2001, and revised in 2002 (Nielsen andMøhl, 2004), whereby notices of successful inspections of retailers were prominently displayed with a graphic of a smiling face of authority. The state showed itself to be the good regulator.

But, in Germany neither shift was complete, as a new Federal Agency for Consumer Protection and Food Safety (BfR) was placed under the Federal Ministry for Consumer Protection, Nutrition *and Agriculture*. Moreover, there has been an intense politicization of the Ministries, making the bureaucratic apparatus closer to political fiefdoms, especially with the role of Renate Künast as the Green Party Minister. The reforms, especially 'The Agricultural Turn', were first of all a matter of reorientation in German agriculture. In Portugal, after a long travail of obstructed reform, an Agency for Food Safety and Quality (AQSA) was first put under the Ministry of Agriculture, and then under the direct responsibility of the prime minister (Domingues, Graça and de Almeida, 2004). By so doing, the agency became more politically charged, and deflected the trust issue from the state bureaucracy to politicians, who, as the survey shows are, as in many other countries, subject to a high level of distrust. This inevitably led to the abolition of the Agency in 2002, when the new government returned responsibility for creating a new model for an agency to the Ministry of Agriculture.

But perhaps the most striking and even surprising comparison is between the United Kingdom and Norway. Although it would be going too far to suggest that Norway represents an entirely static and traditional state architecture of producer-oriented regulation unshaken by crisis and unchallenged by the rise of alternative modes of provisioning, nonetheless it does embody a conception of 'the state authorities know best'. Norway was able to sustain a national autarchy of regulation, although party to the internal market and European food regulation except for the Common Agricultural Policy. After much debate, the main authority of the Ministry of Agriculture over its Food Authority was confirmed.[5] Largely out of public or media gaze, there had been a bitter turf war between departments of health, fisheries and agriculture as to which should have prime responsibility – and the Ministry of Agriculture won (Terragni, 2004). Safety remained the overriding public issue for food. If food is safe, no other issues of trust, at least of public trust, arise. This maintained a traditional alignment between a producer-oriented regulatory architecture and a primary producer-dominated provisioning system. This is a point to which we return, but in this respect two countries characterized by high levels of supermarket shopping and the highest public opinion levels of trust in food are at the opposite ends of a spectrum in terms of the institutional presence of consumers and state regulation of market actors.

The institutional shift embodied in the emergence of the food standards agency model wraps together the key dimensions of comparison, and certainly rearticulates both state–provisioner and state–consumer relationships. The dimensions concerning consumer representation, transparency and accountability; the separation of producer from consumer interests; the range and scope of state regulation are all reflected in the new institutional arrangements. In terms of the institutional bases of trust, these varied rearticulations of the central relationships, and the extent to which consumer distrust is given institutional voice, is a mark of how different societal systems construct a consumer – as distinct from citizen – agency, and particularly around a primary object of consumption, food.[6] But there are additionally some equally important contrasts that can be drawn out.

The United Kingdom reforms involved a highly centralized regulatory authority, corresponding to the high level of national integration of food provisioning. But governmental structures of Germany and Italy, both characterized by devolution and regionalization of powers, as well as a higher level of local and regional provisioning systems, involve quite different forms of state authority. Germany, although embracing European regulatory reform measures, has experienced conflicts of responsibility between regional (Länder) and Federal levels of governance. Italy formally adopted European safety regulation measures – almost as a template on a blank sheet of paper – but implementation and uniformity of application are obstructed by an increasing regionalism resistant to national standards of any kind, quite apart from issues of state corruption.[7] Germany and Italy are thus also peculiarly opposite modes of governance, the one characterized by devolution and negotiated conflict and compromise, the other more by power fragmentation, corruption and distortion. Portugal, with the residues of dictatorship, has a centralization of authority, but a habit of low accountability and transparency combined with bureaucratic inertia frustrating political initiatives to reform. Here state authority may be trusted or distrusted with respect to food regulation for quite different reasons, based upon different historical experience.

These dimensions of deep institutional path dependency, with foundations of course far broader than those required to sustain regulation of food provisioning systems, nonetheless generate tensions and possible destabilization when faced with food crises and longer-term changes taking place in provisioning systems, nationally and internationally. Thus, it can be argued that the BSE crisis worked its way through European market-integrated, international food supply chains, impacting on a national and supra-national scale. This presented particular challenges to regulatory systems that enshrine principles of devolution and regionalization of authority, or are characterized by fragmentation of state authority. Similarly, growth of retailer power, especially nationally integrated supply chains, can develop a tension between market control systems by national-scale market actors to which regional or local state actors may have a less than coordinated response. In terms of the state–market provisioner relationship, these varied sources of tension are critical for consumer trust if mismatches between regulatory and provisioning systems diminish the capability of state regulation.

8.4 Regulation and trust: Comparing national configurations

In the previous chapter, we concluded with an analysis of the core relationship between consumers and provisioners, drawing out contrasts between the six different countries. In this chapter, we have extracted the pole of the state, subjected it to some comparative scrutiny, and analysed variations in state–provisioner and state–consumer relationships. In general, following the BSE crisis, but also many important but on the whole more national, food scandals, there have been major institutional rearticulations of these two relationships. The most radical has certainly been in the United Kingdom, but different institutional responses, shaped both by the institutional path dependency of pre-existing systems and by the very different provisioning systems, have all involved quite substantial changes.

Here we take stock of the analysis so far by constructing our 'triangular affairs' in terms of the societal relationships between institutionalized consumers, provisioning systems, and state regulatory institutions. Before doing so, however, it should be emphasized once more that this is an analytical device. The schematization and simplifications are deliberate. So too are the exclusions from the analysis. If we were to do full justice to the complexity of relationships of trust, many other societal actors would be involved, and there would be a much more differentiated picture of different levels, micro to macro, of relational configurations. For example, the media and science, and the way they are societally institutionalized around the issue of food, have been alluded to, but not analysed or described to any extent. Yet their importance is undeniable. Also national political structures, political parties and democratic institutions, and their variation, if only in relation to the construction of the 'consumer' and 'citizen', are deserving of more attention. It is clear that some parties have different constituencies and allegiances towards actors in the food provisioning system and, depending on the national social structure, this can mean that they are differently implicated in food scandals, or indeed in reforms of state regulation.

That said, and given the complexity even of thinking in terms of triangular relationships, we maintain that this reduction to three central relationships can provide a significant part of the explanation of variations in the institutional bases of trust in food, as well as accounting for the observed and surprising national differences in public opinion revealed in the survey. Triangular affairs involve a complex relationship between consumers and the state regulatory authorities and consumers' evaluation of the relation between state regulatory authorities and market actors. We can now represent this schematically (see Figure 8.3) for each country, and do so in order of the countries' level of trust in food items. Here we are using this schematic representation as a frame for interpretation of public trust as expressed in the survey. In Chapter 9, we will explore more deeply what this means for our understanding of the nature of trust.

The diagrams in Figure 8.3 refer to institutional relations of consumer trust and state–market integration. They intimate the major contrasts between countries in terms of their impact on consumer trust in food. Immediately, some significant contrasts come to the fore. The supermarket-dominated countries, all high trust, now fall into two almost opposite camps. The strength of the trust in the United Kingdom is spread almost evenly between relationships between consumers and the state and consumers and the provisioners (taking into consideration the comparatively low distrust of commercial provisioners for truth-telling, the general sense of improvement across all food issues, and the trust in the safety of food, especially that purchased for the household).

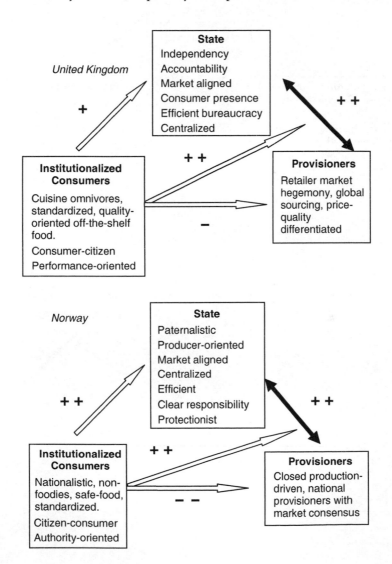

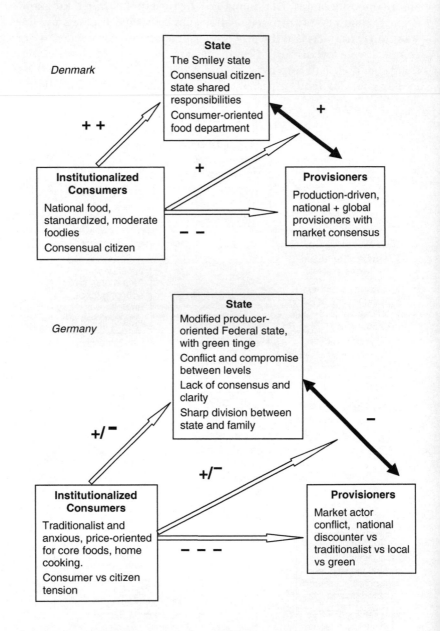

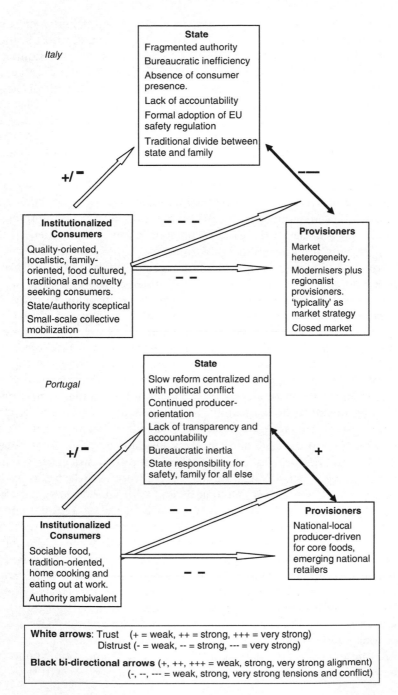

Figure 8.3 Triangular affairs of trust for six countries

The formation of the FSA, with independence, accountability, and an institutionalized consumer voice, has, we believe, enhanced trust in the relationship between state regulation and market provisioning. Moreover this relationship is characterized by a high level of alignment between state regulatory requirements and the hegemonic control exercised by supermarkets over supply chains. But the high levels of trust in the United Kingdom can only partly be attributed to the major institutional transformation of state regulation, and the way it has 'placed the consumer first'. A perceived general improvement of food provisioning, the increase in mass standardized variety and quality, driven by supermarkets, has also led to relatively high direct trust in market actors. Its effectiveness is only intelligible as a triangular affair. In terms of the earlier discussion of the survey (Chapter 5), this interpretation supports a view of the United Kingdom as the country where trust depends most on 'institutional performance'.

Norway and Denmark, the other broadly high-trust countries, display a different basis of trust, in spite of being similarly characterized by high supermarket shopping. Put at its strongest, Norwegians distrust supermarkets and manufacturers and to a lesser extent primary provisioners, and their trust in food is based on an overriding trust in the state to effectively regulate them. Theirs is a state authority-based trust. Moreover, there is a strong alignment between a state-protectionist, producer-oriented regulatory system and the national provisioning system, also largely dominated by producers, even though there is a high concentration of standardized food retailing. Trust is contained within a relatively closed system. Moreover, there is nothing like the extreme polarization between trust in the state and trust in politicians found in the United Kingdom and the low-trust countries. State institutions and politics combine to provide a shared institutional basis of trust, against the forces of the market. Denmark, less paternalistic and with a more active citizen-consumer consensus, is also strongly sceptical of the food provisioning system and reliant on state regulation. But, in contrast to Norway, there has been a significant reorientation of the state towards the citizen consumer, as a counterweight to the representation of producer interests in state regulation. The creation of a Ministry for Consumer Protection and the Family and the visibility of the Smiley system together create a quite different and less-paternalistic authority-based trust in state regulators. As against 'institutional performance', this confirms an interpretation of a strong politico-cultural basis of trust in these countries.

At the opposite end of trust in the food spectrum, it now appears far too simplistic to view the breakdown or absence of trust as a consequence of an erosion of local and traditional provisioning systems in relation to consumer expectations that such traditions will last for ever, with unmodified consumer patterns of behaviour and customary values. The lack of trust in Italy for market provisioners – especially their perception of the deterioration of quality – combines with an endemic distrust of state authorities. The interpretation of this is a double one: first, there is a direct lack of trust in authorities and politicians as such, but, second, there is a distrust in the state's capacity to regulate market provisioners effectively, with the fragmentation of state authority matching to an extent the regionalization of provisioning. The collapse of two of Italy's most renowned food producers, Cirio and Parmalat, has involved a heady brew of fraud, football, the Bank of Italy and politics, unparalleled in Europe. A crisis of the scale and nature of BSE as an external threat is thus particularly threatening, even if the actual impact is quite minor. There is a sense not only of a loss of tradition, but more particularly a lack of confidence in the ability of state and politicians to regulate modernization effectively.

This contrasts with Portugal, the other low-trust country, where there is a much greater sense of a distrust of a centralized state, and its ineffectiveness, combined with a much greater consumer traditionalism in expectations. Partial reforms of the state and the introduction of a food quality and safety authority (AQSA), under direct ministerial control, almost confirms this distrust. The interesting contrast perhaps is with Norway, between a paternalistic and respected traditional state authority, with effective bureaucratic regulation, and Portugal, with a centralized state authority unable to either uphold consumer expectations of the traditions of food provision or develop an alternative future. Portugal is certainly locked in tradition – exemplified by the conservative retreat towards production-oriented state regulation – but enjoys no great faith or affection for that tradition.

Finally, Germany is the most paradoxical case, quite distinctively different from all others. Conflicting norms of consumption – traditional, green, discounting cheap food, familial and manufactured foods – meet a state regulatory system that itself is riven with conflicts and highly politicized state ministries, and disputes between central and regional levels. The scepticism towards provisioners is the most extreme by a margin, and although trust in experts (German science and technology) is high, this does not spread to other public authorities. So there is a disoriented and dislocated relationship between market provisioners and state regulators that perhaps only reinforces consumers' direct distrust of food provisioners. They distrust most what they eat most: processed meat, prepared frozen meals. The conflicts of values in markets, states and consumers, and of their relations to each other, thus seems to result not so much in generalized distrust as generalized disorientation and anxiety.

In conclusion, it is worth remarking on the benefit resulting from an explicitly institutional approach to the interpretation of the survey of public opinion, and in particular the importance for trust of the truth-telling of the main actors presented at the opening of this chapter. It is possible now to suggest a key relationship between truth-telling and power. In high-trust countries, high consumer confidence in truth-telling of at least one actor – state or market – which has power to deliver or control food to satisfactory standards in all its key dimensions appears critical. In the United Kingdom it matters more that consumers trust supermarkets (relative to other countries). In Norway, it matters more that they trust state authorities. Conversely, where there are mismatches or conflicts between state and market actors, for instance as to whether state or market actors should be socially responsible for an aspect of food provisioning and its control, widespread belief in truth-telling of an actor without effective power or control has little impact. Generally, while public experts or consumer organizations are generally deemed to be extremely honest and forthright, it is of little significance if they have no power to make a difference over the quality, safety, price, nutrition or animal welfare aspects within the food provisioning system.

9
Conditions for Trust in Food

9.1 Complex relationships, emergent trust and distrust

In the last two chapters, an interpretation of trust and distrust in food as exhibited in the survey has been developed through an institutional analysis. Different qualities of trust and distrust are seen as emergent properties of differently aligned relationships between differently institutionalized consumers, market provisioners and state regulatory authorities. Analysing the six 'triangular affairs of trust' suggests, at one level, that each set of complex relationships generates distinctive, *sui generis*, emergent properties of trust and distrust. Norwegians do not trust food highly in the same way as consumers in the United Kingdom. Italians do not distrust food in the same way as the Portuguese. The triads emphasize difference, across the board, so that each national case appears unique.

For the sake of economy, these triangular affairs of trust form the core of the explanation, a model for interpreting some of the key dynamics of trust. In this model, trust relations are shown to be non-reciprocal. This departs from assumptions often made with respect to interpersonal or business-to-business relationships, where the parties to the trust relationship are of the same kind, even though the balance within the relationships might be quite asymmetrical.

Consumers, as much as states or market provisioners, are understood as societally institutionalized, although in ways open to change. Practices of food consumption and household provisioning are combined together to form distinctive national patterns of behaviour, expectations and norms. But how consumers of food are variously institutionalized can only be understood in their relationships to the other two poles of the triad, so that the triads as a whole can be seen as historically institutionalized configurations of relationships. It would be wrong either to reduce the poles to the relationships, or the relationship to the poles.

One of the major consequences of this analysis is certainly that it pushes the understanding of levels of trust beyond any simple dichotomy between systems trust and trust based on familiarity. Contrasting Norway with the United Kingdom, for example, suggests that the anonymous, institutional confidence of the former is embodied in authority and tradition within a relatively closed system; whereas the anonymous trust of the latter is one that has become conditional on the effective independent monitoring of the state's performance in relation to a modernizing and open system. Contrasting Italy with Portugal suggests that neither is simply regretting the passing of a nostalgically cosy familiar past. Rather, Italy is failing to cope with conflicts of norms and standards between modernizing tendencies and attachments to local and regional, small-scale consumption and provisioning. There, the state is as much part of the problem as part of the solution. In Portugal, it is more a matter of failure to leave behind a past to which no high cultural value had been attached by the general population.

Nevertheless, the uniqueness of cases is at least in part explained by some underlying common principles of variation. At the crudest level, high trust, even of different kinds, is seen to be a consequence of a 'positive fit' between the relationships of the three poles; low trust is generated by 'negative fit'. So despite their differences, Norway and the United Kingdom share the characteristic of strong alignment between state regulation and market provisioning (the one closed, protectionist and producer-oriented with a producer-dominated provisioning system; the other having supply-chain integrated control, an open system, with centralized regulation). At a broader level, Norway has largely retained a post-war, standardized and national culture of food, protected by a paternalistic state. The United Kingdom has witnessed rapidly expanding globalization of provisioning, an opening up and transformation of mass-food quality, with a regulatory system that adapted quite fundamentally to an extreme crisis symptomatic of modernization. There, a ratcheting up of consumer norms and expectations, both with respect to provisioning and regulation, have to an extent been met by state and market actors.

The analysis of structural reform in European countries in the aftermath of the 'crisis of confidence' provoked by the BSE outbreak suggests that two historical tempos of change are at work, intertwined though they are. On the one hand, there are the longer-term shifts. These have been presented in terms of historical institutional change, the more gradual change in consumer habits,[1] the shifting balance of power and transformation of provisioning systems, and the architecture of institutional regulation, reflecting enduring political power resources and producer interests. On the other hand, there are the immediate crises, provoking remarkably rapid if uneven change across Europe, exemplified by the spread of the Food Agency model, and the shift towards an institutionalization of consumer interest within regulatory bodies. Given these different tempos of change, and given also that different poles of the triad might change at a different pace, the construction of shared norms and expectations in societal relations is continuous and ongoing. Conflicts and tensions are to be expected, and normal. Consequently distrust is normal too, immanent to the process of change. Understanding the impact of scandals, and their various resolutions, becomes essential to an explanation of how trust might turn to distrust, and vice versa.

This points to one possible interpretation of how it is that the country most affected by the BSE crisis in terms of incidence of the bovine disease and human deaths from vCJD has emerged with high trust in food, whereas countries with lower impact (Italy, Germany, Portugal) react very much more strongly towards the scare – a feature repeated in late 2005 with the drop of poultry sales in the different countries in response to the threat of avian flu (very high in Italy and Germany, low in the United Kingdom). The intertwining of different tempos of change has led to more disruption of relationships and their embedded norms and expectations in some countries than others. Norway exhibits high trust because it has been relatively insulated from scandals and has a slow pace of institutional change, whether of consumer habits, provisioning systems or state regulation. The United Kingdom has witnessed quite rapid institutional change, in terms of changing consumer habits and provisioning systems, and the scandal of BSE finally triggered a radical and rapid change in regulatory systems. Denmark in many ways appears closer to the United Kingdom than to Norway in its institutional responsiveness, whether of consumer behaviour or regulatory systems. In Italy both the immediate threats from 'crises' of various kinds, and the longer-term institutional shifts intertwine to maximize disruption of shared norms and expectations – if ever such a state of 'positive fit' existed in post-war Italy. Portugal presents the case of institutional inertia in the presence of short-term crisis, old shared norms and expectations still retaining a residual force in the face of an 'external' threat. And, finally, Germany has witnessed some fairly rapid institutional responses to immediate crises, but not in a direction consistent with longer-term shifts in consumption habits and provisioning systems. This produces a situation of positively conflictual, rather than merely disrupted, norms and expectations. Clearly, this interpretation can only be speculative. But viewed from the relational perspective of 'triangular affairs', trust and distrust are about both profound institutional change and immediate events, crises and scandals.

9.2   Institutionalization and societal configurations

We have demonstrated empirically that there are major institutional differences at each of the three poles of the triangular affairs. The pivotal element of the institutional analysis is consumption. In our triangular affairs, we have concentrated on the relationships between consumers and food provisioners, and consumers and the state. Although significant – particularly in terms of 'fit' – we have not to any extent considered the relationship between provisioners and the state from the point of view of trust, although no doubt such an analysis would be valuable. Given its pivotal significance, therefore, the 'institutionalization of consumption' on the one hand, and the political construction of the consumer on the other, assume a key role in our analysis, and we now turn to our main conclusions in this respect. The distinction between these two aspects, and the societal variations in each of them, contribute to a more nuanced understanding of the dynamic of trust relationships, demonstrating that the consumer, even given huge differences within countries, is not only a social but a societal figure.

Central to our analysis is the notion of 'fit' between the three poles. Relational trust involves shared norms and expectations in terms of behaviours or practices involved, in this instance, in the provisioning, regulation and consumption of food. Distrust emerges with tensions over norms and expectations, as well as conflicts over patterns of behaviour of the respective parties. That is to say, both culture and performance matter. There is no natural or inevitable fit, for example, between the food as provided by the commercial provisioners, the provisioning activities of households, or the consumption patterns of eating. And there is certainly no universal pattern across Europe. However, for high levels of trust, it helps to have 'good relationships' all round. By 'good relationships' we mean that there is consistency and consensus in mutual expectations, coherence within the institutional poles, and consonance between institutional characteristics between poles in each of the three relationships. As shown in the previous chapter, it is also necessary to consider an additional 'relationship between relationships': the impact of the relationship between state and provisioning institutions on the two dyadic relationships of consumers to the state and provisioners. Thus, for example, we have analysed the emergence of the United Kingdom out of the BSE crisis in terms of there being a 'good fit' between regulatory systems for traceability and Hazard Analysis and Critical Control Points (HACCP) and the organization of the provisioning system with its highly integrated supply chains led by supermarkets. This 'good fit' enhanced both the level of trust in the regulatory institutions (the FSA for example) and the retailers. Counter-examples are to be found in Portugal and Italy, where there are blockages to implementation of these traceability and transparency regulations as a result not only of deficits internal to the state regulatory systems, but also through 'mismatches' between regulatory requirements and the organization of the provisioning systems.

This analysis of differently configured 'triangular affairs' provides at least a plausible account of some of the puzzles presented earlier. In particular, it suggests that high trust can be developed, even strengthened, as a consequence of the impacts of a major scandal such as BSE. Moreover, high trust is perfectly consistent with the modernities of supermarkets and globalized food provisioning – *provided that* there is a congruence in relationships with the state and the lifestyles of consumers. A quite different kind of high trust is visible in a traditional paternalistic state and society. And one could assume, or nostalgically regret the passing of, the existence of a prior golden age of high trust based on localism and familiarity, where the state counted for little.[2] Conversely, low trust is generated by conflicts and tensions between the poles, between consumer patterns of consumption and embedded expectations and shifting patterns of provision on the one hand, and between the citizen and the state on the other. Perhaps the most important conclusion, therefore, is that trust in food involves much more than attainment of some putative standard of good or bad food. Different types of relationship, between different types of consumers, provisioners and state authorities generate very different alignments of trust, and indeed distrust.

One further point needs special emphasis. This account challenges any simplistic dualism of state versus market, of regulation and deregulation. There is very little empirical evidence that can support a view of the Anglo-Saxon model as one of 'free markets', as against a continental European social state model. Rather, what the differently configured triangular affairs suggest is different types of concordance or discordance between different types of regulatory frameworks and market provisioning systems. All food provisioning systems, as markets, are highly regulated, at national, European and world trade levels. The contrasts we observe, however, are, first, between the way that different regulatory systems meet and match the organization of provisioning systems. It is significant that new regulatory regimes of traceability from farm to fork and hazards critical point analysis is paralleled by the types of control over production and distribution manifest in integrated supply chains. Second, there are variations both in levels of market coherence and conflict, and in efficiency, transparency and coherence within state regulatory authorities. Some governments have struggled to implement regulatory frameworks in a uniform way across the provisioning systems, themselves often fragmented and very diverse within a given country. This is another source of conflict and tension between regulatory systems and provisioning systems, or simply a lack of efficiency, transparency and coherence in regulation. So between these two poles of our triangular affairs, there are wide variations in 'good' and 'bad' relationships.

The various configurations differ in their ability to tackle problems and to restore trust. Clarity, consensus and transparency seem to be ways of stopping scandals turning to crises; and concealment and deception on the part of authorities (the United Kingdom in 1996 and Germany in the first years of the twenty-first century) seem to be worst case scenarios. It must be emphasized, however, that conditions for trust also have important slow-changing, path-dependent elements. Configurations are, mostly, at least temporarily stable. Nevertheless, they are still subject to change and may sometimes be destabilized quickly, as in the British case. However, in the United Kingdom a new accommodation between producers and regulation re-established significant degrees of trust within a few years.

The notion of configuration captures the uniqueness of cases, focusing on differences rather than similarities between countries. Yet there are many features of institutional arrangements and of conduct which are common to each. A significant number of responses to our questionnaire show very little differentiation across the populations of Europe, for instance, on the importance of many controversial issues.[3] Recognition of problems in the food domain, the safety of different foods, and indeed the relative degree of trust in types of actors are common across countries. People trust market actors least, then public authorities, and the agents of civil society – scientists, consumer organizations – most. Moreover, within the food systems of Europe there are strong forces for convergence. One such is the globalization of the food chain, another is the effect of a single market within Europe. Some strong economic trends impact throughout the European Community. There is also the introduction of regulation. If one of the ironies of the operation of the European Commission is that although its principal objective seems to have been to introduce a single market and to allow more readily free market principles to govern production and exchange, to do so it has introduced more and more sanitary and veterinary regulations, more codification, labelling systems, Public Guardianship Offices (PGOs) and PDIs in order to achieve its goals. These have been concurrent and, at least in intention, equal forces in each of the individual countries. At the same time, different countries implement regulations in different ways, and with different degrees of enthusiasm. More importantly, even if each country implemented a directive in the same way, the effect would be likely to be somewhat different because the impact depends upon the current state of development of the institutions of each. Also, people will have different expectations and experiences, making their responses quite diverse across the countries. An image to keep in mind should be not only convergence towards some imaginary future point but continuous flow in the same direction, but where previously established distances apart may largely be maintained. There is a difference, that is, between convergence and evolutionary development along parallel paths.

9.3   Public opinion and trust

Arguing that trust emerges from institutional configuration affects the nature of causal claims that can be made from comparison. Comparing like with like, as if in a controlled experimental manipulation of discrete factors, is an impossibility. Nevertheless, plausible accounts can be given of variations of trust. We can test – within obvious limits – what accounts will *not* work, or at least not simplistically. To give an example: there might be a presumption that personalized familiar trust, knowing who buys what from whom, a community of consensus within a locality about what matters most about food might produce the highest levels of trust. However, we know from the multiple evidence obtained from both institutional analysis and population survey that this is not the case: Italy and Portugal, where these characteristics are most pronounced, are the most pessimistic, least trustful in relation to many aspects of food. Thus we are not tempted to make the contrary mistake to suggest that because a country has supermarket hegemony it will have high trust. Instead, we use the variation to suggest synchronic variations in the nature of trust on the one hand and, on the other, trust as a temporally dynamic process rather than a steady state, which also varies in relation to different dimensions of what the trust is about (quality, price, safety, nutrition, ethics, etc.). So, the argument is not that the model of localized provisioning and familiar trust does not work, or is not a sufficient social basis of trust. Rather, some types of trust relationship are being eroded in some places, and other types may be emergent or stalled in others, as a consequence of changes in the configuration of regulation, provision and consumption. The result is that we offer 'plausible causal accounts' rather than definitive explanations of the variations in types and foci of trust in terms of societal relations in different configurations.

Our public opinion survey presents many intriguing findings. However, it is necessary to distinguish between trust as manifest in a public opinion survey, and a deeper layer of trust, much less tangible, but nonetheless significant. This is perhaps best illustrated in our assessment of the role of recent food scandals, or the significance of 'immediate and critical events', in a context of major historical shifts in the nature of food, its provisioning and its regulation. Thus, even though BSE was internationalized, the major impact was certainly concentrated in the United Kingdom, in terms of human deaths, animal disease incidence, agriculture and trade. But the results of the survey demonstrated that there is no clear relation between events that might be expected to undermine trust most and the level of trust expressed, notably in relation to food safety. Indeed, overall across Europe, in spite of the succession of scandals, food safety was identified by each of our countries as the area where there was most improvement. Generally, across Europe, although to very different degrees, people thought their food had been getting safer over the past 20 years.[4] Discontent with the perceived price hike following the introduction of the euro was revealed in those countries adopting the new currency, but again the impact was uneven. But above all, the country rocked by the biggest scandal of BSE, as well as a succession of less seismic ones, emerged as the country with the highest public opinion level of trust in food items and the most optimistic view of improvement across the different dimensions of safety, value, quality, nutrition and ethics. How could this be so? And why was Germany – affected insignificantly and indirectly by BSE, and with fewer major food scandals of its own – so shaky in its trust for food, or Italy yet more deeply pessimistic, especially about the future of its food?

The survey, however, did provide some important clues to the ways in which contentious episodes affect trust. In the event of a scandal, trust in the truth-telling proclivities of the different actors directly responsible for, or involved in dealing with, the scandal reveal striking contrasts. Politicians by profession seem least likely to be expected to tell the truth, and market actors (farmers, processors, retailers) are clearly seen to have commercial interests in being economical with the truth. But there are wide differences in trust in these actors between countries, as well as in scientists and regulatory authorities. Most interestingly, it was found that the countries with high levels of trust in food were those that had at least one *powerful* actor with significantly higher levels of expectations to tell the truth than in other countries. In the United Kingdom this was the supermarkets and in Norway, the scientists and authorities. It was of minor consequence whether actors with little power were truthful.

More generally, the state of public opinion on trust in food and in the major actors involved in food production and its regulation shows remarkable and consistent contrasts across the six countries. Whereas at least half of the population in Norway and the United Kingdom were confident that their food was not harmful, less than one in ten in Portugal, or one in seven in Italy, were so trustful. Across a range of food products, fresh and processed, meat, fish, fruit and vegetables, the United Kingdom stands well above other countries in the number of people thinking the different food items were very safe to eat. In Germany, Italy and Portugal less than half as many people are likely to do so. We do not know, and it would be very difficult to measure, a common baseline in time to compare standards between countries. However, in the United Kingdom, substantially more people believe that food is getting better rather than worse *in every respect*, although least so in relation to value for money. In Italy, by contrast, more people think that things are getting worse rather than better in all respects except safety. The overwhelming majority believe price and quality to be deteriorating.

9.4 Institutionalization of distrust

Protest and trust

The development of the food market has throughout history been associated with periods of contestation and social mobilization, which have either been met with some kind of realignment (often re-regulation) or through direct exercise of power. Distribution to urban and national markets meant that food became channelled to groups with high purchasing power, marketization opening up the possibility of speculation in times of under-supply. Conflicts over the fairness of food prices and food distribution formed an important background for the classical food riots which occurred sporadically in Europe until the First World War (Coles, 1978; Frieburger, 1984; Hirdman, 1983; Löwe, 1986; Thompson, 1971). The emergence of industrial processing extended possibilities for fraud and new conflicts over food (Burnett, 1989; French and Phillips, 2000; Levenstein, 1988): chalk and arsenic were employed to whiten bread, contaminated water to dilute milk, and so on. The latter half of the nineteenth and early twentieth centuries saw many conflicts over food quality and the honesty of food suppliers which were eventually settled through the disciplining of market actors. Additives were introduced as cheap and stable ways of preserving food or improving its taste and looks, but they also carried dangers. This had long been an issue, but additives became more contentious during the 1970s, followed by re-regulation. Perhaps more important, the nutrition agenda was turned upside down in this period, from under-nutrition to 'junk' food, overfeeding, obesity and chronic disease on a massive scale. There were strong claims for social and political solutions, but with the emergence of neo-liberalism in the 1980s the responsibility of each private individual became the most dominant response (Kjærnes, 2003). From these accounts, describing both long gone and more recent events, it is reasonable to assume that contestations over food cannot be solved once and for all. A spur of dissatisfaction and distrust will often lead to mobilization. There may be long periods of peace and relative consensus. But technological innovations, new ways of organizing the food commodity chain, and the like will produce new relations and new issues.

However, until the 1980s or even 1990s, tranquillity was not called 'trust', protest was not called 'distrust' and the protesting people were not called 'consumers', even though we now might apply those concepts to describe what was going on. Consumers have been there all along, but only over the last 20 or so years have a number of social problems and conflicts over food been reframed as consumer problems. In the 1980s, problems and discontent became 'concerns', worries that perhaps reflected the individualized privatized understanding of the consumer role. It seems that it was not until some time in the 1990s that these individual concerns were reframed as problems of trust (notably not as distrust). This change of words is clearly not accidental, it must be linked to food issues becoming more politicized, perhaps also that consumer responses became more important to institutional actors.

The Europeanization of the food market and food regulations is in this respect important, bringing up new issues and reconstruing old ones. And the process has not yet been settled in terms of relations between institutional actors and ordinary people. Their role as consumers seems to have become a key point, not only because people are affected as buyers and eaters, but also because this has become a relevant arena for response. The larger and more integrated the sellers become, the more will they rely on reputation. Vulnerability to public criticism is increasingly sensitized and even small drops in demand (even only for a short period) may give rise to 'moral panics'. The confidence of the public becomes more critical, its distrust more consequential.

There is a sense in which in recent years a more critical public has emerged whose trust in food has become more conditional. Publics across Europe express widespread concern about food issues, and their confidence in the main actors in the food provision and regulatory system is, as our survey shows, limited. In response to this situation, we have seen what we would want to call an intensification of 'processes of reassurance'. Corporations and states feel impelled to institute new procedures which acknowledge that consumers might sometimes have grounds for disquiet, that their trust should not be expected to be unconditional. New institutional arrangements have been developed which accept that distrust may in certain circumstances be appropriate and rational. There need to be ways in which consumers can be reassured that they are not subject to malfeasance, misinformation or other forms of mischief on the part of powerful actors. One response to a growing number of situations in which familiar trust or confidence have been destabilized is to establish procedures specifically to restore trust. This reassurance response is one of institutionalizing distrust.

Institutionalization of distrust and the process of reassurance

In the ten years or so after 1990 legitimacy problems were pressing. The BSE crisis was obviously so. From trying to limit the crisis to Britain, it soon became a transnational problem, described as a loss of confidence in food. The framing as a pressing European problem of public welfare was new, requiring urgent action. It represented a threat to the integrity of the European institutions and their programme for integration. But it also gave the EU more freedom to act and to formulate new solutions. The European Commission and the European Parliament panicked and reforms were instigated surprisingly fast. They included key elements like the recognition of consumer concerns for safety, as well as organizational issues of accountability, transparency and independence. Gradually, the issues have receded from the newspaper front pages.

But the European and, especially, the British events cannot be explained merely as the restoration of confidence and re-establishment of the *status quo* through successful social engineering. The consumer has come to stand in a somewhat different relation to the powerful economic and political actors. Institutional means to handle conditionality and instability have become necessary to the reproduction of trust. Distrust not only represents absence of confidence. Rather, we find signs of distrust coming to represent a relevant, dynamic and active option for expressing discontent, feedback and influence on institutional conditions. This distrust is not occasioned by *individuals* becoming more reflexive. Our analysis points to 'fits' and 'misfits' between socially institutionalized actors. As a consequence, particular and new *societal and institutional* configurations of relationships between key actors emerge. Consumer protest is not a new phenomenon, but widespread awareness of a legitimate consumer role or agency is. It certainly means that people are thought to be more self-conscious and willing to become more responsible *as consumers*. But that cannot happen if they do not have the relevant options to act in the market or the necessary channels to express their voice, or if decision-makers disregard their opinions as 'stupid' or 'irrational'. Above all, this is a matter of questioning the distribution of power, and its expression in institutional arrangements. One cannot expect an active and responsible consumer role to emerge without disturbance, conflict and uncertainty among institutional actors. However, we do not attribute this to circumstances where consumer power has grown relative to other major actors – this is nowhere demonstrably the case – but to a realignment of the distribution of power. Thus, acknowledgement and anticipation of consumer demands (or fear of consumer reactions) by the major actors, state and market have had consequences for the recent re-organization of the food system in Europe, both in regulatory arrangements and in the market.

We take the view that what is specifically new about developments over the last decade or so is an intensification of a particular manner of approaching loss or potential loss of confidence. Inspired partly perhaps by the language, the scenarios and the commercial prospects for an industry of risk assessment and risk management, more explicit attention is being paid to how to manipulate trust. This is mostly a matter of seeking channels for the reassurance of sceptical customers. In these new circumstances, crises generate a cycle whereby a sharp loss of confidence is met by introduction of procedures that acknowledge that the consumer may indeed be legitimately disconcerted by the activities of market actors or the state and that it is important to reassure them through fresh institutional structures and safeguards. It is not so much a restoration of the *status quo ante*, but the establishment of trust in a different form. This occurs through the implementation of a new batch of strategies to sustain a process of restoration of confidence.

The ways that distrust has been institutionalized has varied from country to country, but it has happened to some degree everywhere – at least partly because of common EU regulations. To display distrust is not gratuitous trouble-making for it is perfectly rational, on the basis of past experience of food supply, to question the quality of what is made available. Populations are generally aware that food may be contaminated, that governments cover up scandals, and that corporations may pursue profit at the expense of safety and quality (French and Phillips, 2000). Though powerful actors might wish that populations would have undying faith that they would always act in their interests, such unconditional trust is unlikely. For one thing, the actors involved, politicians and corporations, themselves attempt also to mobilize people as 'consumers' – and hence as people whose interests can be damaged by the behaviour of other corporations or other political parties. In such a context, actors merely announcing their own trustworthiness is hardly a viable strategy for allaying scepticism or fear. Hence, we suggest, the extension of institutional arrangements for handling distrust becomes contingently necessary. The means to promote *justifiable* confidence and trust are primarily ones for exercising scrutiny and regulation – monitoring, audit, self-regulation, transparency, involvement of consumer representatives, independent bodies, and so no. Such forms may be conceived as alternative institutional responses to the likelihood that further expressions of distrust will otherwise precipitate ever more costly difficulties. Two strategies have come to prominence, namely 'independence' and 'transparency'.

'Independence' refers to institutional arrangements that allocate to a third party roles and responsibilities for monitoring and auditing the behaviour of organizations. While contracts in market exchange are in principle private and closed, from very early on a third party, usually some kind of public body, has acted both to guarantee accountability and to ensure that general concerns ('externalities'), like food safety, are sufficiently considered. These are the classical roles of market regulation (Wilson, 1980), and the independence of bodies that monitor standards has usually been premised on legitimacy derived from democratic political processes. In recent years, however, the understanding of independence has changed. Public bodies are no longer automatically accepted as independent in all situations (if they ever were). Autonomy not only from economic interests, but also from political control, is increasingly regarded as necessary and requiring of explicit demonstration. Majone (1999) calls this trend 'agencification'. In such agencies, the involvement in decision-making of interested parties as 'stakeholders', including consumers, serves to support negotiation that create consensus and thus legitimacy. These arrangements are not completely new. In several of the countries, there are long traditions of corporative bodies in food policy involving 'concerned parties'. Agencification, however, seems to redirect attention from a traditional focus on issues of implementation and enforcement of procedures towards the formulation of strategies and standards. There has also been a proliferation of non-governmental audit bodies – independent, but often themselves commercialized (Power, 1997) – which ratify corporate accountability. These new forms of independent agencies represent the institutionalization of distrust and involve direct business concerns as well as more general needs of improving legitimacy in the eyes of the public. These new strategies are ambivalent, themselves producing new questions like 'who shall guard the guardians?' (Shapiro, 1987). They vary, however, in how they define independence, whether as independence just from business interests or also from the political machinery of state. In the case of trust in food, the independence issue has been manifest most acutely in terms of the governance of provisioning systems by ministries that are also responsible for promoting the interests of provisioners, or in terms of scientists employed by departments of state.

The second main type of strategy can be labelled 'transparency'. Such strategies cover institutional arrangements that, in principle, make visible to the public how particular problems are handled in the provisioning and regulation of foodstuffs. Third parties, especially public bodies, have traditionally, and particularly in Northern Europe, faced stronger demands for openness, as a matter of democratic control, than have businesses. However, while transparency in a rather direct form seems to have become increasingly important in evaluating food policies in recent years, closely associated to the discussion about independence, this also seems to have become more important for market actors. While corporations prefer closed decisions for competitive reasons, 'sceptical' consumers will demand openness in terms of food composition, origins, processes, social and ethical issues, and so on. Transparency includes a number of different types of arrangements. It can mean internal schemes, such as HACCP, and quality assurance schemes which, through regulation or self-regulation, are made available for monitoring, whether by regulatory bodies and/or the general public. Increasingly, however, these are traceability schemes that have more wide-reaching integrative functions, associated with changing structures of the provisioning chain. In many cases, traceability is directed towards technical needs. The critical questions are whether the information is relevant and whether it is made accessible to consumers and the general public. Such information is often very complicated. Labelling may be seen (as one of its functions) as a way to communicate transparently with ordinary consumer about the contents and origins of food, providing that the information is relevant and reliable. Finally, transparency has also increasingly become a requisite for the independent agencies and governmental regulatory institutions, as in the model of the food standards agencies, where consumers or their representative organizations have freedom of information on all decision-making processes. Arrangements for improving independence and transparency implicitly acknowledge that consumers have valid grounds for distrust of providers and regulators, and provide a foundation now essential to the reconstitution of confidence.

9.5 Trust and distrust and their types

Our analysis of historical developments in Europe suggests something about the applicability of different concepts of trust to the consumer predicament. The most basic distinction in trust literature is between trust relations based on personal interaction and trust in impersonal organizations or systems (Bijlsma-Frankema and Costa, 2005; Guseva and Rona-Tas, 2001; Luhmann, 1988; Seligman, 1997; Uslaner, 2000;). While some, like Bijlsma-Frankema and Costa, and Guseva and Rona-Tas, see organization as an alternative to (personal) trust, others, like Luhmann and Seligman,[5] see a need for trust even in impersonal relations. The two latter authors name trust based on networks and personal relations 'familiarity', while impersonal and generalized trust in institutionalized procedures (or 'systems') is called 'confidence'. In modern societies, institutionalized procedures are increasingly important, and these forms of trust are therefore crucial. However, Seligman suggests that there is a basic difference between a relation based on predictability and shared norms and expectations on the one hand, and a situation where norms and expectations are not shared or are unclear. In the latter situation, if trust is to exist, it will tend to be more explicit, to be negotiated and to be subject to mutual monitoring and review. Seligman referred to this situation only as 'trust' (Seligman, 1997). This has some parallels with Giddens's notion of 'active trust' (Giddens, 1994). In both instances, this specific type of trust is based on mutual negotiation and understanding between two parties to an agreement about appropriate conduct. This form of trust may be more prevalent in relationships between the state and market actors where there is continuous process of consultation, manoeuvre and negotiation around legislation and its implementation. It has more limited relevance to understanding consumer trust. In the case of consumer trust in food there is no mutual requirement for trust; the state and the corporations do not have to trust the consumer, and nor do they negotiate with individual consumers, though they might take account of the views of consumer representatives or sales figures.

Thus we contend that there are two main relevant forms of trust – familiarity and confidence – which, in combination, provide the basis of the general level of distribution or allocation of consumer trust in any country. It is important to emphasize that these different forms of trust are not a matter of individual choice, but depend on the character of the institutionalized relations and their normative and organizational frames. These different types may coexist within a given society, their respective importance depending on the particular context.

We can illustrate how these different types of trust emerge and combine by reviewing the instance of trust in beef, focusing on market exchange between consumers and the provisioning system. Different patterns can be distinguished, depending on the institutionalization of consumption and the structure of the supply chain (see Chapters 5 and 7, also Kjærnes, Poppe and Lavik, 2005). At opposite ends of a spectrum, we have unprocessed beef sold through small butchers, where the interaction is based on personal relations, and we have beef with higher degrees of processing sold through supermarkets, where exchange is based on standardization, labels and other impersonal relations. The contrasts here are Portugal, where the first form prevails, and Norway, where the second form is completely dominant. While trust in beef safety was high in Norway, it was in the medium range in Portugal. For these two countries, trust in beef is established in very different ways. For Portugal, familiarity is the dominant form, while a very generalized form of confidence seems to describe the Norwegian situation well. The Norwegians' trust in beef is taken for granted, based on shared norms and expectations as provided by a predictable, standardized supply and state monitoring. The Portuguese trust neither their food institutions nor people whom they do not know, but they are still able to establish a moderate degree of trust in beef due to the specific character of the Portuguese provisioning system and consumption patterns for beef.

This interpretation may also help to explain the difference in trust in beef between Portugal and Italy. Italians share the Portuguese distrust in food institutions and institutionalized procedures. Italian beef provisioning, however, occurs increasingly via supermarkets, which are growing rapidly in a context of an aggressive food industry, and which together with other aspects of Italian society, make personal, familiarity-based relations less available. This seems to add to the already existing larger tensions in Italian society, where both consumer experiences and the public discourse refer to values embedded in familiarity relations, while people increasingly depend on (too) unpredictable or non-transparent food institutions.

On the other hand, while Italian and British provisioning of beef shares some superficial characteristics, in terms of the proportion of beef bought in supermarkets and the degree of processing of foods, most other institutional conditions are dissimilar, making the outcomes regarding trust fundamentally different. The British display the highest level of trust in beef safety, but the relational foundations seem to be distinctly different even from the Portuguese and the Norwegians. In spite of the high trust, the British situation is much more differentiated; there is a considerable proportion who distrust, trust is more associated with what people do as consumers, both practices and trust responses are more socially differentiated. The supply, especially compared to Norway, is dynamic and varied, and trust has fluctuated over time. The British seem to share the Norwegians' trust in institutionalized procedures, but the character of the trust relations seems more conditional, unstable and individualized. They are, in other words, more dependent upon reassurance. Indeed, the British case might seem most close to the conditions which Giddens describes as 'active trust', where trust relations are 'reflexive' and where trustworthiness has to be actively demonstrated – with the difference that we argue this to be a societal characteristic of institutionalized consumers within a configuration of relationships rather than a feature of individuals.

In the case of beef we can distinguish between more explicitly conditional relations of reassurance in Great Britain and relations based on undisturbed 'confidence' in Norway. In spite of general institutional distrust in Portugal, trusting relationships based on 'familiarity' still prevail, due to the particular character of Portuguese beef provisioning and consumption. The Italian case, however, seems to fail to establish to any large degree any of these types of trust relations.[6] It is not easy to characterize trust relations in the same ways in the German case. 'Disjointed' has already been used to describe German trust relations. It might seem that public responses reflect a 'loss of confidence'; people would like to be protected, but they don't feel protected. As in Norway, survey responses that report a consumer as having little voice are associated with high trust, thus indicating a general confidence in protection by institutions, most likely the authorities. In Italy, people have experienced an erosion of relations of familiarity, but without much success in re-establishing alternative forms of trust. Confidence of the British kind seems to require a recognition of consumers as actors and the existence of appropriate institutional arrangements to reflect that. By contrast, while German consumers are active, there are few institutional arrangements, either in the market or in public regulatory system, which can recognize and deal with consumer agency and feedback.

The case of beef shows that trust, its types and levels, is an emergent property of different types of relationship around exchange. The consumer conditions of existence vary from country to country. They exhibit different types of trust in combination, subject to particular social and economic institutions and trends. We might note in addition that different national experiences may lead to some types of trust being more valued than others.

So, there are different types of trust in play, around different domains. Both familiarity and confidence are embedded and routine, not constantly subject to re-evaluation. Though one is personal and particularized, the other impersonal and generic, both are contingent and conditional. However, typical causes of the deflation of trust level are different. In some situations trust will be more prone to disruption by assessments of performance, as in the United Kingdom; in others, deeper bases of trust are being eroded by external pressure upon institutional arrangements, as in the case of Italy with the impersonalism of the supermarket infiltrating where familiarity was previously primary. In some other instances, even if the conditions for trust are not being met there will be no change in behaviour, because of powerlessness or lack of alternatives. In Hirschman's terms what we see then is only loyalty (Hirschman, 1970).

These types of trust prevail to different degrees. They may alter in level or combination and thereby destabilize the system. Or, the system may change for other reasons, for example EU legislation or a major food scandal, and thus require renewal of trust, perhaps of different sorts. As the corner shop disappears as a result of commercial pressure, there is no way that rebooting personal assurance through reaffirmative efforts will resolve concerns. Indeed, it is interesting that many people think of alternative personalized supply chains as a response to a crisis of confidence; solutions to perceived inadequacies of quality or safety have been to look for local sources, to buy direct from farmers (in the farmers' markets movement) or organic producers, to return to small retailers (Gilg and Battershill, 1998; Hinrichs, 2000; Murdoch and Miele, 1999).

9.6 Configurations and combinations of trust

Finally, let us consider how the different types of trust have manifested themselves within distinctive national configurations. We have shown that the European population is concerned about all sorts of food issues. These are anxious populations. But some countries are affected more than others once that generalized anxiety is transformed into practice and activity. And alleviation of anxiety depends upon how confidence in those institutions (with their competences) and procedures (including representations of their effectiveness), is spread among the populations. One indicator is the trust expressed in key actors; another expressed trust in foods. The latter we consider to be the result of the configuration of institutions (and we have isolated those dimensions of alternative configurations) and therefore it is to considerations of the content of the judgments about the trustworthiness of actors that we turn in concluding this chapter.

In Chapter 8 (see Figure 8.3) we summed up our view of the overall configurations of the relationships that generate different forms and levels of trust. In order to understand consumer trust in particular, we can compare countries on the prevalence and mix of trust accorded to provisioners and regulators (perhaps filtered through the analysis of the relationship between power and truth-telling as in Chapter 8). This in turn allows us brief reflection on the rate and direction of change in the bases of trust.

Norway continues to operate on the basis of high levels of trust in public authorities. A high level of trust in food is in no way attributable to familiar relationships and almost exclusively relies on confidence. Norwegians trust the authorities to manage and regulate corporate actors in whom they have comparatively limited faith. The strong belief in the safety of Norwegian food is almost entirely a matter of generalized confidence in the state as guarantor of the probity of actors in the system of provision. This occurs and is made more possible within a closed and highly protected national food provisioning system. Since confidence has not been subjected to any major crises, there has been no need to introduce means of reassurance. This exhibits some symbiosis with Norwegians' remarkable lack of political or economic consumer activism. Here we see very little sign of individuals asserting their prerogatives as sovereign consumers in the market place. Nor are Norwegians acting as the kind of figure envisaged by analysts who look forward to an active politics of consumption, for this is a particularly non-participatory attitude, delegating power to the official decision-making procedures of government and state bureaucracy. Trust by the consumer is overwhelmingly founded on confidence as a citizen in the Norwegian state.

Denmark exhibits some similarities with Norway in its established modes of political organization. Its tradition of doing politics by consensus, through negotiation among stakeholders, provides a basis for sustaining high levels of confidence in the food system. General political arrangements offer assurance that food matters will be dealt with in a legitimate manner in accordance with some notion of the general interest. As consumers, Danes are somewhat more active than their Norwegian counterparts. They have absorbed a little more of the ethos of the customer as a sovereign consumer. This is partly a result of a much more open economy, where agriculture is a major national industry and where food purchasing occurs through a modernized supermarket system which meets with general acceptance.

Britain, by contrast, occasions a different history and type of high trust, focused on the supermarket and consumer loyalty. More than any other country, the customer-consumer, as described by Cohen (2003), provides the template for action. If Britain is characterized predominantly by the confidence of the customer-consumer, this is within a rationalistic, evidence-based, regulatory framework where the public rules of the state are in relative harmony with the market regulation of the integrated supply chain. Confidence is buttressed by a new state regulatory framework, distanced from the government, with greater transparency and accountability as the grounds for reassurance. A high level of national centralization and integration of both provisioning and state regulatory systems now sustains a restored confidence. However, that is a result of the most radical of programmes of realignment. For here individuals are active over food issues, of both economic and political types, and they seem most powerfully to have incorporated the ideology of the active consumer.

At the opposite extreme, Italy displays considerable dislocation and disruption of its traditional provisioning systems, conflict between European, national and regional state authorities, and a consumer torn between alternative lifestyles of tradition and modernity. There is a nostalgia for familiar trust, and there remain many ways in which the sourcing and management of food depend upon cultivation of personal connections. Yet, now that much food purchase occurs through super-markets, there is need for more general confidence in institutions. For various reasons, this is not forthcoming. Politically, there is suspicion of the effective and legitimate operation of the political system and its regional disarticulation. Economically, the perception is that a modern mass-produced and manufactured food cannot satisfy requirements of quality that are at the centre of culinary culture. Here we see evidence of active response by the population, but without, as yet, channels of reassurance and realignment being established.

Portugal bears some similarity to Italy. However, practically it remains more rooted in relations of familiarity. People buy more of their food from markets and small shops, and there is evidence that these personalized relationships continue to sustain a degree of trust in food. For instance, we have seen that the Portuguese expressed relatively high trust in the safety of their beef. As yet not so subject to the necessity of purchasing standard-ized products in large outlets, there is somewhat less need for confidence; and there has been little evidence of powerful actors pursuing strategies of reassurance. This accompanies relatively little activity on the part of the Portuguese population in the consumer role. This may have been fortu-itous, for there is limited confidence in the performance of authorities or large corporations. This is a land where consumers are still primarily located in traditional exchange relationships based on familiar trust.

Perhaps the most interesting configuration is that of Germany, where there is the unsettled, transitional consumer, sceptical but not overly distrustful, with competing food values and modes of provisioning, and a powerful welfare state, yet one that is less closed than Norway, and with tensions between regional and central governments. Germans are more politically engaged in matters of consumption than any other nationality. They are also active in their role as customers, and as they are increasingly drawn to use large corporate rather than small retail outlets, they come to rely more heavily on confidence to ground trust in food. Yet trust evades them. This is a function of a lack of effective insti-tutional response which would provide the kind of reassurance that has been achieved in, for example, the United Kingdom.

Looking overall at these aspects of configurations, we can draw a couple of general lessons about the role of consumer activism and changing forms of trust.

Since the 1980s, Europeans have been given many lessons in how to be a sovereign consumer. This has had an independent effect on levels and types of trust, depleting confidence and requiring its reconstitution. Reconstitution has drawn on particular forms of reassurance, involving institutional realignments angled towards independence and transparency of regulation of the provisioning system. Consumer activism is highest where reassurance is most prevalent; that is, where there is no longer routine trust based either on familiarity and personal assurance or generalized system confidence. Thus confidence persists in Denmark and Norway; personal assurance is still primary in Portugal. But neither Germany nor Italy has a centralized system in which the population has confidence – there is suspicion at the highest level of both market actors and state. Germans and Italians are relatively highly active, but without bringing forth a satisfactory response by corporations and authorities. They have, so to speak, failed to institutionalize distrust effectively. The United Kingdom, in total contrast, introduced a new system very clearly designed to institutionalize distrust that at present, and in respect of issues of safety, appears to provide appropriate solutions to the problem of the decline of confidence after BSE.

Second, considering the complex dynamics of food provisioning and regulation, it would seem that current ways of restoring trust in situations where familiarity is a primary mechanism of trust are insufficient. Reaffirmation of familiar grounds of trust, once challenged, works sometimes but, increasingly, familiarity provides less of a basis for trust. Increasingly, it seems that there are difficult pressures exerted on familiarity-based trust as the conditions arriving with the organization of modern corporate provisioning and consumption require confidence and the reassurance that is only possible through institutional realignment. While familiarity may have worked satisfactorily once, at least regarding people's food procurement, it seems vulnerable at present, though there is some evidence that where reassurance fails, then there may be some return to alternatives based on familiarity. These include the expansion of farmers' markets, local supply chains and organic cooperatives, but also of forms of pseudo-familiarity, as in a 2006 instance of the leading British supermarket chain putting a photograph of the farmer and his farm on packaged chicken.

Third, we have characterized the predominant means for the reconstitution of trust as 'reassurance'. We will, in the final chapter of the book, discuss whether our observations support the general assumption in many theories of modernity that we are moving towards new, more unstable, active and individualized forms of trust.

10
Explaining Trust in Food

10.1 Food nations

MacDonaldization and globalization. The ubiquitous rise of the supermarket. Whether by big transnational food companies with world-wide brands or globally renowned retailers bringing an ever-expanding variety of counter-seasonal produce from every corner of the world, food transcends national boundaries. So do panics and scandals. Avian flu knows no absolute barriers, geographical or biological. BSE provokes fear in Europe and Japan. And political responses and frameworks have become increasingly transnational. The European single market and the Common Agricultural Policy have been in place for decades. The World Trade Organization regulates growth hormones in beef and the use of genetically modified foods, supervening over national rules and laws.

Yet, remarkably, we find food nations and cultures survive. Deep differences and divergent historical trajectories persist. Discovering that trust and problems of trust are not the same all over Europe has led us to appreciate the significance of the national and societal basis of trust. This is not to argue, of course, that convergence and processes of globalization have no impact on the way different national societies develop. But, whether in terms of public opinion, or the way that food is provided and consumed, or how states respond to change and crises, societal patterns are powerfully shaped within national boundaries.

We find that public opinions on trust in food vary considerably and consistently, most of all between countries. Regional variations are less significant. Country variations are often different from what might initially have been expected. Great Britain, which has experienced the gravest and most disruptive scandals over food in recent years, appears as a country where people display considerable enthusiasm regarding food safety and optimism for a range of other food issues as well. Germany, on the other hand, is marked by widespread public distrust and contention within the food system. It is perhaps not surprising that Danes and Norwegians are generally trusting, but they are so to a lesser degree than Britons. Italy, which is renowned for a strong focus on fresh, high-quality food, is marked by the highest and most consistent levels of distrust regarding all aspects of food and the food system. Finally, and also quite surprising considering the findings in Italy, the Portuguese are considerably less distrustful towards their food, but they are highly sceptical towards authorities and supermarkets, and pessimistic regarding ongoing changes.

Distrust is not necessarily reflected in what people buy and eat. Many happily eat things that they are not sure will be safe, like burgers and restaurant meals. This is especially likely to be the case if the items questioned constitute a major component in the nation's diet and the routines of daily life. Societal norms rapidly reassert themselves. Media attention may in some cases lead to considerable drops in demand, but after a short time demand recovers. But even this kind of turbulence and short-term change appears only in some countries, demand in other countries remaining more or less unaffected. There are societal differences in the way consumers respond to crises.

If, in public opinion, consumers manifest national differences in the way they think, they also differ significantly in what they do in practice from country to country. To some extent this should not be surprising, but, especially in the light of much recent sociological and cultural discussion, nonetheless needs emphasizing. If the Spanish sustain a norm of eating their main evening meal at 10 p.m. and Norwegians their lunch at 11 a.m., there is a logic to these coordinating routines within countries which is uncompelling between countries. While tourists adapt, locals still meet and eat together, in households or wider social networks, within a national social space.[1] Whether to have one or two main meals a day, how often and where to shop, the amount of home food preparation, the use of microwave ovens, and a raft of other aspects of what people do mark differences in behaviours that typify consumers nationally. How much money to spend on food,[2] or whether food safety or quality is the number one issue, express national particularities. For that reason, we speak of an institutionalization of the consumer and consumer behaviours and culture as societal features of different countries. It is not as if these patterns never change – indeed, we find that they are shifting considerably – but they change in different ways in different countries.

This 'institutionalized consumer' does not accord with conceptions of an individual exercising sovereign choice independent of social context, norms or routines. Yet the figure of the Sovereign Consumer dominates contemporary food discourses, functioning as a specific political and normative way of seeing the public, the buyers and the eaters of food. As an analytical concept it is inadequate to the understanding of trust and distrust. Neither public opinion and practice nor 'the consumer' who appears in public discourse is the same everywhere or at all times.

Turning to how food is produced and delivered to consumers, there is no uniform or common 'supermarket phenomenon' across Europe. Certainly, there is evidence in all countries of the growing importance of large-outlet food retailing owned by big chains. But there the similarity stops. Indeed, taking the two countries most dominated by supermarkets, Norway and the United Kingdom, the differences are most extreme, whether in the variety of food, its geographical sourcing, its cultural diversity, its orchestration of food quality, or in the extent to which retailers as such control the whole food chain. Germany divides between price-discounting retail chains and smaller traditional green or quality-oriented outlets. Portugal has experienced a foreign invasion of retail chains, whilst Italy's Coop is just about holding its ground against French supermarkets. More widely, however, the role of farmers and primary producers, often with important political organizations and electoral clout, or of home-country manufacturers, have varying weights and differing profiles from country to country. The provisioning systems of different countries are still primarily national realities.

At the governmental level, since the early 1990s there has been a huge upheaval in the institutional ways of dealing with food, its safety and its quality. The rate of change has been exceptional, and we should expect more in the face of the nutrition crisis because the institutional arrangements for safety are not likely to be sufficient for a new and different type of issue. Here the issue of national versus transnational is certainly complex within Europe, and there is more than an appearance of common models being adopted across the European Community. In response, especially to BSE, the British were the quickest and most radical in their establishment of a Food Standards Agency (FSA), with independence from government and a more prominent institutional role for consumer organizations. The European Commission reorganized its government of food-related issues under a new DG Health and Consumer Protection (DGSanco) and the European Food Safety Authority (EFSA). These were very fast (for governmental bureaucracies) responses to crisis, something which probably has not, and would not, happen in other fields. It seems as if these quick responses, and the way they were done have had the effects of restoring both confidence in markets and the legitimacy of authorities when it comes to food safety. But the Nordic states differ quite significantly between them in the way they regulate food or 'empower' the consumer, and not always in ways that support the current literatures on varieties of states and markets. Norway, for example, remains institutionally unmoved and the producer interest retains its grip, whereas in Denmark, reforms have elevated the consumer into the machinery of governance, reshaping the basis of consensus. Germany responded to the trust crisis – at the state institutional level – in quite a distinctive way, by strengthening – and at the same time redirecting – a producer orientation with the 'greening' of the agricultural ministry. It was an 'agricultural turn'. The Italian response was a further regionalization of responsibilities, while the Portuguese had difficulties making any definitive decisions at all. In each country, national governmental structures have responded to crisis and change in distinctive ways, within existing institutional and political constraints. The result, overall, is certainly not a diminution in differences between national ways of governing food or according consumers a role and representation, and in many ways, differences have sharpened. There is a paradoxical European reality of increasingly common models and frameworks *and* national divergence.

The urgency of the institutional responses when facing a political and a market crisis may indicate that there is a special quality to food, requiring acceptance of societal responsibilities. Food issues easily attract attention, mobilization and, at least in some conditions, disorder, and it seems important to settle contention. These special qualities may, at least in part, refer to the basic, almost trivial, qualities of food; food is a basic need, but potentially hazardous as unstable organic matter and contentious as a product of commercially driven market exchange. How these institutional responses are made at a governmental level, however, is still considerably framed by the organization and capacity of the nation-state.

10.2   Limitations of individualist and risk perspectives

The extent to which countries remain distinctive in their food habits and, as part of that, how trust in food is differently focused and shaped, even when faced by common developments, threats and crises, are a remarkable feature of the contemporary European reality. In the light of this evidence, explanations and conceptions of trust framed in terms of individual resources, cognitive perceptions of risk or some generic modern feature of uncertainty seem inadequate.

While countries display distinct patterns of trust, opinions within countries are often less systematically explicable. Where views within countries are more divided, internal socio-demographic variation appears to play only a minor role. Social structure matters, but primarily as part of societal processes of institutionalization of food consumption. Women are, for example, generally more worried than men, though with noticeable national variations. Such variations are linked to different patterns of gender roles, household division of labour, and labour market participation.

Consistent with our theoretical approach, cognitive perceptions of risk and other psychological issues have not been at the centre of attention in our analysis. They may indeed matter, and no doubt people have their own individual ways of responding emotionally to media output and try to find personal ways to cope. We find a majority all over Europe worrying about a range of food issues. Yet, considering the large, country-by-country variations in responses of trust and distrust, it is highly unlikely that such factors alone can represent major explanations for variation and change in trust. To the degree that psychological processes are influential, they must therefore be understood within particular social and institutional contexts. Personal strategies for procuring satisfactory food are, for example, much more important in some countries than in others (see Chapter 6).

Many analyses of contemporary distrust see it as associated with risk and how risks should be managed, notably through scientifically based risk assessment, risk management and risk communication. For some scholars, distrust as a subject appears primarily in relation to risk communication.

The first problem with that idea is that distrust is frequently linked only to individual responses to information, and to media 'scares' in particular. Our findings imply that the focus on information is wholly insufficient, possibly misleading. Distrust cannot be delimited to individual conceptions or misconceptions of information on risks. Nor are the causes to be found only in how experts and other actors frame risks in the mass media.

A second problem relates to generic concepts of modernity, science and risk, and as a consequence, a rather simplifying view of the role of scientific expertise. Scientists are important in the formulation of public policies, for developing technological and organizational innovations in the food industry, and in giving input to a critical public discourse. But they are not by themselves a key source of trust or distrust in food. Their influence seems to depend on how they are represented in these different capacities in the institutional settings of different countries. The technological factors leading to the BSE outbreak are undoubtedly important in order to understand the political conflict that developed. But we have shown how the crisis and the distrust that emerged were associated with particular decisions and types of inter-relations: how far scientists were viewed as 'government scientists', or whether, culturally, science and technology were accorded high status as an independent source of authority. Scientists contributed to the causes, the formulation of problems, and the development of solutions, but they were not the sole or even main drivers. In some countries it was seen as critical to establish 'scientific independence' on a fresh institutional footing in order to meet expectations of neutrality. These are specific political and national organizational solutions. Unlike Britain, in countries where scientific authority was less impaired, existing institutional arrangements for the place of science in food regulation and provisioning remained bastions of trust. We see that different scientific and technical solutions (culling, vaccination, quarantining, etc.) to new crises (avian flu, foot and mouth, swine fever) are matters of controversy between national experts, shaped partly by their different provisioning realities.

This is not to deny that risks may be framed differently now. Some issues seem to create distrust now that did not do so before, like swine fever and foot-and-mouth disease. Even issues like these, which do not represent a direct threat to human health, are now frequently framed as safety issues. Safety has been at the centre of attention in the debates on distrust and institutional change. At the same time, it is not at all clear whether this means increasing problems, or a ratcheting-up of demands and standards, or whether, instead, changing conditions and relations *per se* form the main background for the contentiousness of these matters.

The third problem is the very widespread misunderstanding that distrust refers only to safety (and environmental) risks and to scientific assessments of those risks. Distrust may have numerous other references. Because it easily overlaps and merges with other issues, like quality, nutrition and ethical concerns, trust in food cannot be considered merely a matter of safety. Issues which we can isolate analytically, pile into one another in the real world. This is evident from our survey and from public discussion. When examined closely, however, people find issues other than safety as generally becoming more problematic. This is particularly so for price (in the euro zone) and quality. So, despite much publicized disquiet about the safety of food (some of which is apparent in all countries in response to attitude questions), discussions of distrust in food and the dynamics of trust cannot be restricted to that. But, more deeply, how safety plays with other dimensions of trust in food is itself a matter of variation between countries. Even the focus on safety is not in itself unambiguous, as the framing and understanding of food safety varies considerably. Safety in Southern Europe is often part of a complex notion of food quality, which encompasses other issues and dimensions like nutrition, ecology, animal welfare and specific local provenance. People in Italy and Portugal are highly worried about the quality of their food, understood in this sense. In Northern Europe, at least in public discourse, the various food issues appear as more separate, each problematized and handled in very different ways.

For all these reasons, therefore, at least in relation to trust and distrust in food, the risk society thesis, with its emphasis on science and modernity on the one hand, and individualized reflexive responses on the other, appears unsatisfactory. The framing and responses to risk, science and safety themselves need to be understood in terms of societal variation.

10.3   Towards a socio-institutional explanation

These considerations led us towards explanations based on the societal characteristics of the different countries. We started out in this study with the assumption that trust in food is influenced by social and institutional conditions. By comparing countries that are not too different historically and politically, we have systematically tried to identify and differentiate different conditions for trust. We find many things by using a comparative method that would not be accessible if we were studying individual countries. Systematic comparison has allowed us to explore aspects that are usually taken for granted within each country context, such as the societal division of responsibilities for key food issues. Cross-country comparisons have also revealed nationally distinct patterns for the institutionalization of food consumption and the role of consumers.

One might say that with our choice of country as the unit of analysis, our methodology will inevitably essentialize the nation-state. Many of the findings might in that way be artefacts in societies that are both globalized and fragmented. In some respects, that is of course true. In contemporary societies national borders are more permeable than before with respect to markets and regulations and public debates and mobilization. We might therefore have paid more attention to both international contexts beyond the EU and influences at the local and regional levels. Nevertheless, everyday food consumption is delimited in time and space. The institutions to which we relate as food consumers share important characteristics within each national context. Even the far-going, exceptional regionalization that we find in Italy impacts on all Italians' trust, or rather distrust, in food. Indeed, the North–South divide in Italy is part of what makes Italy overall societally distinctive, even when compared to a recently unified Germany with its East–West divide and federalization. These are, respectively, Italian and German realities.

We started out with surveys of popular trust. Throughout, however, we have viewed public opinion as an aggregate social and political phenomenon and have therefore searched for macro-level national patterns. At this aggregate level of analysis we find considerable consistency in response patterns between survey questions and other indications of consumer trust, as expressed in public discourse, in fluctuations in demand or in interviews with key informants. This gives us confidence that our characterizations of high- and low-trust settings are valid and reliable.

When we ask who trusts whom about what with respect to food, therefore, we are identifying and analysing relationships at the societal level – although, of course, relationships may be analysed at other levels as well. These societal relationships are broad features of the countries we examined. Everywhere, in terms of trust in food people tend to distinguish strongly between different types of actors, but in each country, even though the cast of actors may be listed under the same names (farmers, scientists, retailers, consumers, politicians, journalists, etc.) their characters and performances play out quite distinctively national dramas. Different roles, expectations and types of inter-relations are evidently involved.

In treating trust as an emergent aspect of these societal relationships, three aspects are especially important: the societal division of responsibilities between actors; the matches and mismatches between the norms and expectations of the various actors, especially in relation to their practices and performances; and the societal 'configurations' of these relationships, or how the relationships fit together.

The first aspect, involving the division of responsibilities for key food issues, is crucial for understanding trust in terms of social relationships between actors. There is no one particular type of division of responsibilities that we can say will produce trust or distrust. The relationship between state and market actors differs according to their respective responsibilities as they have been institutionalized in different countries. In the area of food, new roles of the state as well as of the market are emerging; for example, by making direct monitoring and inspection a market responsibility, while public authorities take on a more indirect role as auditor. What we see is a process of re-regulation rather than the generally declining role of the state. How, for example, are consumer expectations towards food quality to be met in highly competitive markets that are expanding in scale? And how can ethically and socially framed consumer concerns be included in complex supply chains with innovative advanced technologies and technical traceability schemes?

Shifting responsibilities may also establish new boundaries between the public and the private. Responsibilities may be redistributed between market actors, the state and private households. Policies that centre upon 'the consumer' as a private and individual figure tend towards the privatization and individualization of responsibilities, and thus potentially the de-politicization of food issues. However, the very fact of their being consumer policies implies the politicizing of consumption. Handling consumer distrust then pulls food consumption out of the private and into the public sphere.

Shared norms and expectations are not easily established when organizational arrangements for the distribution of responsibilities change. This introduces the second important aspect of a socio-institutional explanation. The distribution of economic and political power is crucially important. There are no given, automatic or infallible matches between responsibilities and power. Increasingly powerful supermarket chains may engage in fierce price competition only if they ensure an acceptable level of safety, and in some cases quality. Mismatches and failures to deliver produce distrust. Increasing consumer choice cannot alleviate the problem.

Divisions of responsibilities vary not only between countries, but also between key food issues. And they change over time. While the responsibility for food safety was an urgent issue all over Europe some years ago, it seems less pressing now – notably at the EU level – and more so in some countries than in others. The handling of avian flu may bring it up again. However, responsibilities for other issues are far less clear, including food quality, nutrition and ethical issues. New issues raise new questions, and perhaps tensions, and require new institutional solutions to the division of responsibilities because current institutions are ill-prepared to handle the issues or the distrust associated with them. Nutrition and the recent concern with obesity is one example. Public efforts towards solving nutritional problems have over the last decades been curbed by concerns for individual freedom and the privacy of the family. The potential scale of the problem of obesity, and the inadequacy of current channels for dealing with it, raises big questions about the division of responsibilities. Existing solutions are no more than relatively modest programmes for nutritional education. In all six countries there seem to be weak and unsettled institutionalization around nutrition issues. This is not only due to concerns for individual or family freedom, but also because more active advice may easily affect commercial interests. Controversy around the responsibility for nutrition in relation to school meals represents a prominent example: how shall responsibility be divided between state, private companies and parents? Another crucial question is whether the power and control that individuals and households have over the nutritional quality of food is sufficient to allow them to assume effective responsibility. There is no general answer to that. But expectations that are not met may in any case cause distrust; for example, following a realization that school meals are not healthy.

If only with respect to the shifting societal divisions of responsibilities for different food issues in different countries, there is an ever-present potential for the mismatches and tensions between the norms and expectations that consumers have and those of the other societal actors, state and market. Distrust seems to be associated with such mismatches and contention, and with shifting or uncertain responsibilities. Broadly, we have distinguished between long-term underlying changes in relationships between actors resulting from shifts in responsibilities, including changing norms and expectations of the different actors that arise from developments in food provisioning, and 'scandals' as a more episodic phenomenon. But scandals are themselves signs of underlying tensions. 'Scandals' in societal relationships test the strength of norms and expectations that bind actors together. When a Minister of State made a public pronouncement on the safety of beef in the midst of the BSE crisis, this created a scandal in the societal relationship: it threatened, and eventually undermined, trust in a range of institutions, scientific, regulatory and political, in a quite generalized manner. It was not just anybody making a statement to an atomized population of consumers, each responding in an individualized manner. It was a societal event, testing a relationship *shared* by consumers in a national context to the state, market actors, media and scientists. For this type of reason, one of the most striking conclusions from this type of analysis is that scandals happen differently in different societies, not only in terms of magnitude of impact, but equally in terms of institutional response or consumer protest. A food crisis may even reinforce trust if its resolution is achieved through meeting consumers' pre-existing norms and expectations of those it holds responsible for handling crises.

A crisis about food may be the occasion in which tensions and mismatches between actors' norms and expectations become manifest, discussed publicly and in the media. But it is longer-term changes in consumer behaviour, in the way food is provisioned, or the way the state is governed, that often constitute the underlying dynamics of trust and distrust. After all, BSE was a scandal that broke at a particular time and in relation to a particular threat to human health, but it was predicated on developments in agricultural technologies and production methods that had been taking place on an historical scale.

Quality of food, likewise, can easily become a focus of mismatches in norms and expectations between consumers and producers. One example of this might be from the production side: how does the local and traditional quality of foods survive the massive expansion of markets, requiring a massive scaling-up and automation of production. Consumers of the world may all delight in Parma ham or Roquefort cheese. But new methods of standardization and mass production, possibly alongside the older small scale and local, necessarily develop to meet that demand. Mass-produced, sliced and pre-packaged Parma ham is not at all the same as ham from a small butcher in a village in the Parma region. Not all consumers can have it both ways, the 'old' traditional in the 'new' world markets. But consumers want many different things, and in their changing worlds and lifestyles may develop quite contradictory, even irreconcilable, desires. The growing interest in, or even need for, convenience and ready-made food can easily go together with a nostalgia for traditional home-cooking, and an expectation for a distinctive quality of food that cannot be matched by providers of mass-produced foods. Pizzas from fast-food outlets meet a demand for instant satisfaction, but conflict with a desire for individually crafted, traditional oven-baked versions. Consumers may want their cake (traditional quality) and eat it (ready-made). Indeed, many producers and retailers of mass-produced food play on this ambivalence in their styling, presentation and advertising.

These then are examples of longer-term shifts in norms and expectations between consumers and the other actors of food provisioning and regulation. They are taking place unevenly across Europe, and from different food traditions and starting points. When we find that Italians are distrustful, especially about quality, or that the Norwegians are trustful, especially about safety, the explanation is in terms of stability or instability, the pace and direction of changes, and the emergence of crises and scandals at the societal scale of matches and mismatches between norms and expectations.

Finally, as the third aspect of a socio-institutional explanation, we turn to the way relationships fit together amongst the cast of actors involved in food provisioning and consumption. Given that we are seeking explanations at the societal level and looking at national configurations, we have privileged three main actors: consumers with their shared national characteristics; the market food provisioners; and the state actors (regulatory bodies, experts, etc.). The national configurations between these three relational poles were described in terms of 'triangular affairs'. Between the societally institutionalized consumers, national provisioning systems, and the state endowed with different modes of governance and organization of responsibilities, there are shared and nationally typical relationships between consumers and provisioners; consumers and state; and state and provisioners.

We argue that how the relationships fit together in the overall configuration is more important than the strength of trust embodied in any one of the relationships taken separately. Even though Norway and the United Kingdom are so different in terms of each of the three principal relationships, consumers manifest high levels of trust in food because of the concordance between norms and expectations running between them. Simplifying: what really matters is that everyone expects everyone else to be doing what they should be doing with respect to everyone else in the triangular affair. What is actually expected of whom in Norway and Britain, and how responsibilities are organized, how and what different actors do, matters much less than consistency and conformity of norms and expectations between our three polar actors. Governments, retailers and manufacturers must do what they are expected to do – and what they are doing must be acceptable to people as consumers and citizens.

Likewise for distrust: actors differ between each other both with respect to what they expect of each other, and in the norms of what they do in relation to each other. Again, we can contrast two countries to make the point. Germany displays relatively high levels of distrust, and, using the configurational approach, we argue that conflicts of expectations and norms arise not only between consumers and the other two poles, but also in what the state expects of consumers and market actors. Its support of green and local food against the mass-standardized foods of discount retailers aggravates the tensions. Italy presents quite a different configurational basis for even higher levels of distrust: a distrust of state regulation and, more importantly, of rules imported from the European Community meets a consumer torn between modernizing lifestyles and conserving tradition, conceptualized as the local, the 'typical'. In the event of a potential crisis like avian flu, it is not only that farmers and food manufacturers might be distrusted for pursuing commercial interest above safety, but also that the state is not seen as capable of ensuring that standards, inspections and control are uniformly exerted throughout the country. The result is a combination of these distrusts, intensifying their effects. In this analysis, distrust is much more than an absence of harmony and concordance between actors and their norms and expectations. There are positive conflicts, reflecting the historical capacity of food to generate controversy, now fuelled by the rapid changes in consumption, regulation and provision of food.

We have in this book addressed a quite distinct and long-standing debate about the mechanisms that produce trust, asking whether trust emerges through slowly changing cultural solidarity, social networks and interpersonal relations or, instead, through an instrumental and rational assessment of institutional performance. Cultural processes might, by their nature, be expected to be very general, while institutional performance would refer more directly to the current behaviour of food institutions, state and market. Institutional performance may well matter, but more in relation to changing social norms and expectations than evaluations of performance by each and every individual consumer.

In an empirical study of food, it is not easy to disentangle one from the other. The formation of institutionalized relationships between the major actors or 'poles' certainly have strong cultural, path-dependent elements, influencing the division of responsibilities and expectations. But we have also seen that performance matters, not only in the short run, but also in the more long-term development of these relationships. From the evidence, it appears that in some countries (for example, Norway), a culturally founded general trust dominates, whereas in others, notably the United Kingdom, after experiencing a period of change and crisis, institutional performance appears more significant. In general, however, these do not appear to be alternatives. But, whether they are complementary and mutually reinforcing or not may be an outcome both of the particular phase of crisis and change, and of the particular societal circumstances of different countries. National variations are far from static and a situation of widespread distrust regarding particular issues may relatively rapidly turn into a situation of trust – and vice versa. A country such as Italy exhibits high levels of cultural distrust (narrow familialism) alongside low expectations of institutional performance continuously reinforced by experience. Although well beyond the scope of this book, there can be assumed to be strong interactions between the cultural and institutional performance aspects of societal relations between consumers and other actors, state and market. Variations in trust seem to some degree to reflect differences in social and political conditions at a very general level. But in order to understand responses of distrust in food, one has to recognize major influences from institutions and relations that are specific to the food sector.

10.4   Establishing and restoring confidence

Given that we understand trust and distrust to be emergent properties of relations within particular configurations, what does this mean for the concept of trust itself? Basically, we distinguish between two forms of trust – 'familiarity' and 'confidence'. These forms of trust[3] may coexist, but it is not a matter of individuals choosing which to adopt. Processes of institutionalization ensure that they will usually not appear as explicit alternative strategies. The relative importance of these forms switch, depending on institutional trajectories.

In the field of food, both forms of trust are characterized by non-reciprocity, but the degrees of asymmetry are different. Even though the distribution of power, resources, information and competence between consumers and other actors is generally biased against the consumer, the balance may differ considerably. Still, it is consumers who trust or distrust supermarkets or public authorities, and not vice versa. Different forms of trust are based on distinct sets of norms and expectations, including different modes of accordance or investiture of trustworthiness. Both forms are contingent, but the way contingency operates is different.

Familiarity relies on long-term personalized, experience-based and particular relations that involve knowledge of the shop, often also particular persons, and specific knowledge of the origins and qualities of the food. Resources acquired in personal social networks will therefore be of value. Expectations are communicated and modified through the personal encounter. But note that when talking about market exchange, familiarity refers to instrumental, single-purpose relations, *not* multi-purpose, mutual relations where exchange of food might be more like a form of gift-giving. For this reason, and given that food is overwhelmingly acquired through market exchanges, familiarity-based trust in food is at most 'thin familiarity', and, in the big picture, has for a long time been marginal and is becoming more so. Much more common is the phenomenon of mass-marketed pseudo-familiarity, localism and traditionality based on symbols rather than forms of interaction.

Confidence, on the other hand, relies on impersonal inter-relations with formal institutions. The impersonal and highly asymmetrical inter-relations make generalization a basic feature of confidence. Instead of specificity and particularity, prioritized properties are standardization and predictability. Expectations and evaluations are based on generalized public opinion and codified, often formalized, types of information, such as labels. Confidence does not only build on the immediate trust-worthiness of institutional actors, but also, and sometimes predominantly, on beliefs in the legitimacy and effectiveness of institutionalized procedures such as standardization, traceability schemes, monitoring programmes, and so on.

The two forms are not static. Mismatches, tension, contention and, perhaps above all, poor performance may lead to episodes and periods of distrust. If not handled directly through better performance and improved match between actors and expectations, episodes of distrust may lead to more generalized and embedded forms of distrust, whereupon distrust becomes part of routinized inter-relations among institutional actors.

Such episodes or periods may also generate a crisis and initiate a phase of reconstitution, characterized by issues and solutions being openly and explicitly contested. In such circumstances, consumer trust cannot be taken for granted. Trust and distrust appear instead as clear options in relatively unstable situations. Notably, distrust and demands for change are recognized by consumers themselves and by other actors. Phases of reconstitution are nothing new. However, the effects of distrust and phases of reconstitution are very different whether starting out with trust based on familiarity or on confidence.

Distrust, mismatches and challenges to relations based on familiarity may result in reconstitution through directly *reaffirmative* efforts that can either strengthen consumers' immediate control in existing relations or lead to new, perhaps even more specific, relations. Increasing asymmetry and reliance on complex institutions will, on the other hand, make that difficult. Our empirical findings suggest that reaffirmation occurs in pursuit of increased personal control when distrust in institutions is high; for example, by buying fresh, organic food from a specific shop or market stall where you know precisely the place or farm of origin – or even going directly to the farmer. But, the restoration of familiarity-based trust is almost a contradiction in terms. First, in response to a generalized crisis, a generalized reconstitution of familiarity undermines its defining feature: particularity and local difference. Second, it is politically difficult to create new institutional arrangements that feel as if they had always been there. Once broken, familiarity is hard to fix. Reaffirmative efforts appearing within contexts of widespread institutional distrust provide a refuge rather than a viable alternative.

After a breakdown of confidence, reconstitution of trust involves, on the one hand, a *realignment* between new norms and expectations and, on the other hand, *reassurance* through explicit political debates, often concerning transparency, neutrality and independence from contaminating influences. In describing this overall process of reconstitution as a 'phase of reassurance', we therefore imply a combination of different processes. For problems are understood as social and political, and therefore organizational arrangements are the focus of attention, with both criticism and proposed solutions. Realignment of the societal configuration of relationships is at stake, forcing new ways of doing things (regulating, consuming, provisioning) and stimulating the emergence of newly concordant norms and expectations. But in the transitional phase, before the new relationships again become taken for granted, discourses of reassurance and contestation often highlight their novelty or emphasize the possibility of alternative arrangements.

Successful realignment will gradually re-embed confidence through the establishment of routines, conventions and institutionalized interrelations. Even though the history of food crises repeatedly demonstrates this, each reconstitution of confidence emerges with a new institutional basis and new kinds of conditionality. New periods of calm and consensus can be expected; but with their in-built specific tensions and weaknesses. A phase of reconstitution can be highly disruptive and confusing, but is potentially positive and constructive. What eventually emerges, however, involves a realignment of norms and expectations and a new configurational institutional basis of confidence.

Institutionalization of distrust has constituted a major element of recent processes of realignment and the development of new bases for confidence. Consumer distrust has been recognized explicitly as a problem and new arrangements set in place to reflect the fact that people do not trust actors, processes or procedures. In other words, the new organizational forms recognize the asymmetry of the interrelations and the possibility of malfeasance detrimental to consumers. Recently, that has meant emphasis on arrangements for third-party monitoring to ensure that consumer and public interests are properly considered. Such third-party presence, first of all represented by public authorities, has historically played a major role in protecting food consumers and ensuring accountability. Measures to ensure transparency are generally important as a way of demonstrating and monitoring that public concerns and interests are actually being properly considered.

Processes of the reconstitution of trust tend to be irreversible, whether they refer to familiarity or confidence. What may have worked in an earlier historical period, might be quite inadequate to meet new circumstances of crisis and distrust. We have already said that reaffirming familiarity is problematic in a modern, globalized food market. But also conditions for reconstituting confidence are changing. Previous political approaches to realignment now appear 'statist', with governments passing legislation and providing for enforcement bodies to control private interests in the name of society. The protective state represented a general consumer interest less controversially, accepting that less organized individuals had less power. Problems and minor crises may in fact strengthen rather than threaten this type of institutional order. We find this model still works sufficiently in Norway; but in other cases, like the United Kingdom, such solutions have been seriously undermined.

More generally, though, the current phase of reconstituting confidence is characterized by a special emphasis on the rights or legitimate expectations of the consumer within a context of more complex inter-relations. This produces demands for new forms of governance and ways of institutionalizing distrust, including:

- representation in decision-making of the public in their capacity or role as consumers;
- independence which is not only independence from business interests, but also from political influence (agencification and non-governmental audit organizations may have that purpose);
- transparency through democratic monitoring becoming insufficient, processes and decisions must be open for scrutiny by the general public, among other things to demonstrate independence and sufficient consideration of consumer interests. Transparency may also involve monitoring the internal procedures of business organizations.

Such developments are the basis for a realignment of the relationships that generate trust within national configurations. They do not imply a new form of trust, rather just another episode in a long series of recurring phases of reconstitution of confidence in food through institutional realignment. This confidence is based on more complex institutional arrangements than before, and therefore also more complex conditions for the investiture of trustworthiness.

But this new institutional basis for confidence assumes neither more reflexivity on the part of individuals nor any basically new way of understanding and handling food risks. The dynamic of consumer trust in food is an outcome of changes in particular relations of power, interests and responsibilities within the food sector, rather than general, inherent conditions for trust characteristic of post- or second modernity. We suspect that trust in many other spheres of provisioning is likewise a confidence rooted in complex institutional arrangements.

Notes

2 Trust and Food Consumption: Theoretical Approaches

1. The theory of planned behaviour is very often used as the main theoretical frame of reference (Ajzen, 1991; Ajzen and Fishbein, 1980).
2. See also Lagerspetz (1998), who sees tacitness as a basic feature of trust.
3. Mistzal (1995, 14) makes a parallel distinction between seeing trust as a property of a social system on the one hand, and trust as a property of social relationships, on the other.
4. Dulsrud (2002) has shown that such particular and network-based trust relations can prevail even over long distances, as exemplified by traditional distribution systems for fish. To extend such long-distance network-based relations to include even consumers will be very demanding, especially within a modern context of mass distribution.
5. The range of issues can be much larger than for personal exchange of fresh food, due to the complexity of the inter-relations and the procedures as well as the higher degrees of processing. As already indicated, GM food, for example, introduced a number of new issues, so do global sourcing systems.

3 Enquiring into Trust: Some Methodological Considerations

1. In order to provide for a systematic analysis of the institutional conditions of trust, we paid special attention to two items within the food system. One item has been examined that is a source of controversy – beef – which illustrates aspects of consumer distrust and the ways in which institutions seek to handle crises and scares. This was compared with a product around which there is less controversy – tomatoes – so that we can examine how systems work in normal times when consumers routinely exhibit trust.
2. This material, compiled as six country studies and a study of the EU arrangements have been published in the project working paper series available at www.trustinfood.org.
3. For example, centralized versus decentralized responsibility for food safety; presence or absence of trade protection; global versus national versus local sourcing of food products.
4. In this exercise there is nothing objectionable about using survey-generated data to add to the relevant characteristics of each country. Nor is it obligatory to make the outcome variable according to some measure of public opinion drawn from the population survey (PS). The balance of public opinion on various topics is just as much an institutionalized factor as is the degree of centralization of the regulatory system or the integration of the supply chain.

5. We developed the method *post hoc*, but there would be gains from developing this tool at the earliest possible stage, because it would involve much more systematic gathering and organizing of data, making the outputs more robust. It requires a degree of consensus about concepts, empirical indicators and explanatory frames that would have been very challenging in an exploratory exercise like ours. Early meetings between collaborators would need to devote considerable time to developing this, and one would expect this to be an iterative process which develops the tool in the course of the research.

6. The topic in question, trust in food, may also be sensitive to public events and debates. As part of the country studies of institutional and social conditions, all teams were asked to monitor the media carefully in the period just before and during the survey data collection and to record significant occurrences.

7. The results of the regression analyses, in addition to correlation analyses, are reported in other publications from the project (Kjærnes, Poppe and Lavik, 2005; Poppe and Kjærnes, 2003).

4   Variations in Popular Trust

1. In our statistical analyses we have kept the eastern and western parts of Germany separate. This is because we are interested in whether East Germany, as a former Eastern European country, has different dynamics of trust from the western part. As will become evident, trust levels are very similar, but the processes behind them are partly different (see also Chapter 5).

2. Checks for consistency have been made, using Cronbach's alpha, that the reliability of the indices are satisfactory. See also Poppe and Kjaernes (2003).

3. The order of the items was rotated, so that the order would not influence the answers.

4. The distribution of answers on this question is quite consistent, compared to other questions. We therefore believe that the scale reflects trust–distrust distinctions.

5. Proportions of those who answered 'very safe' for each item were added up, divided by the number of food items and multiplied by 100.

6. Underlining this is the observation of the British very positive evaluations of food safety, which are clearly higher than in the Eurobarometer survey from 1998 (Berg, 2000a,b). In both studies, the British made much less clear distinctions between fresh and processed food items.

7. The test was a linear regression analysis, using the trust in food index as the dependent variable, and the questions of change regarding the five key food issues as independent variables. The results are reported in Poppe and Kjærnes (2003, 75).

8. The summary index is based on dummy variables, distinguishing between proportions saying the various actors would tell the whole truth, and those saying they would tell parts of the truth or withhold information. For each respondent, all truth-telling items are added up. Next, this is divided by the number of indicators and multiplied by 100. The additive index varies between 0 and 100, where 0 denotes that none of the eight actors are

believed to tell the whole truth in case of a food scandal, and 100 denotes that all of them are.

9. The notion 'food experts' is very broad and may include experts working for the food industry, for authorities and in independent academic positions. Their ranking here suggests that food experts were taken to have some independence to express their own results and opinions.

10. *Variable definitions*: All the independent variables are dummies, coding 1 for those believing that a given actor will tell the whole truth in case of a food scandal, and 0 otherwise. Index 1 is a variable summing up the 'very safe' categories on 12 food items. *Index means*: Calculated as the mean of the predicted average scores for each geographical area. For further definitions, see Poppe and Kjaernes (2003).

5   Culture and Performance: Trust in Meat

1. This is an additive index made up of six dummy indicators of safety related to as many specific meat products, all scoring 1 if the given food item is considered 'very safe' to eat and 0 otherwise. Each individual score is divided by 6 and multiplied by 100 to produce a variable that varies between 0 and 100 index points. Needless to say, scoring 0 on the index means that none of the six meat items are regarded as 'very safe' to eat while a score of 100 implies that all of them are. As indicated by the alpha values reported in Table 5.2, the internal consistency of the index is moderate to high in all countries (Ringdal, 2001).

2. *Variable definitions*: *Trust in Most People*: A dummy scoring 1 for 'can be trusted', 0 otherwise. *Confidence in own food*: A dummy scoring 1 for 'High degree', 0 otherwise. *Evaluation of change*: Additive index made up by five dummy indicators of food issues, each *scoring* 1 for 'worse' and 0 otherwise. These include 'prices', 'taste quality', 'farming methods', 'nutrition' and 'safety'. *Truth-Telling*: Additive index made up by eight dummy indicators of institutional actors, each scoring 1 for 'whole truth' and 0 otherwise. The actors in question are 'consumer organizations', 'food experts', 'food authorities', 'media', 'farmers', 'supermarket chains', 'politicians' and the 'processing industry'. *Trust in meats*: Additive index made up by six food item indicators, scoring 1 for 'very safe' and 0 otherwise. The meat products included are 'beef', 'organic beef', 'pork', 'chicken', 'sausages' and 'burgers from outlets'. *Index means*: Calculated as the mean of the predicted average scores for each geographical area. Like the dependent variable, both indices are standardized to produce variables that vary between 0 and 100 index points.

3. To illustrate, in the BSE case, people could adapt to the new situation by either turning to a supplier believed to be safer, drawing upon personal networks for safe beef provisions or buying other types of meat than beef – or even drop eating meat and turn to other types of food. None of these options were blocked in any BSE area. Cf. Kjærnes (1999).

4. The score for non-confident and non-trustful Italian respondents is given by the constant. Cf. Chapter 4.

5. A similar analysis was run using the full index for trust in 12 food items (see Chapter 4) as the dependent variable. The analysis showed the same national

tendencies in terms of how much the four variables added to the explanation of trust in food/meat (Poppe and Kjærnes, 2003, 123). The general tendency is that the analysis explains somewhat more of the variation when the 12 foods index was used. Noticeable, however, is that these differences in explained variation between the two analyses are most evident for the performance related variables, less for the 'cultural' variables. This difference underlines the point made above, that these pairs of questions refer to different dimensions or mechanisms of trust. It is probably not surprising that performance-related questions seem more specific or conditional than those that refer to cultural, underlying dimensions.

6. For Denmark and Norway, the calculation is as follows: the coefficient value [–0.08 * 100] = 8 index points. For Italy the corresponding computation yields the value 7.

6   Mobilizations of the Consumer

1. It is thus only the duty aspects of citizenship that Cohen emphasizes, not rights or consumer demands expressing common interests and general welfare issues. Such collective issues framed as consumer interests have in periods been prominent on the agenda in Europe as well as America when it comes to food.

2. The power relations lying behind these shifts are made more apparent by Jacobs (2000) and Cross (2000) who document the ways in which conservative republican business interests cemented in law their prejudice in favour of free markets. This debate has been driven by concern with social democratic politics and the decline of welfare provision, by the ways in which state behaviour/politics has changed, and has paid rather too little attention to how commercial organizations have also adapted their behaviour (i.e., as if there was only one way in which capitalist organizations could work).

3. We considered these as nominal categories of response and set about comparing the first and the second, and the third and the second. Multinomial regression analysis was deployed to show how much more likely people with particular characteristics – socio-demographic, procurement habits, political engagement and general attitudes towards trust (see the analysis in chapter 4 for the attitudes) – were to express trust or distrust. There were thus two parallel calculations, the one estimating likelihood of saying 'very safe' as opposed to 'rather safe', and 'not very safe' as opposed to 'rather safe'. The comparison showed that the effects of the independent variables were not symmetrical in these two exercises. Different factors disposed respondents to choose 'very safe' than to choose 'not very safe'. We take this as an indication that processes producing high trust may be different from those producing distrust.

4. As we shall see later in this chapter, these are also the countries with the most active consumers.

5. The German food retailing system is very heterogeneous. These alternative forms may be 'hidden' in answers saying that food is bought in small shops and food markets. For example, organic food is sold mainly through special shops instead of (as in Britain) in supermarkets.

6. Note that the sample is different from that which was presented in Chapters 4 and 5. We here include respondents from all countries into one sample, where each country has the same weight. Therefore, unlike analyses presented so far, individual characteristics are controlled for effects of the country of residence.
7. The independent variables used in the models have mostly been used in earlier parts of our inquiry (see Chapters 4 and 5). We have constructed one new, strategically interesting variable which describes shopping habits. We asked those respondents who said that they did at least sometimes shop for food and who also sometimes bought tomatoes and beef, where they purchased these items. We identified four possible patterns of shopping, distinguishing between those who bought both beef and tomatoes in a supermarket (44 per cent of all the relevant respondents to the survey), those who bought tomatoes but not beef in the supermarket (25 per cent), those who purchased beef but not tomatoes in the supermarket (8 per cent), and those who bought neither product in the supermarket (22 per cent). We then created an indicator of supermarket shopping which contrasted the first pattern, buying both items in the supermarket, from the rest.

7   Buying into Food

1. Trusting the state over taxation has similar asymmetric and non-reciprocal characteristics, as Daunton (2001, 2002) has argued in a way that parallels much of the approach developed here. Citizens distrust/trust the state as a legitimate taxation authority, rather than vice versa, partly by virtue of the asymmetric relationship between state as the taxing agent and citizen as the object of taxation (and state expenditure). Institutional conditions for trust, such as alignment between taxation systems and economic organization, are combined with relational conditions, such as equity between different interest groups.
2. One should assume a relatively high base-line of patriotism, as the opposite bears the implication of disloyalty. This may be especially true of countries with relatively high agricultural employment.
3. Only 15 per cent had switched stores in the previous 12 months (Competition Commission, 2000, 17).
4. By traditionalism, we are referring to patterns that during the interwar period, and especially the immediate post-war period, not to some dim and distant agrarian paradise.

8   The State and Triangular Affairs of Trust

1. These are the 'protected geographical indications' (PGI, where at least one part of the production process must involve the indicated geographical context: Normandy cider where the apples may come from somewhere else, or Newcastle Brown Ale, likewise, are examples) and the much more powerful 'protected designation of origin' (PDO) where every part of the production process must take place in the geographical area according to production specifications, and involving particular local know-how: Parma ham is a prime example). These were enshrined in a European directive in 1992 (regulation 2081/92/EEC).

2. Aside from well-known manufacturer brands, for example, own-label supermarkets in the United Kingdom have attempted to establish their own superior quality brands, in many cases superposed on branding by PDO or PGI, for example, Tesco 'Finest', Sainsbury 'Taste the Difference'.
3. It is noteworthy that where national regulatory systems exist for PDO and PGI, they generally come under Ministries of Agriculture, and are producer-led regimes of quality (Barjolle and Sylvander, 2000)
4. For organics, this was Regulation 2092/91/EEC.
5. There was a major institutional reform, where bodies for control of animal production, fish and fish farming, plant production, animal health, food safety and drinking water were merged. This led to a reorientation towards primary production rather than retail sale to consumers. Quality, animal welfare, and so on are included, but first of all within this overall focus on primary production.
6. To make the point in another way, the Food Standards Agency model has yet to spread into other areas of consumption, such as transport, media, housing, energy, and so on. In that respect, the FSA and EFSA cannot be readily understood as examples of 'agencification' in the general sense of being rationalized instruments of operational functions responsible to Ministries (Jordana and Levi-Faur, 2004; Pollitt and Talbot, 2003).
7. This has most recently been reflected in the Cirio and Parmalat fraud scandals, two of Italy's largest food producers: the Parmalat collapse has been described as 'Europe's Enron', *Financial Times*, 21 December 2003. Subsequently, the fraud scandals have extended their tentacles to the football clubs they owned (Lazio and Parma, respectively).

9   Conditions for Trust in Food

1. This is not to suggest that consumer habits are by nature conservative and resistant to change: the rapid expansion of consumption of pizza across Europe is an example of changed ways of what, how, when and where food is eaten.
2. It is not possible from our study to say whether this situation was ever very successful in producing high trust or whether, instead, social coherence and order was obtained through other mechanisms of authority and power.
3. There was very little difference in answers to questions like: how important is it that beef or tomatoes are tasty?; also regarding whether particular actors exercise hygienic control; also regarding some shopping habits, like checking the date stamp, sticking to special brands; also regarding political or consumer protest, where there is of course very limited activity in most countries; and, most striking, there is widespread agreement about reasons to be concerned about food issues, across the countries a very substantial majority agreed that currently contentious food issues are important matters.
4. This was supported also by time-series data (see discussion in Chapter 4).
5. Durkheim's concept of 'precontractual trust' is an early parallel (Durkheim, 1989).
6. The Danish case is in many respects similar to Norway, particularly regarding the generalized, taken-for-granted confidence in the role of the authorities

regarding food safety issues. However, the provisioning system displays a more open and differentiated character, as reflected even on the consumer side and in public discourse, thus suggesting that more active, conditional relations of confidence are becoming increasingly important.

10   Explaining Trust in Food

1. Even regional or class differences in eating times are nonetheless societal, distinguishing one country from another.
2. The money spent on food of course also reflects the level of income and the relative level of food prices.
3. We see 'trust' as a more encompassing concept including different forms, unlike for example Luhmann and Seligman, who have used 'trust' to characterize a third, more contemporary form.

Bibliography

Ajzen, I. (1991) 'The theory of planned behaviour', *Organisational Behaviour and Human Decision Processes*, 50(2): 179–211.

Ajzen, I., and Fishbein, M. (1980) *Understanding Attitudes and Predicting Social Behaviour* (Englewood Cliffs, NJ: Prentice-Hall International).

Allaire, G. (2004) 'Quality in economics. A cognitive perspective', in M. Harvey, A. McMeekin and A. Warde (eds), *The Qualities of Food. Alternative Theories and Empirical Approaches* (Manchester: Manchester University Press), pp. 61–93.

Almås, R. (1999) 'Food trust, ethics and safety in risk society', *Sociological Research Online*, 4(3): 1–9.

Appadurai, A. (1988) 'How to make a national cuisine: Cookbooks in contemporary India', *Comparative Studies in Society and History*, 30: 3–24.

Argenbright, R. (1993) 'Bolsheviks, baggers and railroaders: Political power and social space, 1917–1921', *The Russian Review*, 52(4): 506–28.

Ballantine, B. (2003) 'Improving the quality of risk management in the European Union: Risk communication', *EPC Working Paper No. 5* (Brussels: The European Policy Centre).

Banfield, E. C. (1958) *The Moral Basis of a Backward Society* (New York: Free Press).

Barbagli, M., and Saraceno, C. (1997) *Lo stato delle famiglie in Italia* (Bologna: Il Mulino).

Barber, B. (1983) *The Logic and Limits of Trust* (New Brunswick, NJ: Rutgers University Press).

Barjolle, D., and Sylvander, B. (2000) *PDO and PGI Products: Market, Supply Chains and Institutions* (Brussels: European Commission).

Barling, D., and Lang, T. (1999) 'European public policy on genetic modification of agricultural products and food', *European Journal of Public Health*, 9(3): 163–5.

Barrientos, S., and Perrons, D. (1999) 'Gender and the global food chain: A comparative study of Chile and the UK', in H. Afshar and S. Barrientos (eds), *Women, Globalisation and Fragmentation in the Developing World* (Basingstoke: Macmillan – now Palgrave Macmillan).

Bauman, Z. (1988) *Freedom* (Buckingham: Open University Press).

Beck, U. (1992) *Risk Society: Towards a New Modernity* (London: Sage).

Beck, U. (1999) *World Risk Society* (Cambridge: Polity Press).

Beck, U., and Beck-Gernsheim, E. (2002) *Individualization. Institutionalized Individualism and Its Social and Political Consequences* (London: Sage).

Beck, U., Bonss, W., and Lau, C. (2003) 'The theory of reflexive modernization: Problematic, hypotheses and research programme', *Theory, Culture and Society*, 20(2): 1–33.

Beck, U., Giddens, A. and Lash, S. (1994) *Reflexive Modernization: Politics, Tradition and Aesthetics in the Modern Social Order* (Cambridge: Polity Press).

Becker, G. (1977) *The Economic Approach to Human Behavior* (Chicago: Chicago University Press).

Bennett, T., Grossberg, L., and Morris, M. (eds) (2005) *New Keywords: A Revised Vocabulary of Culture and Society* (Oxford: Blackwell).

Berg, L. (2000a) *Trust in Food in Europe: Focus on Consumer Trust in Norway, England and Belgium*, Working Paper No. 15 (Oslo: The National Institute for Consumer Research).

Berg, L. (2000b) *Tillit til mat i kugalskapens tid*. Report No. 15 (Oslo: The National Institute for Consumer Research).

Berg, L., Kjærnes, U., Ganskau, E., Minina, V., Voltchkova, L., Halkier, B., and Holm, L. (2005) 'Trust in food safety in Russia, Denmark and Norway', *European Societies*, 7(1): 103–30.

Bergeaud-Blackler, F. (2003) *Institutional Report: The European Union*, Trust in Food Working Paper, available at: www.trustinfood.org.

Bergeaud-Blackler, F. (2004) 'Institutional Report: European Union', *Trust in Food Working Paper Series No. 9* (Manchester: www.trustinfood.org2004).

Berger, P. L., and Luckmann, T. (1976) *Den samfundsskabte virkelighed. En vidensociologisk afhandling* (Copenhagen: Lindhardt og Ringhof).

Bevir, M., and Trentmann, F. (eds) (2004) *Markets in Historical Context: Ideas and Politics in the Modern World* (Cambridge: Cambridge University Press).

Bijlsma-Frankema, K., and Costa, A. C. (2005) 'Understanding the trust-control nexus', *International Sociology*, 20(3): 259–82.

Blaikie, N. (1993) *Approaches to Social Enquiry* (Cambridge: Polity Press).

Block, F., (2003) 'Karl Polanyi and the Writing of the Great Transformation', *Theory and Society*, 32: 275–306.

Böcker, A., and Hanf, C. H. (2000) 'Confidence lost and – partially – regained: Consumer response to food scares', *Journal of Economic Behavior and Organization*, 43(4): 471–85.

Boltanski, L., and Thévenot, L. (2006) *On Justification: Economies of Worth* (Princeton, NJ: Princeton University Press).

Borre, O. (2000) 'Critical issues and political alienation in Denmark', *Scandinavian Political Studies*, 23(4): 285–309.

Boyer, R. (1997) 'The variety and unequal performance of really existing markets: Farewell to Doctor Pangloss', in J. R. Hollingsworth and R. Boyer (eds), *Contemporary Capitalism: The Embeddedness of Institutions* (Cambridge, Cambridge University Press), pp. 55–93.

Braithwaite, J. (1998) 'Institutionalizing distrust, enculturating trust', in V. Braithwaite and M. Levi (eds), *Trust and Governance* (New York: Russel Sage Foundation), pp. 343–75.

Breck, T. (2000) 'The risk of BSE cannot be compared to that of cycling', Fødevarenyt (May): 8–11.

Brobeck, S., Mayer, R. N., and Herrmann, R. O. (1998) 'The consumer movement today: An encyclopedic view', *Consumer Interests Annual*, 44: 190–3.

Brown, C. (1998) 'Consumer activism in Europe', *Consumer Policy Review*, 8(6): 209–12.

Brown, N., and Michael, M. (2002) 'From authority to authenticity: The changing governance of biotechnology', *Health, Risk and Society*, 4(3): 259–72.

Bruce, D. M. (2002) 'A social contract for biotechnology: shared visions for risky technologies?', *Journal of Agricultural and Environmental Ethics*, 15: 279–89.

Burgess, A. (2001) 'Flattering consumption: creating a Europe of the consumer', *Journal of Consumer Culture*, 1(1): 93–118.

Burnett, J. (1989) *Plenty and Want: A Social History of Food in England from 1815 to the Present Day* (London: Routledge).

Burnett, J., and Oddy, D. J. (eds) (1994) *The Origins and Development of Food Policy in Europe* (Leicester: Leicester University Press).

Busch, L. (2000) 'The moral economy of grades and standards', *Journal of Rural Studies*, 16(3): 273–83.

Cohen, L. (2000) 'Citizens and consumers in the United States in the century of mass consumption', in M. Daunton and M. Hilton (eds), *The Politics of Consumption: Material Culture and Citizenship in Europe and America* (Oxford: Berg), pp. 203–20.

Cohen, L. (2003) *A Consumers' Republic: The Politics of Mass Consumption in Postwar America* (New York: Knopf).

Coleman, J. C. (1990) *Foundations of Social Theory* (Cambridge, MA: The Belknap Press of Harvard University).

Coles, A. J. (1978) 'The moral economy of the crowd: Some twentieth-century food riots', *Journal of British Studies*, 18(1): 157–76.

Competition Commission. (2000) *Supermarkets. A Report on the Supply of Groceries from Multiple Stores in the United Kingdom* (London: HMSO).

Coppin, C. A. and High, J. (1992) 'Umpires at bat: Setting food standards by government regulation', *Business and Economic History*, 21: 109–18.

Cross, G. (2000) 'Corralling consumer culture: Shifting rationales for American state intervention in free markets', in M. Daunton and M. Hilton (eds), *The Politics of Consumption: Material Culture and Citizenship in Europe and America* (Oxford: Berg), pp. 283–300.

Cvetkovich, G., and Löfstedt, R. E. (1999) *Social Trust and the Management of Risk* (London: Earthscan).

Daunton, M. (2001) *Trusting Leviathan: The Politics of Taxation in Britain, 1799–1914* (Cambridge: Cambridge University Press).

Daunton, M. (2002) *Just Taxes: The Politics of Taxation in Britain, 1914–1979* (Cambridge: Cambridge University Press).

Daunton, M., and Hilton, M. (2000) *The Politics of Consumption: Material Culture and Citizenship in Europe and America* (Oxford: Berg).

Davis, M. (2001) *Late Victorian Holocausts: El Nino Famines and the Making of the Third World* (London: Verso).

Deakin, S., Michie, J. (eds) (1997) *Contracts, Co-operation, and Competition. Studies in Economics Management and Law* (Oxford: Oxford University Press).

Domingues, M., Graça, P., and de Almeida, M. D. V. (2004) 'Portuguese consumers' trust in food: An institutional approach', *Trust in Food Working Paper Series No. 7* (Porto: www.trustinfood.org).

Dulsrud, A. (2002) *Tillit og transaksjoner. En kvalitativ analyse av kontraktsrelasjoner i norsk hvitfiskeksport*, Doctoral Thesis (Oslo: Department of Sociology and Social Geography, University of Oslo).

Durkheim, E. (1989) *The Division of Labour in Society* (Basingstoke: Macmillan).

Elster, J. (1989a) *Nuts and Bolts for the Social Sciences* (Cambridge: Cambridge University Press).

Elster, J. (1989b) *The Cement of Society* (Cambridge: Cambridge University Press).

Elvbakken, K. T. (1997) 'Offentlig kontroll av næringsmidler. Institusjonalisering, apparat og tjenestemenn', *Rapport nr. 50* (Bergen: Institutt for aministrasjon og organisasjonsvitenskap, Universitetet i Bergen).

Esping-Andersen, G. (1990) *The Three Worlds of Welfare Capitalism* (Cambridge: Polity Press).

European Commission. (2000) *White Paper on Food Safety* (Brussels: European Commission).

European Commission. (2004) *Protection of Geographical Indications, Designations of Origin and Certificates of Specific Character for Agricultural Products and Foodstuffs. Guide to Community Regulations* (Brussels: European Commission).

European Commission – European Coordination Office. (1998) *Eurobarometer 49 on Food Safety* (Brussels: European Commission DG XXIV).

European Opinion Research Group. (2003) *Consumer Protection in the EU: Special Eurobarometer 59.2, Special Report 193* (Brussels: European Commission).

Ferretti, M. P., and Magaudda, P. (2004) 'Italy: between local traditions and global aspirations', *Trust in Food Working Paper Series No. 4* (Bologna: www.trustinfood.org).

Fife-Schaw, C., and Rowe, G. (1996) 'Public perceptions of everyday food hazards: A psychometric study', *Risk analysis*, 16(4): 487–500.

Foster, R. B. (2000) 'Enhancing trust in institutions that manage risk', in M. P. P. R. P. T. Cottam (ed.), *Foresight and Precaution: Proceedings of ESREL* (Rotterdam: A. A. Balkema), pp. 3–7.

Freitag, M. (2003) 'Beyond Tocqueville: The origins of social capital in Switzerland', *European Sociological Review*, 19(2): 217–232.

French, M., and Phillips, J. (2000) *Cheated not Poisoned? Food Regulation in the United Kingdom, 1875–1938* (Manchester: Manchester University Press).

Frewer, L. J., Howard, C., and Shepherd, R. (1997) 'Public concerns in the United Kingdom about general and specific applications of genetic engineering: Risk, benefit, and ethics', *Science, Technology and Human Values*, 22(1): 98–124.

Frewer, L. J., Scholderer, J., and Bredahl, L. (2003) 'Communicating about the risks and benefits of genetically modified foods: The mediating role of trust', *Risk analysis*, 23(6): 1117–33.

Frieburger, W. (1984) 'War prosperity and hunger: The New York food riots of 1917', *Labor History*, 25(2): 217–39.

Gabriel, Y., and Lang, T. (1995) *The Unmanageable Consumer: Contemporary Consumption and its Fragmentations* (London: Sage).

Gagnier, R. (2000) *The Insatiability of Human Wants: Economics and Aesthetics in Market Societies* (Chicago: Chicago University Press).

Gambetta, D. (ed.) (1988) *Trust: Making and Breaking Cooperative Relations* (Oxford: Basil Blackwell).

Giddens, A. (1991) *Modernity and Self-identity. Self and Society in the Late Modern Age* (Cambridge: Polity Press).

Giddens, A. (1994) 'Living in a post-traditional society', in U. Beck, A. Giddens and S. Lash (eds), *Reflexive Modernization: Politics, Tradition and Aesthetics in the Modern Social Order* (Cambridge: Polity Press), pp. 56–109.

Gilg, A. W., and Battershill, M. (1998) 'Quality farm food in Europe: A possible alternative to the industrialised food market and to current agri-environmental policies: Lessons from France', *Food Policy*, 23(1): 25–40.

Goldthorpe, J. H. (1997) 'Current issues in comparative macrosociology: A debate on methodological issues', *Comparative Social Research*, 16: 1–26.

Gough, C., Darier, E., De Marchi, B., Funtowitz, S., Grove-White, R., Pereira, A. G., Shackley, S., and Wynne, B. (2003) 'Contexts of citizen participation', in B. Kasemir, J. Jäger, C. C. Jaeger and M. T. Gardner (eds), *Public Participation in Sustainability Science* (Cambridge: Cambridge University Press), pp. 37–61.

Granovetter, M. (1985) 'Economic action and social structure: The problem of embeddedness', *The American Journal of Sociology*, 91(3): 481–510.

Green, K., Harvey, M., and McMeekin, A. (2003) 'Transformations of Food Consumption and Production Processes', *Journal of Environmental Policy and Planning*, 5(2): 145–63.

Greenberg, C. (2004) 'Political consumer action: Some cautionary notes from African American history', in M. Micheletti (ed.), *Politics, Products and Markets: Exploring Political Consumerism, Past and Present* (New Brunswick, NJ: Transaction Publishers), pp. 63–83.

Gronow, J., and Warde, A. (2001) *Ordinary Consumption* (London and New York: Routledge).

Guseva, A., and Rona-Tas, A. (2001) 'Uncertainty, risk, and trust: Russian and American credit card markets compared', *American Sociological Review*, 66: 623–46.

Halkier, B. (1999) 'Consequences of the politicization of consumption: The example of environmentally friendly consumption practices', *Journal of Environmental Policy and Planning*, 1(1): 25–41.

Halkier, B., and Holm, L. (2006) 'Shifting responsibilities for food in Europe', *Appetite*, Special Issue, 47(2): 127–204.

Hansen, J., Holm, L., Frewer, L., Robinson, P., and Sandoe, P. (2003) 'Beyond the knowledge deficit: Recent research into lay and expert attitudes to food risks', *Appetite*, 41(2): 111–21.

Hardin, R. (2001) 'Distrust', *Boston University Law Review*, 81: 495–522.

Harvey, M. (2002) 'Markets, supermarkets and the macro-social shaping of demand: An instituted economic process approach', in A. McMeekin, K. Green, M. Tomlinson and V. Walsh, *Innovation by Demand: An Interdisciplinary Approach to the Study of Demand and its Role in Innovation* (Manchester: Manchester University Press), pp. 187–207.

Harvey, M., and Randles, S. (2002) 'Market exchanges and "instituted economic process": an analytical perspective', *Revue d'Economie Industrielle*, 101: 11–30.

Harvey, M., Quilley, S., and Beynon, H. (2003) *Exploring the Tomato: Transformations of Nature, Society and Economy*. (Northampton, MA, and Cheltenham: Edward Elgar).

Helstosky, C. (2004) *Garlic and Oil: Politics and Food in Italy*. (Oxford and New York: Berg).

Hilton, M. (2003) 'The fable of the sheep; or, private virtues, public vices: The consumer revolution of the 20th century', *Past and Present*, 176: 222–56.

Hilton, M. (2004) 'Models of consumer-political action in the twentieth century: Rights, duties and justice', in I. Theien and E. Lange, *Affluence and Activism: Organised Consumers in the Post-War Era* (Oslo: Oslo Academic Press), pp. 21–40.

Hinrichs, C. C. (2000) 'Embeddedness and local food systems: Notes on two types of direct agricultural market', *Journal of Rural Studies*, 16(3): 295–303.

Hirdman, Y. (1983) *Magfrågan. Mat som mål och medel Stockholm 1870–1920* (Stockholm: Rabén and Sjögren).

Hirschman, A. O. (1970) *Exit, Voice and Loyalty. Responses To Decline in Firms, Organizations and States* (Cambridge, MA: Harvard University Press).

Hoffmann-Riem, H., and Wynne, B. (2002) 'In risk assessment, one has to admit ignorance. Explaining there are things we can't know could improve public confidence in science', *Nature*, 416 (14 March): 123.

Hogan, D. G. (1997) *Selling 'em by the Sack: White Castle and the Creation of American Food* (New York: New York University Press).

Hooker, N. H. (1999) 'Food safety regulation and trade in food products', *Food Policy*, 24(6): 653–68.

Ilmonen, K., and Stø, E. (1997) 'The "consumer" in political discourse: Consumer policy in the Nordic welfare states', in P. Sulkunen, J. Holmwood, H. Radner and G. Schulze (eds), *Constructing the New Consumer Society* (Basingstoke: Macmillan Press), pp. 197–217.

Inglehart, R. (1997) 'Postmaterialist values and the erosion of institutional authority', in J. S. Jr. Nye, P. D. Zelikow and D. C. King (eds), *Why People Don't Trust Government* (Cambridge, MA, and London: Harvard University Press), pp. 217–36.

Isserman, A. M. (2001) 'Genetically modified food: Understanding the societal dilemma', *American Behavioral Scientist*, 44(8): 1225–32.

Jacobs, M. (2000) 'The politics of plenty: Consumerism in the 20th century United States', in M. Daunton and M. Hilton (eds), *The Politics of Consumption: Material Culture and Citizenship in Europe and America* (Oxford: Berg), pp. 223–40.

Jensen, H. R. (1984) *Forbrugerpolitik og organiseret forbrugerarbejde* (Copenhagen: Akademisk Forlag).

Jensen, K. K. (2004) 'BSE in the UK: Why the risk communication strategy failed', *Journal of Agricultural & Environmental Ethics*, 17: 405–23.

Jordana, J., and Levi-Faur, D. (2004) 'The politics of regulation in the age of governance', in J. Jordana and D. Levi-Faur (eds), *The Politics of Regulation: Institutions and Regulatory Reforms for the Age of Governance* (Cheltenham: Edward Elgar), pp. 1–32.

Kaase, M. (1999) 'Interpersonal trust, political trust and non-institutionalised political participation in Western Europe', *West European Politics*, 22(3): 1–21.

King, D., and Rothstein, B. (1994) 'Government legitimacy and the labour market: A comparative analysis of employment exchanges', *Public Administration*, 72: 291–308.

Kjærnes, U. (1995) 'Milk: Nutritional science and agricultural development in Norway 1890–1990', in A. den Hartog (ed.), *Food Technology, Science, and Marketing: The European Diet in the 20th Century* (Scotland: Tuckwell Press), pp. 103–16.

Kjærnes, U. (1997) 'Framveksten av ernæringspolitikk i Norden', in U. Kjærnes (ed.), *Utfordringer i ernæringspolitikken. Nord-Rapport 619* (København: Nordisk Ministerråd), pp. 73–88.

Kjærnes, U. (1999) 'Food risks and trust relations', *Sosiologisk tidsskrift*, 7(4): 265–84.

Kjaernes, U. (2001) *Eating Patterns: A Day in the Lives of Nordic Peoples*, Report No. 7 (Oslo: The National Institute for Consumer Research).

Kjærnes, U. (2003) 'Food and nutrition policies of Nordic countries: How have they been developed and what evidence substantiates the development of these policies?', *Proceedings of the Nutrition Society*, 62: 563–70.

Kjærnes, U., Poppe, C., and Lavik, R. (2005) *Trust, Distrust and Food Consumption: A Study in Six European Countries, Project Report No. 15* (Oslo: The National Institute for Consumer Research).

Kjørstad, I. (2005) 'Consumer concerns for food animal welfare: Part IA. Literature Reviews', in: J. Roux and M. Miele (eds), *Farm Animal Welfare*

Concerns: Consumers, Retailers and Producers, Welfare Quality Reports No. 1 (Cardiff: Cardiff University, School of City and Regional Planning), pp. 3–53.

Klein, N. (2000) *No Logo: Taking Aim at the Brand Bullies* (New York: Picador).

Klingemann, H.-D., and Fuchs, D. (1995) *Citizens and the State* (Oxford: Oxford University Press).

Krippner, G. (2001) 'The elusive market: Embeddedness and the paradigm of economic sociology', *Theory and Society*, 30: 775–810.

Lagerspetz, O. (1998) *Trust: The Tacit Demand* (Dodrecht: Kluwer Academic Publishers).

Lamont, M., and Thévenot, L. (eds) (2000) *Rethinking Comparative Cultural Sociology: Repertoires of Evaluation in France and the United States* (Cambridge: Cambridge University Press).

Lane, D. (2005) *Berlusconi's Shadow: Crime, Justice and the Pursuit of Power* (London: Penguin).

Leach, M., Scoones, I., and Wynne, B. (2005) *Science and Citizens: Globalization and the Challenge of Engagement* (London and New York: Zed Books).

Lenz, T. (2003) *Consumer First? Shifting Responsibilities in the German Food System in the Light of European Integration and the BSE Crises*, Trust in Food Working Paper, available at: www.trustinfood.org.

Levenstein, H. A. (1988) *Revolution at the Table: The Transformation of the American Diet* (New York and Oxford: Oxford University Press).

Levi, M., and Stoker, L. (2000) 'Political trust and trustworthiness', *Annual Review of Political Science*, 3: 475–507.

Lewis, J. (1997) *Lone Mothers in European Welfare Regimes: Shifting Policy Logics* (London and Philadelphia: Jessica Kingsley Publishers).

Lie, J. (1991) 'Embedding Polanyi's market society', *Sociological Perspectives*, 34(2): 219–35.

Lie, J. (1992) 'The concept of mode of exchange', *American Sociological Review*, 57(4): 508–23.

Light, D. W., Castellblanch, R., Arredondo, P., and Socolar, D. (2003) 'No exit and the organization of voice in biotechnology and pharmaceuticals', *Journal of Health Politics, Policy and Law*, 28(2–3): 473–507.

Listhaug, O., and Wiberg, M. (1995) 'Confidence in political and private institutions', in H.-D. Klingemann and D. Fuchs (eds), *Citizens and the State* (Oxford: Oxford University Press), pp. 298–322.

Löfstedt, R. (2004) 'Risk communication and management in the 21st century', *International Public Management Journal*, 7(3): 335–46.

Löfstedt, R. E., and Frewer, L. (1998) 'Introduction', in R. E. Löfstedt and L. Frewer (eds), *The Earthscan Reader in Risk and Modern Society* (London: Earthscan Publications), pp. 3–27.

Löwe, H.-D. (1986) 'Teuerungsrevolten, Teuerungspolitik und Marktregulierung im 18.Jahrhundert in England, Frankreich und Deutschland', *Saeculum*, 37(3–4): 291–312.

Luhmann, N. (1988) 'Familiarity, confidence, trust: Problems and alternatives', in D. Gambetta (ed.), *Trust: Making and Breaking Cooperative Relations* (New York: Basil Blackwell), pp. 94–108.

Luhmann, N. (1979) *Trust and Power: Two Works* (Chichester: John Wiley & Sons).

Lyon, J. D. (1998) 'Coordinated food systems and accountability mechanisms for food safety: A law and economics approach', *Food And Drug Law Journal*, 53: 729–76.

Mahoney, J. (2004) 'Comparative historical sociology', *Annual Review of Sociology*, 30: 81–101.

Majone, G. (1999) 'The regulatory state and its legitimacy problems', *West European Politics*, 22(1): 1–24.

Maurice, M., and Sorge, A. (2000a) 'General introduction', in M. Maurice and A. Sorge (eds), *Embedding Organizations: Societal Analysis of Actors, Organizations and Socio-Economic Context* (Amsterdam: John Benjamins), pp. 1–6.

Maurice, M., and Sorge, A. (2000b) *Embedding Organisations: Societal Analysis of Actors, Organisations, and Socio-Economic Context* (Amsterdam: John Benjamins).

Maurice, M., Sellier, F., and Silvestre, J.-J. (1986) *The Social Foundations of Industrial Power: A Comparison of France and Germany* (Cambridge, MA: MIT).

Maurice, M. (2000) 'The paradoxes of societal analysis: A review of the past and prospects for the future', in M. Maurice and A. Sorge (eds), *Embedding Organizations: Societal Analysis of Actors, Organizations and Socio-Economic Context* (Amsterdam: John Benjamins Publishing Company), pp. 13–36.

McCracken, G. (1988) *Culture and Consumption: New Approaches to the Symbolic Character of Consumer Goods and Activities* (Bloomington: Indiana University Press).

Micheletti, M., Follesdal, A., and Stolle, D. (2003) *Politics, Products, and Markets: Exploring Political Consumerism Past and Present* (New Brunswick, NJ: Transaction Publishers).

Michelsen, J. (2001) 'Recent development and political acceptance of organic farming in Europe', *Sociologica Ruralis*, 41(1): 3.

Micklitz, H.-W. (1992) 'The international dimension of product safety', in M. Fallon and F. Maniet (eds), *Product Safety and Control Processes in the European Community* (Brussels: Centre de Droit de la Consommation).

Miele, M., and Murdoch, J. (2002) 'The practical aesthetics of traditional cuisines: Slow food in Tuscany', *Sociologica Ruralis*, 42(2): 312–28.

Miles, S., and Frewer, L. J. (2001) 'Investigating specific concerns about different food hazards', *Food Quality and Preference*, 12(1): 47–61.

Miller, A. H., and Listhaug, O. (1998) 'Policy preferences and political distrust: A comparison of Norway, Sweden and the United States', *Scandinavian Political Studies*, 21(2): 161–87.

Mintel. (2003a) *Food Retailing – Denmark*, Report.

Mintel. (2003b) *Food Retailing – Norway*, Report.

Mintel. (2003c) *Food Retailing – Portugal*, Report.

Mintel. (2005a) *Food Retailing – Italy*, Report.

Mintel. (2005b) *Food Retailing – UK*, Report.

Mintel. (2005c) *Food Retailing – Germany*, Report.

Mintel. (2005d)*Microwave Ovens – UK*, Report (April).

Mintz, S. W. (1996) *Tasting Food, Tasting Freedom: Excursions into Eating, Culture, and the Past* (Boston, MA: Beacon Press).

Mishler, W., and Rose, R. (2001) 'What are the origins of political trust? Testing institutional and cultural theories in post-communist societies', *Comparative Political Studies*, 34(1): 30–62.

Misztal, B. (1995) *Trust in Modern Societies: The Search for the Bases of Social Order* (Cambridge: Polity Press).

Morgan, D. (1979) *Merchants of Grain* (London: Weidenfeld & Nicolson).

Murdoch, J. and Miele, M. (1999) '"Back to nature": Changing "worlds of production" in the food sector', *Sociologia Ruralis*, 39(4): 465–82.

218   *Bibliography*

Nestle, M. (2002) *Food Politics: How the Food Industry Influences Nutrition and Health* (Berkeley: University of California Press).

Nielsen, A. and Møhl, T. (2004) 'A decade of change in the Danish food system', *Trust in Food Working Paper Series No. 5* (Copenhagen: www.trustinfood.org).

Pharr, S. J., and Putnam, R. D. (2000) *Disaffected Democracies: What's Troubling the Trilateral Countries?* (Princeton, NJ: Princeton University Press).

Pira Market Report. (2005a) *Packaging's Place in Society.*

Pira Market Report. (2005b) *Ruling the Waves.*

Pollack, M. A., and Shaffer, G. C. (2000) 'Biotechnology: The next transatlantic trade war?', *The Washington Quarterly*, 23(4): 41–54.

Pollitt, C., and Talbot, C. (2003) *Unbundled Government – A Critical Analysis of the Global Trend to Agencies, Quangos and Contractualisation* (London: Routledge).

Poortinga, W., and Pidgeon, N. F. (2004) 'Trust, the asymmetry principle, and the role of prior beliefs', *Risk analysis*, 24(6): 1475–86.

Poortinga, W., and Pidgeon, N. F. (2005) 'Trust in risk regulation: Cause or consequence of the acceptability of GM food?', *Risk analysis*, 25(1): 199–209.

Poppe, C., and Kjaernes, U. (2003) *Trust in Food in Europe: A Comparative Analysis*, Professional Report No. 5 (Norway: The National Institute for Consumer Research)

Powell, D. A. (2000) 'Food safety and the consumer – perils of poor risk communication', *Canadian Journal of Animal Science*, 80(3): 393–404.

Power, M. (1997) *The Audit Society: Rituals of Verification* (Oxford: Oxford University Press).

Putnam, R. D. (1993) *Making Democracy Work: Civic Traditions in Modern Italy* (Princeton, NJ: Princeton University Press).

Ragin, C. (1987) *The Comparative Method: Moving beyond Qualitative and Quantitative Strategies* (Berkley, Los Angeles and London: University of California Press).

Ragin, C. (1992) 'Casing and the process of social research', in C. Ragin and H. Becker (eds), *What is a Case?* (New York: Cambridge University Press), pp. 217–26.

Ragin, C. (1994) 'Introduction to qualitative comparative analysis', in T. Janoski and A. Hicks (eds), *The Comparative Political Economy of the Welfare State* (Cambridge: Cambridge University Press), pp. 299–319.

Ragin, C. (1995) 'Using qualitative comparative analysis to study configurations', in U. Kelle (ed.), *Computer-Aided Qualitative Data Analysis: Theory, Methods and Practice* (Newbury Park: Sage), pp. 170–89.

Ragin, C. (1997) 'Turning the tables: How the case-oriented research challenges variable-oriented research', *Comparative Social Research*, 16: 27–42.

Raynolds, L. T. (1994) 'Institutionalising flexibility: A comparative analysis of Fordist and post-Fordist models of third-world agro-export production', in G. Gereffi and M. Korzeniewicz (eds), *Commodity Chains and Global Capitalism* (Westport, CT: Praeger), pp. 143–61.

Renn, O., and Rohrmann, B. (2000) *Cross-Cultural Risk Perception: A Survey of Empirical Studies* (Dordrecht, Boston, MA, and London: Kluwer Academic Publishers).

Ringdal, K. (2001) *Enhet og mangfold. Samfunnsvitenskapelig forskning og kvantitativ metode* (Oslo: Fagbokforlaget).

Rothstein, B. (2000) 'Trust, social dilemmas and collective memories', *Journal of Theoretical Politics*, 12(4): 477–501.

Salvatore, A., and Sassatelli, R. (2004) 'Trust in food: A theoretical discussion', *Trust in Food Working Paper Series No. 1* (Bologna: www.trustinfood.org).

Sassatelli, R., and Scott, A. (2001) 'Wider markets, novel food and trust regimes', *European Societies*, 1(2): 231–63.

Scholderer, J., and Frewer, L. J. (2003) 'The biotechnology communication paradox: experimental evidence and the need for a new strategy', *Journal of Consumer Policy*, 26: 125–57.

Scholfield, R., and Shaoul, J. (2000) 'Food safety regulation and the conflict of interest: The case of meat safety and E. coli', *Public Administration*, 78(3): 531–54.

Seligman, A. B. (1997) *The Problem of Trust* (Princeton, NJ: Princeton University Press).

Shapiro, S. P. (1987) 'The social control of impersonal trust', *American Journal of Sociology*, 93(3): 623–58.

Siegrist, M., and Cvetkovich, G. (2001) 'Better negative than positive? Evidence of a bias for negative information about possible health dangers', *Risk Analysis*, 21(1): 199–206.

Slovic, P. (1999) 'Trust, emotion, sex, politics, and science: Surveying the risk-assessment battlefield', *Risk Analysis*, 19(4): 689–701.

Smart, J. (1986) 'Feminists, food and the fair price: The cost of living demonstrations in Melbourne August–September 1917', *Labour History* (Australia), 50: 113–31.

Southerton, D. (2003) 'Squeezing time: Allocating practices, co-ordinating networks and scheduling society', *Time and Society*, 12(1): 5–25.

Sparks, P., and Shepherd, R. (1994) 'Public perceptions of the potential hazards associated with food production and food consumption: An empirical study', *Risk Analysis*, 14(5): 799–806.

Strasser, S., McGovern, C., and Judt, M. (eds) (1998) *Getting and Spending: European and American Consumer Societies in the Twentieth Century* (Cambridge: Cambridge University Press).

Swidler, A. (1986) 'Culture in action: Symbols and strategies', *American Sociological Review*, 51(2): 273–86.

Sztompka, P. (1999) *Trust: A Sociological Theory* (Cambridge: Cambridge University Press).

Terragni, L. (2004) 'Institutional strategies for the production of trust in food in Norway', *Trust In Food Working Paper Series No. 3* (Oslo: www.trustinfood.org).

Theien, I., and Lange, E. (2004) *Affluence and Activism: Organised Consumers in the Post-War Era* (Oslo: Oslo Academic Press).

Thompson, E. P. (1971) 'The moral economiy of the English crowd in the eighteenth century', *Past and Present*, 76–136.

Tilly, C. (1975) 'Food supply and public order in modern Europe', in C. Tilly (ed.), *The Formation of National States in Western Europe* (Princeton, NJ: Princeton University Press), pp. 380–455.

Tilly, L. A. (1983) 'Food entitlement, famine, and conflict', in R. I. Rotberg and T. K. Rabb (eds), *Hunger and History: The Impact of Changing Food Production and Consumption Patterns on Society* (Cambridge: Cambridge University Press), pp. 135–51.

Trentmann, F. (2004) ' "Beyond" consumerism: New historical perspectives on consumption', *Journal of Contemporary History*, 39(3): 373–401.

Trentmann, F. (2006) *The Making of the Consumer: Knowledge, Power and Identity in the Modern World* (Oxford: Berg).

Uslaner, E. M. (1999) 'Trust but verify: Social capital and moral behavior', *Social Science Information*, 38(1): 29–55.

Uslaner, E. M. (2000) 'Producing and consuming trust', *Political Science Quarterly*, 115(4): 569–90.

Uusitalo, L. (2005) 'Consumers as citizens – Three approaches to collective consumer problems', in K. G. Grünert and J. Thøgersen (eds), *Consumers, Policy and the Environment: A Tribute to Folke Ölander* (New York: Springer), pp. 127–50.

Vogel, D., and Kagan, R. (2002) *Dynamics of Regulatory Change: How Globalization Affects National Regulatory Policies, International and Area Studies Digital Collection, Edited Volume 1* (Berkeley: University of California Press).

Völker, B. and Flap, H. (2001) 'Weak ties as a liability: The case of East Germany', *Rationality and Society*, 13(4): 397–428.

Wales, C. (2004) 'Country report: United Kingdom.' *Trust in Food Working Paper Series No. 6* (Manchester: www.trustinfood.org).

Ward, N., and Almås, R. (1997) 'Explaining change in the international agro-food system', *Review of International Political Economy*, 4(4): 611–29.

Wilson, J. Q. (1980) *The Politics of Regulation* (New York: Basic Books).

Winch D. (2006) 'The problematic status of the consumer in orthodox economic thought', in F. Trentmann (ed.), *The Making of the Consumer: Knowledge, Power and Identity in the Modern World* (Oxford: Berg), pp. 31–52.

Wong, R. B. (1983) 'Food riots in China and Western Europe', *Annales Economies, Societés, Civilisations*, 38(2): 234–58.

Wynne, B. (1996) 'May the sheep safely graze? A reflexive view of the expert-lay knowledge divide', in S. Lash, B. Szerszynski and B. Wynne (eds), *Risk, Environment and Modernity: Towards a New Ecology* (London: Sage), pp. 44–83.

Wynne, B. (2005) 'Reflexing complexity: Post-genomic knowledge and reductionist returns in public science', *Theory, Culture and Society*, 22(5): 67–94.

Index

active trust, 33, 179
actors
  categories, 43
  power of, 171
  relationships between, 44–5
  and trust, 12, 29–30, 42–3, 71–5,
    143–4, 181–4
  see also institutional actors
additives, 172
agencification, 176, 201
Agency for Food Safety and Quality
  (AQSA), Portugal, 153, 161
agents *see* actors
Aldi, 134, 135
Asda, 133
Auchan, 135
authorities (public food), 68–71, 73,
  76, 175–6
  see also institutional actors

Bauman, Z., 10
Beck, Ulrich, 21–2
beef
  consumption, 123–4
  demand for, 78–9
  food safety, 61–4, 185
  organic, 61–4, 80
  shopping habits, 99–102, 127
  trust in, 80, 178–80
  see also meat
Belgium, 3
Bijlsma-Frankema, K., 177
Boltanski, L., 51
box schemes, 110
Britain *see* United Kingdom
BSE (bovine spongiform
  encephalopathy)
  dimensions of trust, 3–4
  fall in demand for beef, 79
  reflection of trust configuration, 46
  regulatory changes resulting from,
    150–5
  societal event, 194–5

state response, 146, 149
  and trust, 165, 167, 170
burgers, 46–7, 61–4, 80, 186

Carrefour, 135
case-oriented research, 49–50
CATI (Computer-Assisted Telephone
  Interviews), 54
chicken, 61–4, 79, 80
  see also meat
Christian Democratic Union, 134
Cirio, 161, 208
civic ethos, 112–15
Codex Alimentarius, 2
cognitive process, 19–21, 26
Cohen, L., 96–7, 182
Common Agricultural Policy
  (CAP), 13, 135, 136, 145, 146,
    154, 185
concealment, 168
confidence
  in institutions, 31, 35, 39
  national expressions of, 4–5
  in own food, 85–6, 88
  restoring, 198–202
  type of trust, 177–8, 199
consumer organizations, 68–71, 72,
  76, 104–5, 108–11
  see also institutional actors
consumers
  economic perspective, 25, 93–4
  and food provisioners, 118, 138–41,
    156–62
  institutionalization of, 120–30, 187
  perceptions of change, 111–15
  political action, 93–4, 102–3,
    105–11, 115–17
  responsibilities, 106–7
  role of, 11, 94–9, 172–4, 201
  sociologists' perspective, 25
  as stakeholders, 176
  and the state, 143–4, 148, 150,
    151–5, 156–62